THE EDUCATION DEBATE

Stephen J. Ball

First published in Great Britain in 2008 by

The Policy Press
University of Bristol
Fourth Floor, Beacon House
Queen's Road
Bristol BS8 1QU

Tel +44 (0)117 331 4054
Fax +44 (0)117 331 4093
e-mail tpp-info@bristol.ac.uk
www.policypress.org.uk

British Library Cataloguing in Publication Data
A catalogue record for this book is available from the British Library

Library of Congress Cataloging-in-Publication Data
A catalog record for this book has been requested

ISBN 978 1 86134 920 0 paperback

Cover design by In-Text Design, Bristol.
Front cover: photograph kindly supplied by www.corbis.com
Printed and bound in Great Britain by Henry Ling Ltd, Dorchester.

Contents

List of tables, figures and boxes

Tables

Figures

Boxes

List of abbreviations

APU	Assessment of Performance Unit
ARK	Absolute Return for Kids
ASEAN	Association of Southeast Asian Nations and Japan
AST	Advanced skills teacher
BSF	Building Schools for the Future
CCT	Compulsory competitive tendering
CLEA	Council of Local Education Authorities
CRE	Commission for Racial Equality
CTC	City Technology College
DES	Department for Education and Science
DCSF	Department for Children, Schools and Families
DfEE	Department for Education and Employment
DfES	Department for Education and Skills
DIUS	Department for Innovation, Universities and Skills
DTI	Department of Trade and Industry
EAZ	Education Action Zone
EFA	Education for All
EiC	Excellence in Cities
EU	European Union
FE	Further education
FEFC	Further Education Funding Council
GATS	General Agreement on Trade in Services
GATT	General Agreement on Tariffs and Trade
GDP	Gross domestic product
GEMS	Global Education Management Systems
GTC	General Teaching Council
HE	Higher education
HEFCE	Higher Education Funding Council of England
HLTA	Higher-level teaching assistant
HMI	Her Majesty's Inspector
ICT	Information and communications technology
ILAs	Individual learning accounts
ILEA	Inner London Education Authority

IMF	International Monetary Fund
IT	Information technology
ITT	Initial teacher training
LEA	Local education authority
LMS	Local management of schools
LPSH	Leadership Programme for Serving Headteachers
MP	Member of Parliament
NAHT	National Association of Headteachers
NAO	National Audit Office
NCC	National Curriculum Council
NCSL	National College for School Leadership
NFER	National Foundation for Educational Research
NGO	Non-governmental organisation
NIS	National innovation system
NNVS	National Nursery Voucher Scheme
NPM	New public management
NPQH	National Professional Qualification for Headship
NUT	National Union of Teachers
NWA	National Workload Agreement
ODPM	Office of the Deputy Prime Minister
OECD	Organisation for Economic Co-operation and Development
Ofsted	Office for Standards in Education
PFI	Private finance initiative
PISA	Programme for International Student Assessment
Plasc	Pupil level annual school census
PMSU	Prime Minister's Strategy Unit
PPP	Public–private partnership
PRU	Pupil Referral Unit
PSLN	Primary Strategy Learning Network
PWC	PricewaterhouseCoopers
QAA	Quality Assurance Associates
QCA	Qualifications and Curriculum Authority
QTS	Qualified teacher status
RAE	Research Assessment Exercise

RoAs	Records of achievement
SAP	Structural adjustment programme
SATs	Standard assessment tasks
SCAA	School Curriculum and Assessment Authority
SEAC	Schools Examination and Assessment Council
TAs	Teacher assessments
TES	*Times Education Supplement*
TGAT	Task Group on Assessment and Testing
TTA	Teacher Training Agency
Ufi	University for Industry
UNESCO	United Nations Educational, Scientific and Cultural Organization
WTO	World Trade Organization

About the author

Stephen J. Ball is Karl Mannheim Professor of the Sociology of Education at the Institute of Education, University of London. His work is in 'policy sociology' and he has conducted a series of ESRC funded studies which focus on issues of social class and policy. He has an honorary doctorate from Turku University, Finland, is Visiting Professor at the University of San Andrés, Argentina and is a Fellow of the British Academy.

Acknowledgements

This book could not have been written and written so quickly without help. Michael Hill, Kate Hoskins, Marie Lall and Carol Vincent read and commented on chapters; Brian Davies read, commented on and corrected almost everything above and beyond the call of duty, for which I am very grateful. The inefficacies that survive are mine. Heidi Mirza and Dave Gillborn helped me sort out some analytic problems with 'race' policy. Robin Chen undertook searches for me. Trinidad gave me technical and emotional support that I value beyond words, and my brother Terry was staunch through difficult times.

In developing this series of books I indicated that I wanted critical but not simplistic analyses of contemporary policy issues. Stephen Ball's book fully meets that brief.

Michael Hill
Series Editor

Forthcoming titles include:
The health debate by David J. Hunter
The sustainable development debate by Michael Cahill

Introduction: education education education policy

This chapter's title is drawn from former Prime Minister Tony Blair's pre-election speech in 1996 that signalled a decisive repositioning of education onto the centre of the policy stage in England. Education has become a major political issue, a major focus of media attention and the recipient of a constant stream of initiatives and interventions from government. The same is true in many other countries around the globe. Education is now seen as a crucial factor in ensuring economic productivity and competitiveness in the context of 'informational capitalism'. In other words, education policy is increasingly thought about and made within the context of the 'pressures' and requirements of globalisation. While clearly the 'path dependency' of individual nation-state education systems remains important, global trends and convergences are discernible – a new 'global policyspeak' (Novoa, 2002). The effects and implications of this 'policyspeak' are crucial to any understanding of contemporary national education policies (see below).

English education has played a particular role in the development and dissemination of the education 'global policyspeak' as a social laboratory of experimentation and reform. Policies like school-based management, parental choice, information and accountability systems and privatisation are now being 'exported' around the world by English education businesses and 'policy entrepreneurs'. However, English education policy has also been an 'importer' of policies – the influence of US policy ideas like charter schools has been important, and the World Bank, Organisation for Economic Co-operation and Development (OECD) and European Union (EU) have also had an impact on thinking about issues such as public sector reform, the use of quasi-markets, quality assurance and education as a business opportunity.

The terms 'England' and 'English' are used here, and this is important. Both historically and currently there are significant differences between

the English education system and English education policy and the rest of the UK. Much of the 'policy' discussed in this book does not apply in the rest of the UK. While Scotland, Wales and Northern Ireland are not exempt from the pressures of globalisation, they mediate those pressures differently, they balance them differently against other priorities and face different social and economic problems.

While this book examines general trends in education policy it concentrates on school policies and politics with asides to and examples from other sectors where relevant. Because of the sheer volume of current education policy it is impossible to do justice to all four sectors (preschool, school, further education [FE] and lifelong learning, and higher education [HE]) in one book, although many of the policy 'levers' and 'technologies' discussed in what follows can be traced through the specifics of policy in these other sectors. In 2007, following Gordon Brown's takeover as Prime Minister, the Department for Education and Skills (DfES) and the Department of Trade and Industry (DTI) were abolished and restructured into two separate departments. The Department for Children, Schools and Families (DCSF) is now responsible for those areas of policy with which this book is primarily concerned and Ed Balls, former economic adviser to Gordon Brown, became Secretary of State. Post-compulsory education is now the responsibility of the Department for Innovation, Universities and Skills (DIUS) with John Denham as Secretary of State.

In the past 20 years education, like many other areas of social policy, has become subject to 'policy overload', or what Dunleavy and O'Leary (1987) call 'hyperactivism'. The 'depth, breadth and pace of change' and 'level of government activity' in education is 'unprecedented' (Coffield, 2006, p 2). In part this is tactical. It is about the dynamism of government (see Chapter One), about being seen to be doing something, tackling problems, 'transforming' systems. As Hyman (2005, p 2) explains in his account of his time as Tony Blair's speech writer: 'modern politics is all about momentum. Stagnate, drift, wobble, and the media or, if strong enough, the opposition, will pounce'. This kind of dynamism and the necessities and language of change are never more evident than at moments of political change. So in his last

Preface

Education is a central pillar of welfare policy and a subject close to the hearts of anyone with children or grandchildren going through the education system. It is also an area of hyperactive policy change and, even though I have worked within higher education for many years, I find much that is going on in the organisation of modern British education bewildering. I welcome Stephen Ball's book as a guide through the twists and turns of recent policy. From the beginning his long list of abbreviations warns us of the complexity ahead, but he takes us through the maze with clarity and vision.

While the statements of some of our politicians suggest an education revolution – setting aside the untidy old themes and replacing them with bright modern ones – Stephen's analysis shows us that the old problems are still there. Moreover, even as I write this preface new research is challenging some of the government's claimed achievements. Stephen argues that we must continue to address educational inequality, and indeed to recognise that it takes new complex forms. He also discusses the important but uneasy relationship between education and the economy. His analysis of policy debates shows how some of these concerns are evaded by our politicians, and highlights some often ill-focused adaptations to education policy.

If, as I do, you want to see the challenge to traditional values in education sustained but are concerned about the individualisation and fragmentation of the system, the dominance of benchmarks and indices, and the expectation that education can simply be a servant of the economy, this book will be invaluable reading. Gone are the days when radical thinkers naively thought there could be progressive advance through the reform of the education system – this sophisticated analysis indicates that there is no easy way forward. In any case, we need first a realistic analysis of how we have got to where we are now, and where we may be going; and this excellent book offers that.

major speech before taking over as Prime Minister in 2007 Gordon Brown began to outline his 'new approach' to education policy: 'The foundation of our new approach is that for the first time young people in Britain will be offered education to 18 and for the first time also a clear pathway from school to a career' (Brown, 2007). He also signalled in a variety of ways the increasingly close-knit relationship between the processes of education and the requirements of the economy and what he called the 'biggest transformation in the skills of our economy for more than a century'.

To give some sense of the sheer volume of education policy, the 'Monthly listing of official publications related to the work of the Department for Education and Employment', as it was then called, for July 2000, contained 106 items, including 39 Statutory Instruments. For teachers and FE lecturers in particular, policy is currently experienced as a constant flood of new requirements, changes, exhortations, responsibilities and expectations. These sometimes bear down heavily (see Box 1.1). In the course of this book we have to find our way through this welter of policy but also avoid becoming mired in the detail of particular initiatives, schemes and legislation, while identifying the main tendencies and patterns and key moments and significant developments. We also have to attend to the 'joining up' of education policy within a broader framework of social care and 'childcare' initiatives such as, for example, the Sure Start programme, parenting education and the development of 'full service' schools with after-hours and homework clubs (see Chapters Three and Four). Increasingly schooling is being joined up, in another sense, with other educational experiences as part of lifelong learning (see Edwards, 2002). One effect of these changes and others discussed later is that the traditional time–space configuration of schooling is being significantly reworked by policy. The ecology of education, what it looks like, when and where it happens, is being changed and, as a result, so too is the learner.

Box 1.1: The pressures of policy

A former union leader and primary school headteacher broke down in tears yesterday after revealing that work stress had caused him to leave the profession. Delegates at the National Union of Teachers (NUT) conference in Torquay heard how work pressure and 'government bullying' had led John Illingworth to take extended sick leave. In an emotional speech receiving a standing ovation, Mr Illingworth said that mental illness is likely to affect a third of those currently in the profession. He said: 'My illness has been caused by cumulative stress of work over many years which became beyond my capacity to manage.... I have always felt bullied by government'.

Mr Illingworth has been a teacher for 33 years and has been a head for seven years of that period.

Source: Rebecca Smithers, *The Guardian*, Tuesday, 18 April 2006 (www.guardian.co.uk/)

Policy sociology

The method and approach of this book is that of 'policy sociology' (Ball, 1997). Sociological concepts, ideas and research are used as tools for making sense of policy. In some cases these are heuristic devices, not definitive accounts of 'how things are' but methods for thinking about 'how things may be'. The book also contains a number of different sorts of arguments, ideas and lines of thought about education policy – how it works, what it does, whose interests it serves. One recurring theme is the relationship of education policy to the needs of the state and the economy, that is, to the contradictory requirements and necessities of the management of the population and in particular the problems of social authority, citizenship and social welfare over and against the role of the state as the 'midwife' for economic competitiveness. Another is the relationship between education policy and social class.

The book's emphasis is on presenting an analytic description and developing a set of tools that could be made use of in other contexts. This differentiates the book from many of the existing education policy texts. However, sociological jargon will be kept to a minimum and where concepts are used they will be explained. One particular aspect of the sociological emphasis of the text will be the attention given to the language of policy – policy rhetorics and discourses. This is done not in terms of a focus on language for its own sake but rather as a way of seeing how policy discourses work to privilege certain ideas and topics and speakers and exclude others. Policy discourses also organise their own specific rationalities, making particular sets of ideas obvious, common sense and 'true'. Discourses mobilise truth claims and constitute rather than simply reflect social reality. In other words, 'Language is deployed in the attempt to produce certain meanings and effects' (Edwards et al, 1999, p 620). Discourses also produce social positions 'from which people are "invited" (summoned) to speak, listen, act, read, work, think feel, behave and value' (Gee et al, 1996, p 10) – for example, parents, choosers, leaders, consumers, managers, lifelong learners and entrepreneurs. Policies are very specific and practical regimes of truth and value and the ways in which policies are spoken and spoken about, their vocabularies, are part of the creation of their conditions of acceptance and enactment. They construct the inevitable and the necessary. Within the processes of policy discourse individuals and groups of 'policy intellectuals' play an important role in establishing credibility and 'truthfulness' and some of these people will be identified as a way of putting 'faces' to policies. At moments of crisis or change such intellectuals play a key role in discursive struggles and, as Jessop calls it, in the 're-narration of the public sector … to consolidate an unstable equilibrium of compromise among different social forces around a given economic, political and social order' (2002, p 6) – they provide ways of thinking and talking about policies that make them sound reasonable and sensible as solutions to social and economic problems.

So, as part of the presentation and interrogation of policy this book will examine how policies are represented and disseminated through 'policy texts', that is, the documents and speeches that 'articulate' policies and policy ideas, which work to translate policy abstractions like globalisation and the knowledge economy and public sector reform, into roles and relationships and practices within institutions that enact policy and change what people do and how they think about what they do.

In a different sense, the use of language is a problem throughout the book. Many of the terms in use in policy analysis and in policy texts are slippery and consequently clear meanings are often elusive. As you will see there are a variety of terms in common policy usage – such as globalisation, or choice, or modernisation – that should be subject to critical examination. In particular, terms or ideas that are presented in the text in 'quotation marks' should be treated with critical care, or are being signalled as analytic metaphors. The contemporary 'dispersed' form of education policy also means that a perplexing variety of abbreviations are used and a list of these is included in the prelims. However, not all of these organisations and systems, nor all of the policy initiatives referred to, are explained fully in the text; space does not permit that, but the wonders of the internet and such sites as Wikipedia mean that details can be found very easily.

It is important to recognise that the book offers one set of interpretations of education policy, its history and contemporary manifestations, but these are not the only ways of looking at or thinking about policy. This is a selective account, as indicated already; comprehensive coverage is impossible and issues, moments and processes have been chosen that seem to be of particular significance.

Something should also be said about what is meant by 'policy'. 'Policy' is one of those obvious terms we all use but use differently and often loosely. The meaning of policy is something that has been written about at length (for example, see Hill, 2005), and the issues will not be rehearsed in detail here. For the most part, a common-sense concept of public policy as something constructed within government (in the broadest sense) – what we might call big-P policy (Evans et al, forthcoming: 2008) that is 'formal' and usually legislated policy – is being used here. But we need to remain aware that policies are made and remade in many sites, and there are many little-p policies that are formed and enacted within localities and institutions. Furthermore, policy that is 'announced' through legislation is also reproduced and reworked over time through reports, speeches, 'moves', 'agendas' and so on. Therefore, policy is not treated as an object, a product or an outcome but rather as a process, something ongoing, interactional and unstable:

> In a sense everything in the policy world is really just process, the movement of people and programs around common problems such as education, transport and employment. None of the initiatives in these fields stays fixed for very long because the problems themselves keep moving and changing. We cannot afford, therefore, to view policy as just a study of decisions or programs. The specific decisions which often interest us are merely important punctuation marks within this flow – not the thing itself. (Considine, 1994, pp 3-4)

Policies are contested, interpreted and enacted in a variety of arenas of practice and the rhetorics, texts and meanings of policy makers do not always translate directly and obviously into institutional practices. They are inflected, mediated, resisted and misunderstood, or in some cases simply prove unworkable. It is also important not to overestimate the logical rationality of policy. Policy strategies, Acts, guidelines and initiatives are often messy, contradictory, confused and unclear. I often write about education policy as education reform, as though they were the same thing. In a sense education policy has always been about reform, about doing things differently, about change and improvement. Policy is an enlightenment concept, it is about progress, it is about moving from the inadequacies of the present to some future state of perfection where everything works well and works as it should. Since the 1970s the current phase of education policy has been about 'radical' change (an overused but significant term here), about changing the principles on which education has functioned previously, for example, unsettling the welfare state 'settlement' of which comprehensive education was a part. Reform in this period is not just about changing the way things are organised or done; it is about changing teachers and learning, and educational institutions and their relations to the economy (and to information and communications technology [ICT]) and to international economic competitiveness. It is about rethinking, or 'reimagining', education. When the term 'education reform' is used it is to this sort of conception of policy change to which I refer. However, one of the simple but important points repeated several times in the text is that when we focus our attention on change, or reform, we must not lose sight of what stays the same, the continuities of and in policy.

The book is organised as follows: Chapter One introduces a set of key concepts that are then used and referred to in the rest of the book. In particular this chapter puts education reform and education policy into a global context and in relation to 'the knowledge economy', and outlines a set of generic policy technologies that are deployed in an enormous variety of different national settings to reform and re-form education. The main multilateral 'players' in global education policy are also introduced and the 'necessarian logic' of New Labour, which relates education very directly to the demands and inevitabilities of globalisation, is examined. Chapter Two deals with the history of English education policy, a history of the present, and how we got to where we are today. This cursory history of education policy is used as a way of explaining some of the contemporary patterns of the English education system and why the system we have looks like it does; in the concluding chapter some parallels are drawn between contemporary education policy issues and those in play at the beginning of education policy in the mid-19th century and some of the generic themes, continuities, recurrences, patterns and trends in education policy. Chapter Three explores some of the specifics of current education policy through the perspective of a particular document *The UK government's approach to public service reform* (Cabinet Office, 2006), a document that outlines a 'joined-up' model of reform based on performance management, voice and choice, contestability and workforce 'remodelling'. This is supported by a set of genealogies of policy that trace various policy 'moves' within each of these mechanisms, from the Conservative governments (1979-97) to New Labour (1997-2007). Chapter Four focuses on the issue of equity and policy by looking at performance and participation in education in relation to 'race', gender and social class; the emphasis given to the moral responsibilities of parenting and the problem of social exclusions; and the school policies of academies and trusts as 'solutions' to underachievement in socially disadvantaged areas. The final chapter, Chapter Five, as noted already, focuses on some of the circularities and discontinuities within education policy and points up for further attention some of the recurring themes in the book as a whole:

- the changing form and modalities of the state
- the production of 'new learners'
- the subordination of education to economic imperatives
- policy convergence, across countries and across sectors
- the 'privatisation' of public sector education
- the 'joining up' of social and educational policies.

Much more needs to be said, however, about things such as special needs and disability, refugee education, FE and HE, childcare and parenting, citizenship, school building and funding issues, extended education and in particular the curriculum, but because there is now so much education policy, one book is not enough to cover it all. However, the idea of this book is that, as well as offering a substantive account of current policy trends, and some ways of making sense of what is happening to our experience of education, as learners, as teachers, as parents and as citizens, a number of analytic tools will be introduced that may have a more general usefulness in the interpretation of policies which are not dealt with directly.

1

Introduction to key concepts: education policy, economic necessity and public service reform

> But we should not forget why reform is right, and why, whatever the concerns over individual benefits, most people know it is right. Above all, the system must change because the world has changed beyond the recognition of Beveridge's generation.... We need a system designed not for yesterday, but for today. (Blair, 1998a, p 1)

This chapter provides the groundwork for the analysis and presentation of policy in the book as a whole and introduces topics that are taken up more fully or in more specific ways later. The central theme of the chapter is education reform and in relation to this it emphasises in particular the global and international context of education policy, issues of policy transfer and 'borrowing',[1] 'convergence' and the changing spatial configurations of policy and policy making. As part of these processes of reform, the various ways in which education and education policy have become dominated by the perspective of economics will be demonstrated. That is, the role of education as a producer of labour and skills and of values, like enterprise and entrepreneurship, and of commercial 'knowledge', as a response to the requirements of international economic competition. Within policy, education is now regarded primarily from an economic point of view. The social and economic purposes of education have been collapsed into a single, overriding emphasis on policy making for economic competitiveness and an increasing neglect or sidelining (other than in rhetoric) of the social purposes of education. Cowen (1996, p 151) writes about this as the 'astonishing displacement of "society" within the late modern educational pattern'. Education is increasingly subject to 'the normative assumptions and prescriptions [of] economism' (Lingard et al, 1998, p 84). This is evident across a whole variety of policy texts. The 1998 Green Paper, *The Learning Age* (DfEE, 1998a, p 1), began: 'Learning is the key to prosperity – for each of us as individuals, as well as for the nation as a whole. This is why the Government has put learning at the heart of its ambition'. Or, as Tony Blair put it in a speech early in his time as Prime Minister (1997-2007):

> … education is our best economic policy…. This country will succeed or fail on the basis of how it changes itself and gears up to this new economy, based on knowledge. Education therefore is now the centre of economic policy making for the future. What I am saying is, we know what works within our education system, we can learn the lessons of it. The key is now to apply those lessons, push them right throughout the education system, until the young children, whether they are growing up here in the constituency of Sedgefield, or in the inner city urban estates of London, or Liverpool, or Manchester, or Newcastle, wherever they are, they get the chance to make the most of their God given potential. It is the only vision, in my view, that will work in the 21st century. (Blair, 2005a)

The chapter also introduces the key concepts that are deployed in the analysis of education policy and the 'reform' of education – globalisation/glocalisation, the knowledge economy and policy technologies (the market, management, performativity). Most of the discussion in this chapter is fairly abstract but the concepts are grounded in the specifics of policy in the following chapters. It is, to some extent, a counterbalance to the point made in the introduction about the Englishness of this account. Here there is a primary emphasis on a set of policies, an ensemble of *generic policies*, which have global currency in the reform of education and particular attention will be given to the increasing role in the policy of multilateral organisations but some of the ways that the discourse of globalisation and its relationships to education reform are played out within the policy rhetorics of New Labour will also be explored.

As we shall see, the *discourses* that are currently in play, in a whole variety of diverse policy settings, are important in two ways. First, in their contribution to the construction of the need for reform, particularly in the case of globalisation and international economic competition and the requirements of the knowledge economy, and, second, in providing and making obvious and necessary 'appropriate' policy responses and solutions. These constructions and their rationales privilege particular social goals and human qualities and currently give overwhelming emphasis to the economic role of education. Policies are both systems of values and symbolic systems, ways of accounting for and legitimating political decisions. In both respects the language of policy is important. Part of the work of policy is done in and through policy texts, written and spoken, and the ways in which these represent policy subjects – teachers, learners, managers, etc. Policies to greater or lesser extents have a semantic and ontological force. They play their part in the construction of a social world of meanings, of causes and effects, of relationships, of imperatives and inevitabilities. By attending to the changing language and rhetorical constructions of education policy we can begin to see the ways in which policies have histories and the way that they 'join up' within and across different policy fields. Such attention also highlights the contradictions and incoherences that are embedded within policy. Nonetheless, policy also works in very practical and material ways through the installation of policy devices or 'technologies', such as choice, performance management and competition.

New Labour education and the rhetorics of education reform

We can see the processes and discourses of the 'economic perspective' being 'played out' very clearly in and through New Labour policy talk and policy texts. The 'necessities' of these are connected in turn to the 'need for' public services reform. Olssen et al (2004, p 245) argue that 'globalisation and education comprise the dual mantras of "third way" politics', and indeed it was one of Tony Blair's declared aims to 'make this country at ease with globalisation' (Blair, 2005b).

Education reform began in the policies of the UK Conservative governments during 1979-97 (see Chapter Two) and has been developed in the policies of New Labour since 1997. In particular, within the complex and expansive political rhetoric of New Labour the ideas of transformation, modernisation, innovation, enterprise, dynamism, creativity and competitiveness are key signifiers in education and public sector reform. They often appear in texts as co-occurrences, that is, they are linked together as an ensemble and signify the sense of the pace, movement and constant change that is taken to define globalisation, and the globalised economy. They are set over and against the supposed inadequacies, particularly the slowness and unresponsiveness and risk aversion, of the public sector prior to reform. The shift from the latter to the former is taken to be necessary and inevitable and related primarily to economic rather than social pressures and needs, as a response to the urgent demands of globalisation and international competitiveness:

> Complaining about globalisation is as pointless as trying to turn back the tide. Asian competition can't be shut out; it can only be beaten. And now, by every relative measure of a modern economy, Europe is lagging. (Blair, *Newsweek*, 29 January 2006, www.msnbc.msn.com)

This is a key part of the 'necessarian logic of New Labour's political economy' (Watson and Hay, 2003, p 295). 'The accepted need', as

McCaig (2001, p 189) calls it, 'for flexible workforces in the knowledge economy of the future obliges New Labour to be socially and educationally interventionist. This means, in compulsory education offering the kinds of specialism which will produce a differentiated and flexible workforce'. The public sector must be remade in order to respond to the exigencies of globalisation and to play its part in the economics of international competition. Individual and institutional actors and their dispositions and responses are tied to the fate of the nation within the global economy:

> The purpose of the reforms is to create a modern education system and a modern NHS where within levels of investment at last coming up to the average of our competitors, real power is put in the hands of those who use the service the patient and the parent; where the changes becoming self-sustaining; the system, open, diverse, flexible, able to adjust and adapt to the changing world. ('The then Prime Minister Tony Blair reflects on "pivotal moment" for education', Monthly Press Conference, 10 Downing Street, 24 October 2005)

There is an easy-to-grasp narrative here, an 'insistent singularity' that links the reform of educational practices (for example, the use of choice as a change mechanism in this case) to the global economy. The lack of clarity and coherence that is sometimes evident in such statements, how the elements are joined up in practice, seems unimportant and is overcome by reiteration in and across policy texts. Within these texts there is a dialogue that places the 'old' public sector in contrast to a 'modern' public sector and the 'new' economy and that treats the 'old ways' of working as a threat to competitiveness and reiterates the need for 'radical change' – modernisation and transformation:

> Do we take modest though important steps of improvement? Or do we make the great push forward for transformation? Let me spell it out. In education ... we open up the system to new and different ways of education.... There's nothing

> wrong with the old principles but if the old ways worked, they'd have worked by now. (Blair, 2002)

Terms such as 'modernisation' and 'transformation' are 'used to signal the need to bring the political world into line with changes conceived to have occurred in other domains, principally, society, economics and culture' (Kenny and Smith, 2001, p 239). The rhetoric within which they are used conjures up the need for new kinds of policy (the technologies outlined below) and new kinds of government (changes in the role of the state), and that 'new' is of course New Labour itself. The assertion is that the 'imagination' of new policies will ensure a new 'creativity' in public service delivery:

> We must let the systems change and develop. The old monolithic structures won't do. We can't engineer change and improvement through bureaucratic edict. Hence the reform programme.... It is not our tax and fiscal positions which are holding us back as a nation. It is productivity and the state of our public services. (Blair, 2001)

Education is very much to the centre of all of this and the use of the term 'productivity' is a simple indicator of the new lexicon within which education is conceived, a language drawn from business and from economics:

> ... to thrive in the global knowledge economy it is going to be important to change the whole educational system to ensure a wide base of knowledge workers who understand and use these information technologies. Thus, education is a key, in order to ensure the skills for the knowledge economy exist in abundance. It is important that there be an army of skilled technical experts who understand and can apply technical knowledge. These workers are the underpinnings of the knowledge economy. (www.egovmonitor.com/)

However, the rhetoric of reform often also manages to couple improvements in social justice and equity, of a particular kind, and the maximisation of social, educational and economic participation, to enterprise and economic success, in particular through the idea of meritocracy (see Chapter Four), the argument being that modernisation and change are meritocratic and just insofar as they are an escape from old social divisions that subordinated talent to social status. This is also presented as a form of liberation that will allow creativity and passion to flourish unhampered. Here individual and collective well-being are totally elided. Equity and enterprise, technological change and economic progress are tied together within the efforts, talents and qualities of individual people and the national collective – the 'us' and the 'we':

> It is to modernize our country, so that, in the face of future challenges, intense and profound for us and like nations, we are able to provide opportunity and security for all; not for an elite; not for the privileged few; but for all our people, whatever their class, colour or creed. It is to build on the platform of economic stability, the modern knowledge economy, with the skills, dynamism, technological and scientific progress a country like Britain needs. And above all, they are about realizing the enormous creative energy and passion that people feel in all walks of life for education; for its liberating power; for its unique ability to correct the inequalities of class or background. (Blair, 2006a)

Education reform then is intimately tied through the development of skills and 'new knowledge' to the requirements of the knowledge economy, that is, forging 'a nation where the creative talents of all people are used to build a true enterprise economy for the 21st century – where we compete on brains, not brawn' (Tony Blair, Colorado Alliance for Arts Education, www.artsedcolorado.org/). The dynamic of transformation and the need to seize opportunities, to constantly innovate and constantly improve performance are everywhere:

> Schools at the cutting edge of innovation and collaboration will be selected from amongst the country's best schools as a lever to transform secondary education, to engineer the growth of collaborative learning communities and federations, and to promote innovation research and development to push the boundaries of current teaching practice. (www.standards.dfes.gov.uk/leadingedge/)

Such a discourse works in a variety of ways to redraw boundaries, label heroes and villains, create space for action, exclude alternatives, legitimate new voices (like those of the private sector), attribute cause and effect and make some things seem natural and others inevitable, that is, to construct events into sequences – narratives – and thus rewrite history. The public sector is reimagined and within this and as part of the reform process public sector institutions are to 'be more businesslike' and 'more like business', and business itself, the private sector, is to have an increasing role in the management and delivery of public services – this is something to which I will return in more detail in Chapter Three.

Despite all of this, Labour's education policies cannot be read off in their entirety from a global educational agenda nor is it the case that Labour has no control over its policy decisions, set as they are within the logic of the global market. There are many education policies that are not in any way obviously related to the economics of globalisation. However, there is exemplification here of what Fejes (2006) calls 'planetspeak discourses',[2] a limited set of possibilities for speaking sensibly about education, which recur in many, very different national contexts, with the effect of 'convergence' – the deployment of policies with common underlying principles and similar operational methods (for a discussion of convergence see also Whitty and Edwards, 1998, pp 39-42).

Knowledge economy

> Today's most technologically advanced economies are truly knowledge-based (Department of Trade and Industry, 1998, *Our competitive future: Building the knowledge-driven economy* (www.dti.gov.uk/comp/competitive))

The 'knowledge economy' is a much-used term in relation to contemporary education policy but as a concept it is elusive and misleading. It derives from the idea that knowledge and education can be treated as a business product, and that educational and innovative intellectual products and services, as productive assets, can be exported for a high-value return. The idea of the knowledge economy was first introduced in a book by Drucker, *The effective executive* (1966), in which he described the difference between a manual worker and a knowledge worker. Manual workers work with their hands and produce 'stuff'. Knowledge workers work with their heads and produce or articulate ideas, knowledge and information. In the current stage of economic development it is argued that *information* and *knowledge* are replacing capital and energy as the primary wealth-creating assets, just as the latter two replaced land and labour 200 years ago, that is, technological developments in the 20th century have transformed the majority of wealth-creating work from physically based to 'knowledge-based' – a new stage of capitalism (Leadbeater, 2000a). Technology and knowledge are now the key factors of production. With increased mobility of information through information technology (IT) systems and a global workforce, knowledge and expertise can be transported instantaneously around the world, and any advantage gained by one company can be eliminated by competitive improvements overnight. The only comparative advantage a company or more generally a nation can attain will be its processes of innovation – combining market and technology know-how with the creative talents of knowledge workers to solve a constant stream of competitive problems – and its ability to derive value from information. These are sometimes called national innovation systems (NIS). An NIS is a well-articulated network of firms, research centres, universities and think-tanks that work together to take advantage of the growing stock of global knowledge, assimilate and adapt it to local needs and create new technology. Increasingly tertiary education systems (FE and HE) figure prominently in NIS, providing not only high-level skills but also operating as the main locus of basic and applied research (see below). Charles Leadbeater, New Labour policy adviser (Demos think-tank associate), describes this as 'living on thin air':

> Three forces are driving modern economies – finance, knowledge and social capital. It is no coincidence that all are intangible: they cannot be weighed or touched, they do not travel in railway wagons and cannot be stockpiled in ports. The critical factors of production of this new economy are not oil, raw materials, armies of cheap labour or physical plant and equipment. These traditional assets still matter, but they are a source of competitive advantage only when they are vehicles for ideas and intelligence which give them value. (Leadbeater, 2000b)

In short, then, the development of the knowledge economy can be understood in terms of the increasing role of knowledge as a factor of production and its impact on skills, learning, organisation and innovation. Innovation systems and their 'knowledge distribution power' are critically important. This has a whole variety of implications for education and education policy.

One example of the translation of these ideas into a form of education policy, and an exemplification of the role of multilateral agencies in 'making' education policy, comes from the World Bank Education for the Knowledge Economy Programme. This refers to World Bank assistance aimed at helping developing countries equip themselves with the highly skilled and flexible human capital needed to compete effectively in today's dynamic global markets. Such assistance is based on the assumption that the ability to produce and use knowledge has become a major factor in economic development and critical to a nation's competitive advantage. Education is increasingly viewed primarily in these terms. It is also clear how the idea of the knowledge economy is translated into and articulated through national education policies (see above). For example, in the UK's White Paper *Our competitive future: Building the knowledge driven economy* (DTI, 1998), a knowledge-based economy is defined as:

> ... one in which the generation and the exploitation of knowledge has come to play the predominant part in the creation of wealth. It is not simply about pushing back the frontiers of knowledge; it is also about the more effective use and exploitation of all types of knowledge in all manner of activity. (www.dti.gov.uk/comp/competitive/wh_int1.htm)[3]

The significance of the knowledge economy is also evident in the policy discourse of other countries:

> ... a well-educated graduate is the fundamental building-block of a knowledge-based economy. (Ministry of Education of Pakistan, 2004)

> ... the education system is currently undergoing reforms in order to meet the current and future needs and challenges of the socio-economic developments of the country as well as the imperatives of the global knowledge economy. (Ministry of Education of Bangladesh, 2004)

There are generally three sorts of responses to and criticisms of the knowledge economy among policy analysts, each of which treats the idea of the knowledge economy differently in terms of its reality, and if it is real, its effects. One of the arguments levelled against the effects of the knowledge economy discourse as it works in and through national education policies is that it constructs a narrow, instrumental approach to the economics of knowledge and to intellectual culture in general; in other words, that knowledge is commodified. What that means is, in fetishising commodities, we are denying the primacy of human relationships in the production of value, in effect erasing the social. Our understanding of the world shifts from social values created by people to one in which '… everything is viewed in terms of quantities; everything is simply a sum of value realised or hoped for' (Slater and Tonkiss, 2001, p 162). This shift is neatly captured in the title of a book by Slaughter and Leslie (1997), *Academic capitalism*. The term describes the phenomenon of universities' and their staff's increasing attention to market potential as the impetus for research, based on what the DTI document quoted earlier calls the 'exploitation' of knowledge. According to Slaughter and Leslie, globalisation has worked to efficiently link the status of universities and their research funding income to the marketability of the knowledge they produce from research, and they see this trend being exploited by governments as grants are replaced with 'market money' which is linked to performance indicators. Increasingly universities must earn their budgets from outside commercial funding or through competition for government contracts or in relation to their research performance, as in the UK's Research Assessment Exercise (RAE) system – a mechanism of *performativity* (see below):

> The Research Assessment Exercise is conducted jointly by the Higher Education Funding Council for England (HEFCE), the Scottish Funding Council (SFC), the Higher Education Funding Council for Wales (HEFCW) and the Department for Employment and Learning, Northern Ireland (DEL). (www.rae.ac.uk/)
>
> The primary purpose of the RAE 2008 is to produce quality profiles for each submission of research activity made by an institution. The four higher education funding bodies intend to use the quality profiles to determine their grant for research to the institution which they fund with effect from 2009-10. (www.hefce.ac.uk/)

Willmott's (1995) discussion of developments in UK HE takes this further when he describes the 'commodification of academic labour as its use value, in the forms of its contribution to the development of the student as a person, as a citizen or at least as a depository and carrier of culturally valued knowledge, becomes displaced by a preoccupation with doing those things which will increase its exchange value in terms of the resources that flow, directly or indirectly, from a strong performance on the measures of research output and teaching quality' (p 1002). In relation to this, he goes on to say 'students have been explicitly constituted as "customers", a development that further reinforces the idea that a degree is a commodity that (hopefully) can be exchanged for a job rather than as a liberal education that prepares students for life' (Willmott, 1995, p 1002). Here then we have various aspects of the transformation of social relations into a thing and further aspects of the subordination of the purposes of education to economics. Furthermore, as universities compete to maximise their income by seeking new 'markets' and reorienting themselves to the student-customer, new forms of 'delivery' and consumption of HE are being created that can result in learning becoming increasingly fragmented and combined in novel ways with no guarantee of internal coherence. Increasingly learning can be transferred as 'credits' – made 'readable' in the jargon of the Bologna Declaration – between institutions and countries. Lyotard (1984, p 38), in his review of HE, refers to this as a process of 'exteriorisation' that is summed up in his terms as a shift from the questions 'is it true?' and 'is it just?' to 'is it useful, saleable, efficient?'. Knowledge is no longer legitimated through 'grand narratives of speculation and emancipation' (Lyotard, 1984, p 38) but, rather, in the pragmatics of 'optimization' – the creation of skills or of profit rather than ideals.

The second point of criticism is rather different and raises questions about the real significance of the knowledge economy. The empirical evidence for the knowledge economy is still weak at best. Keep (1997, p 461) makes the point that: 'Research suggests that the impact of globalisation on the British economy and the job market is being both over-emphasised and over-simplified ... many parts of the domestic economy, especially in the service sector, remain relatively insulated from global economic competition'. The main areas of recent economic growth and expansion of jobs in countries like the UK and the US rest not on knowledge but on 'service'. Service employment accounts for two thirds or more of total employment in the US and Europe and 85% or so of female employment, although the service sector itself is very diverse. Figures from the Department for Education and Employment (DfEE) website (www.coi.gov.uk/coi/depts/GDEJuly 1999) indicate that service work now accounts for 75% of total employment in the UK. In particular, the 'hospitality industry', as it is called (hotels, tourism and catering), has been the major growth area in the UK economy since the 1980s and has accounted for the majority of the falls in unemployment since the mid-1990s. The proportion of economic activity involving new technologies and 'new science' (for example, bioengineering) remains relatively modest. In the US, the IT share of nominal gross domestic product (GDP) grew from just 4.9% in 1985 to 8.2% in 1997.

The third point of criticism is that developments in relation to the knowledge economy, both in terms of technological developments, investments in innovation and research and in educational expansion, are together reinforcing systematic social inequalities and exacerbating economic and social polarisation. In part this is the point that there is a 'wired world' and an 'unwired world' – many people and many countries are not 'connected' electronically and do not participate in a real sense in the knowledge economy. These gaps and inequalities are evident within as well as between countries. In India, per capita annual income in 1995 was $340: the majority of the population of 900 million lived on less than one dollar a day. At the same time, India hosts a major offshore software centre for the rest of the world. Software production in 1997 was a US$2 billion industry, employing 260,000 people (Quah, 1998).

Globalisation/glocalisation

> We can already see how important education and skills are for individual and collective prosperity.... On a global scale, half the increase in the annual growth of productivity comes from new ideas and ways of doing things. The fastest-growing cities in America and Europe are those with the highest proportion of knowledge workers. (Blair, 2000)

Globalisation is key here in two senses. First, as an articulation of the 'problems' of policy and, second, as a spatial frame within which policy discourses and policy formulation are now set. On the one hand, talk about globalisation – what it means, how it impacts on the nation-state – produces a set of imperatives for policy at the national level and a particular way of thinking about education and its contemporary problems and purposes. On the other, as a result of particular aspects of the process of globalisation, the nation-state is no longer adequate, on its own, as a space within which to think about policy. Policies are 'made' in response to globalisation and those responses are variously driven or influenced by their take-up of supranational agencies, the policy work of intellectual and practical policy 'fads' and the resulting 'flow' of policies between countries. Education is very particularly implicated in the discourse and processes of globalisation through the idea of the *knowledge economy* (see above). However, the idea of globalisation has to be treated with care and is subject to extensive debate.

Broadly speaking most writers on globalisation deploy one of two general forms of interpretation. One is what we can call the 'one world' thesis. The other is a 'relational' or 'vernacular' interpretation of globalisation. The nub of the 'one world' thesis rests on the question of the future of the nation-state as a political and cultural entity. The thesis is articulated through four closely interrelated literatures addressing, respectively, economic, political, cultural and social changes, with precedence given to the role of economics. In the case of the first two the focus is on whether, within the context of global economic change, individual nation-states retain their capacity to steer and manage their own economies in the face of the power of 'rootless' multinational corporations, the ebb and flow of global financial markets, facilitated by ICT and trade deregulation, and the spread of modern post-Fordist industrial production. Clearly, in the past 30 years:

> The capacity of any government to command a particular firm to take a specified task in supporting public policy, such as settling in a backward region or holding down a key price, has been reduced; large firms now have a capacity that they never had before for choice between competing nations. (Vernon, 1977, p 63)

Economic globalisation has a number of key characteristics and drivers. The global communications revolution has been of major significance but has been accompanied by a widespread movement to economic deregulation, including:

- the reduction of tariff and non-tariff barriers on trade in both goods and services;
- the floating of currencies and deregulation of financial markets more generally;
- the reduction of barriers to foreign direct investment and other international capital flows, and of barriers to technology transfers;
- business procedures becoming increasingly integrated and standardised with the aim to diminish friction losses – or transaction costs – in production processes. Consequently, the location of the production of goods and services becomes less important;
- the deregulation of product markets in many countries, particularly in terms of the reduction in the power of national monopolies in areas such as telecommunications, air transport and the finance and insurance industries.

Alongside all of this is the issue whether individual nation-states are also losing their political autonomy more generally to the increasing range and influence of supranational organisations such as the World

Bank, World Trade Organization (WTO), OECD and regional states and organisations, like the EU or Association of Southeast Asian Nations and Japan (ASEAN).

In terms of culture, again the main issues revolve around the question of the continuing vitality and independence of national and local cultures in the face of the unifying and homogenising effects of westernisation or Americanisation and the production of a generic consumer who knows and responds to 'global brands', such as Nike, McDonald's, Gap, Coca-Cola, HSBC, GameBoy, etc, the argument being that we are experiencing the creation of a 'McWorld' driven by the interests of the global cultural industries and disseminated by global media – television, film and the internet. And, finally, socially, the question is whether the nature of personal social experience has been fundamentally altered by the space–time compressions and changing economic flows of globalisation, such as labour migration.

The point about social change is succinctly made by Giddens (1996, p 367), who argues that 'Globalisation is not just an "out there" phenomenon. It refers not only to the emergence of large scale world systems, but to transformations in the very texture of everyday life'. The rhythm and content of daily life has become both more ephemeral and volatile and commodity production increasingly emphasises the values and virtues of instantaneity and disposability. What is important here is both that globalisation changes the way that we as individuals engage in and experience the world, and how we experience ourselves; that is, globalisation changes the ways that people talk about themselves and others, changes their consciousness, dispositions and affects. This is what Elliott and Lemert (2006) call 'the emotional costs of globalisation'. As they explain:

> … globalisation, involving very different patterns of transnational interactions, flows and networks, remains above all about people. Global transformations are deeply inscribed in people's sense of their own individualism, at once demanding significant levels of psychic commitment and reorganization. (Elliott and Lemert, 2006, pp 90–1)

For a very small number of individuals globalisation has created a whole new space and set of possibilities for living based on instantaneous communications and speed of travel, a form of life that has no necessary relationship to national identity or traditions and is 'structured to its core by high exposure to the intensity of global networks' (Elliott and Lemert, 2006, p 105). This is a form lived by people Zygmunt Bauman calls 'globals' and involves new forms of work within the knowledge economy – what Reich call 'symbolic analysis': 'Symbolic analysts solve, identify, and broker problems by manipulating symbols. They simplify reality into abstract images that can be rearranged, juggled, experimented with, communicated to other specialists, and then, eventually, transformed back into reality' (Reich, 1991, p 178). This is work as 'articulation' rather than as 'creation'. Potentially these changes have very significant consequences for education systems. Education and skills, as 'human capital', are 'traded' in the global marketplace, as, for example, Indian or Korean software engineers are 'imported' into California, South African nurses and eastern European doctors and Spanish pharmacists are 'attracted' to the UK (one in two doctors and nurses currently recruited to the UK health service comes from abroad, while at the same time UK nurses move to Australia):

> With a population of just 20 million people, the [Australian] economy faces a chronic skills shortage. To sustain its present levels of growth, the economy needs an influx of skilled workers – skilled workers who ideally speak fluent English. With Britain offering that pool of labour, it is a win-win for both parties. So Australia has been welcoming British skilled workers in record numbers over the past three years. In 2005, 21,780 UK nationals left Britain to settle in Australia, a 30% rise on the year before. (http://news.bbc.co.uk/2/hi/uk_news/6175345.stm)

European students increasingly move around within the EU and others are attracted to EU universities from countries around the world – educational services are an increasingly important international trade commodity (see below). In 2001 the OECD estimated that globally student mobility was worth US$50 billion. Overseas students and other 'educational services' are an important source of income for UK universities – in 2003-04 UK education and training 'exports' were worth £28 billion, more than financial services (worth £19 billion).

Elliott and Lemert (2006) go on to make another point about individuals and their relation to globalisation that is often lost in some of the exaggerated versions of the globalisation debate:

> The central conceptual and political limitation of conceptualizing globalisation purely as an external force, however, is that it prevents us from seeing with sufficient clarity the myriad ways in which individuals engage, respond, escape, reproduce or transform the whole gamut of globalizing forces that they necessarily encounter in their everyday lives. (p 94)

To put it another way, in thinking about these issues we need to be wary of what Harvey (1996) calls 'globaloney'. Both empirically and conceptually many of the basic tenets of the globalisation thesis have been subject to stern criticism. Globalisation can be used to 'explain' almost anything and, as we have seen, is ubiquitous in current policy texts and policy analysis. It is certainly possible to overstate the case and succumb to what Weiss (1997) calls the 'myth of the powerless state', which seems particularly difficult to sustain since 9/11 and the Iraq war. Also, the analysis of the flow and influence of policies between nations needs to be addressed with care. Ideas, knowledge, culture and artefacts are not assimilated uncritically or unreflexively into diverse national settings. Furthermore, nations are positioned differently in relation to the structures and effects of globalisation. As Lingard and Rizvi (2000, p 2100) express it: 'globalisation does not impinge on all nation-states and at all times in exactly the same way' and domestic state capacities differ. Some states are more able and more likely to deflect or mediate global policy trends while others, as we shall see, are required to accept and respond to external reform imperatives.

With some oversimplification the outcome of the debate around globalisation has been the development of a *relational* position, that is, a move away from a deterministic logic to a recognition that:

> Globalisation invades local contexts it does not destroy them; on the contrary, new forms of local cultural identity and self-expression are causally bound up with globalising processes. (Giddens, 1996, pp 367-8)

This is, in Robertson's terms, 'the simultaneity and the interpenetration of what are conventionally called the global and the local' (1995, p 100), or what he calls 'glocalisation'. Indeed, national policy making is inevitably a process of bricolage, a matter of borrowing and copying bits and pieces of ideas from elsewhere, drawing on and amending locally tried-and-tested approaches, cannibalising theories, research, trends and fashions, responding to media 'panics' and not infrequently a flailing around for anything at all that looks as though it might work. Most policies are ramshackle, compromise, hit-and-miss affairs, that are reworked, tinkered with, nuanced and inflected through complex processes of influence, text production, dissemination and ultimately recreation in diverse contexts of practice (Ball, 1994). In short, national policies need to be understood as the product of a nexus of influences and interdependencies, resulting in 'interconnectedness, multiplexity and hybridisation' (Amin, 1997, p 129), that is, 'the intermingling of global, distant and local logics'.

In relation to all this, one of the tensions that runs through all varieties of policy analysis is that between the need to attend to the local particularities of policy making and policy enactment and the need to be aware of general patterns and commonalities or convergences across localities (see Whitty and Edwards, 1998). In each of its main dimensions – economic, political and cultural – it is possible to see globalisation as reducing the autonomy and specificity of the national and the local, while at the same time policy ideas are received and interpreted differently within different political architectures, national infrastructures, national ideologies[4] and business cultures.[5] In some fields of policy analysis the identification of such differences has led to attempts to develop typologies of societies (see Hill, 2005, pp 90-5).

We can note, for example, Taylor et al's (1997) case studies of education policies in Papua New Guinea, Malaysia and Australia. They conclude that: 'there is no essential determinacy to the ways in which globalisation pressures work, since for various globalisation pressures there are also sites of resistance and counter movements' (p 72). (For a similar argument see Colclough and Lewin, 1993, p 256.) In other words, generic global policies are polyvalent, they are translated into practice in complex ways. They interact with, interrupt or conflict with other policies in play in national and local settings and with long-standing indigenous policy traditions to produce particular versions or mediations of policy. This is what is called 'path dependency', a self-reinforcing process that maintains and reinforces heterogeneity. Past choices condition present preferences but do not preclude policy innovation entirely. Jones (2007) enters a further word of caution when he notes that 'the impact of globalisation on actual classroom practice has not been as great as one might imagine' (p xv). Here we can understand the relations of states to globalisation, while recognising variations in autonomy, not as a process of making the nation-state redundant but a 'reconfiguration' and 'reshaping' of the role of states. We need to find a subtle balance between what may be common across states, and be related back to processes of globalisation, and what needs to be understood in terms of the particularities of the nation-state. In this chapter the emphasis is on the former; in the following chapter that emphasis will be redressed, to some extent, with an attempt to account for some English particularities in the history of education policy.

In order to begin to understand better some of the influences and mediations of globalisation on education policy and some of the new scales and spaces of policy making, we will look briefly at the work and impact of four multilateral 'agencies': the World Bank, OECD, WTO and EU. In different ways each organisation acts directly and indirectly on national education policy making to reframe policy thinking and in some cases to rework the political and economic possibilities within which such thinking is set.

Education and the World Bank

For the past two decades the World Bank has increased its economic and ideological influence in setting the educational policy agenda, particularly in relation to less developed countries. 'The World Bank lies at the centre of the major changes in global education of our time.... It has served as a major purveyor of western ideas about how education and the economy are, or should be connected' (Jones, 1992, p xiv). The economic crises in sub-Saharan Africa and Latin America in the 1980s, alongside the reduction of bilateral forms of educational aid, created the 'opportunity' for the World Bank through its structural adjustment programmes (SAPs),[6] and loan conditionalities (that is, policy commitments that are required of borrower countries as conditions for loans), to become an influential actor in the process of educational globalisation. Specifically, 'Its commitment to education has been no less than a celebration of human capital theory' (Jones, 1992, p 233) and a 'vigorous' promotion, as Jones puts it, of privatisation, as a response to declining public budgets for education, especially in Africa. This is based, as the World Bank sees it, on the one hand, on 'the willingness of households to contribute resources directly to education' and, on the other, on the inefficient use of resources in schools 'reinforced by the lack of competition between schools' (World Bank, 1986, p 27). Jones notes that 'fewer and fewer Bank loans by the end of the 1980s were free of the obligations imposed by loans conditionality to promote the privatisation of education through the building up of a system of private institutions and the expansion of user charges in the public sector' (1992, p 249). Indeed, this approach to funding policy and the transformation of public sector organisations became an 'inviolate orthodoxy', as ex-World Bank chief economist Joseph Stiglitz calls it (Stiglitz, 2002, p 43). Indeed, the World Bank and International Monetary Fund (IMF) in particular are firmly committed to what is sometimes called the Americanisation of the world economy. Their staff are primarily North American, their headquarters is in the US and most of their funding comes from the US Treasury: 'Building free capital markets into the basic architecture of the world economy had long been, in the words of the US Treasury's (then) Deputy Secretary Lawrence Summers "our most crucial international priority"' (Wade, 2001, p 125). Stiglitz, reflecting on his time as chief economist at the World Bank, describes major decisions taken by the IMF as 'made on the basis of what seemed a curious blend of ideology and bad economics, dogma that sometimes seemed to be thinly veiling special interests' (2002, p xiii).

During the 1990s the World Bank policy hegemony in the economic, social and educational policies for development was subject to serious challenge as SAPs as a mechanism for achieving economic growth appear to have had little positive effect. However, 'while there are some movements in the World Bank agenda, the theory, principles and expected outcomes of the World Bank education policy remain unaltered' (Bonal, 2002, p 5). Jones (2007, p xvi) makes the same point: 'If anything, the Bank has become increasingly insistent, even strident, although it has made serious attempts to moderate its language, soften its image and mollify its critics'.

Education and the Organisation for Economic Co-operation and Development

> If the World Trade Organization (WTO), International Monetary Fund (IMF) and World Bank are the body of globalisation's dark side, the Organisation for Economic Co-operation and Development (OECD) is its head. Although not such a post-Seattle household name as the others, the OECD is the source of the ideology which drives them. It is the crude, lumbering think-tank of the most wealthy nations, bulldozing over human dignity without pause for thought. Its tracks, crushed into the barren dereliction left behind, spell 'global free market'. (Opening passage from a May 2002 non-governmental organisation [NGO] electronic

article 'The OECD's crocodile tears', www.flyingfish.org.uk/articles/oecd/tears.htm)

The OECD's educational policy work is based mainly on research and supranational information management – the instruments of which are published country-by-country and as comparative analyses, statistics and thematic reviews. The OECD differs in particular from other supranational organisations in that its influence over the education policy of the 30 member states is based on the collection, processing, classification, analysing, storing, supplying and marketing of education policy information. The OECD is unable to take any legally binding decisions or issue obligatory education policy recommendations. However, the OECD has developed an advisory role to policy makers at the highest level and thereby exerted a widespread influence on the social and economic policies of its member states in multiple but indirect ways. Policy instruments such as evaluation studies and 'quality monitoring' have sometimes had considerable influence on national education policy. It is 'a globalising agency', an instrument of, forum for and actor in policy, with a central role in the flow of international educational ideas:

> Countries cling to supranational guidelines because accepting the recommendations offered by the OECD, its funding activities, research and reports, and disseminating its end products appear to offer easy, effective and reliable solutions to common problems. This development is especially apparent in the smaller, so-called peripheral member countries of the EU and the OECD. (Rinne et al, 2004, p 476)

The OECD operates through a form of rational peer pressure to disseminate 'what works' in policy terms (see below on UK public sector reforms), in particular policies that have proven to be 'successful' responses to international competition – again the primacy of the economic imperative. However, the OECD does not have a singular educational agenda. Indeed, it represents its educational position in broad terms arguing for instance that education 'will play its crucial role all the better by awakening and sharpening critical intelligence and allowing individuals to move beyond fear, introversion and ethnocentrism' (OECD, 1998, p 117). Nonetheless, of particular prominence in the OECD orthodoxy are what Henry et al (2001) term 'the hollowed out logic of performativity' (p 159) and 'an ascendant neo-liberal paradigm of policy' (p 175), and these are aspects of international policy convergence fostered by the adoption of the organisation's imperatives.

Perhaps one of the simplest and yet most effective of the OECD's policy instruments has been the three-yearly Programme for International Student Assessment (PISA) study results (first published in 2003) carried out in 41 countries (www.pisa.oecd.org/). The 2003 results identified Finland as the industrialised world's most successful education system, followed by Japan and Korea. The result has been an enormous amount of attention by policy makers from many different countries to what Finland is 'doing right'.[7] Countries whose students performed less well are involved in critical self-examination and subjecting themselves to reform. For example:

> Two years on, Germany is still reeling from the shock of the international Pisa study which placed their school children in the bottom third of 32 industrialised countries in reading, mathematics and science. (BBC News Online, 11 May 2004, news.bbc.co.uk/)

Education and the World Trade Organization

The third of the powerful 'multilaterals' in education is the WTO, which replaced the General Agreement on Tariffs and Trade (GATT) in 1995, and which provides a legal and institutional framework for international trade. The WTO is based permanently in Geneva. The Ministerial Conference meets every two years, and appoints the WTO's director-general. By 2001, the WTO had 142 member nations. The outlook underpinning the WTO is deregulation, with incremental 'freedom for transnational capital to do what it wants, where and when it wants' (Tabb, 2000, p 5). As part of the work of the WTO the General Agreement on Trade in Services (GATS) seeks to open up 160 services sectors to international capital – 70% of world economic activity is in the form of services. Specifically, it aims to create a 'level playing field', thereby avoiding discrimination against foreign corporations entering national service markets like education. WTO members committing themselves to opening up primary and secondary education through GATS (as the UK has) must show any limitations on access for foreign suppliers, and then these can be challenged through the WTO Disputes Panel by commercial organisations. Grieshaber-Otto and Sanger have argued:

> At first glance, the GATS does not appear to pose serious or immediate threats to public education.... [Yet it] would be wrong to conclude, however, that WTO rules do not affect public education. The treaty already casts a long shadow over it. The effects of the current treaty, already significant in themselves, can be expected to become more important in the future. (Grieshaber-Otto and Sanger, 2002, p 45)

As yet external private penetration of the UK 'education services market' is fairly limited but foreign companies, like Skanska (Sweden) and Kajima (Japan), are extensively involved in infrastructure work, through private finance initiative (PFI) schemes. The US company Edison (see Saltman, 2005) has a small UK subsidiary that is involved in school improvement work, and in 2007 it was awarded a contract to run a secondary school in Enfield. And 3Es, another small education services contractor, which manages two state schools in Surrey, among other activities, is now owned by General Education Management Systems (GEMS), a Dubai-based company. On the other hand, UK multinational service companies such as SERCO, Capita and Mouchell Parkman have widespread overseas involvements (see Crump and See, 2005; Ball, 2007). The Tenders Electronic Daily Service (www.scottish-enterprise.com/sedotcom_home/about_se/procurement/

tenders/teds.htm) estimates the total value of the public procurement market (contract for public sector work of all kinds) across the EU at £500 billion annually.

Within the EU[8] (see below) 'partnerships' with business are seen as 'an effective framework for mobilizing all available resources for the transition to the knowledge based economy' (EU, 2000, para 41). As Robertson (2002, p 2) explains: 'For key economic actors, like the large transnational firms IBM, Cisco and Nokia, amongst others, participating in the creation of a European educational space means generating the conditions for their investment in the lucrative education market without the impediments of existing institutional arrangements'. These partnerships blur the boundary between the public and private sectors and can work to colonise government and public bodies with ideas and concepts from the private sector and remake public sector actors as entrepreneurs.

Similar developments are evident within policy making in England. Representatives of the private sector are in regular conversation with government and are now part of the 'policy creation community' (Mahony et al, 2004) in much the same way as the teacher trade unions and local education authorities (LEAs) were in the 1950s and 1960s. Companies are now involved within government, giving advice, doing paid consultancies and evaluations of policies or programmes or reviews of departments or functions, or running national programmes and services on contract. In some of these capacities there can be very fine or barely discernible lines between advice, paid work and business advantage. This is part of a process that Mahony et al (2004, p 277) call 'the privatization of policy'.

Education and the European Union

Like the OECD, the EU does not enact education policies as such; this is formally beyond its remit. However, some EU programmes and initiatives (the Bologna Declaration is a case in point) act in effect as policies across EU countries through the process of *harmonisation*. These education policies work towards the creation of a 'European educational space', which is being shaped by various supranational administrative bodies, networks and cultural and economic projects. The 1992 Maastricht Treaty, in which education was formally recognised as one of the central areas of responsibility for the EU, was a turning point in this respect. Again, substantively, this is part of a general shift of emphasis towards a 'knowledge-based economy' and is intended to develop strategies both to increase the production of high-skills workers and to attract overseas students into EU educational institutions. The Lisbon Conference in 2000 mandated the EU to a vision of the 'Europeanisation' of education and the 'European educational model', in which lifelong learning and information play a central role. Increasingly conscious of the importance of education and training for their economic and social objectives, EU member states began working together (using the legislative process known as the 'open method of coordination'). This is referred to as the Education and Training 2010 Programme. The open method rests on soft law mechanisms such as guidelines and indicators, benchmarking and sharing of best practice. This means that there are no official sanctions for those who lag behind. Rather, the method's effectiveness relies on a form of peer pressure and naming and shaming, as no member state wants to be seen as the worst in a given policy area. The member states aim to respond coherently to common challenges, while retaining their individual sovereignty in the field of education policy. The EU also funds educational, vocational and citizenship-building programmes that encourage EU citizens to take advantage of opportunities to live, study and work in other countries.

What we see here is an increasingly complex and increasingly significant set of global and regional influences, pressures and dynamics that impinge on and are embedded in national systems of educational policy making – processes of policy harmonisation, convergence, transfer and borrowing, which are confronted by and enter into diverse local political and cultural histories. In policy analysis the problem is to understand how these policy processes work at a national level. As noted previously the emphasis in this chapter is primarily on the identification of the commonalities and in particular the role of economic imperatives within education policy. The economics of globalisation is an increasingly important point of reference in national educational policy making. Education policies are formed and developed in relation to the supposed pressures of international economic competition; other purposes or outcomes from education are threatened with subordination to economic 'necessities'. The meaning of education and what it means 'to be educated' are changed and a new kind of *flexible, lifelong learner* is articulated by policy in relation to the knowledge economy. In addition, as indicated, education services are now an important international economic commodity in their own right. There are profits to be made from the privatisation of education and from contracts to deliver public education services, and government spending cuts can be traded off against 'other income' earned by public sector educational organisations. In all these ways, education policy can no longer be understood within the limited framework of the nation-state or separate from economic policy.

The focus now turns to the idea of the globalisation of education policy.

Policy epidemics

There is a discernible process of convergence, or what Levin (1998) calls a 'policy epidemic', in education. An unstable, uneven but apparently unstoppable flood of closely interrelated reform ideas is permeating and reorienting education systems in diverse social and political locations with very different histories. This convergence has given rise to what can be called a *generic global policy ensemble* that rests on a set of basic and common *policy technologies*. Below the components of this ensemble and the workings of these technologies will be outlined – *the market*, *management* and *performativity* – and once again one of the recurring themes of this book will be highlighted – the increasing colonisation of education policy by economic policy imperatives.

In outlining the elements of the policy epidemic the aim is not to mount a counter-offensive to the position of relational or vernacular globalisation discussed above. The intention is neither to reassert a simple deterministic logic nor to deny what the deep-seated historical traditions are that are institutionalised in the structures, practices and institutional cultures of each nation, but rather to identify significant 'commonalities within difference'. Furthermore, if these commonalities can be identified, they need then to be interrogated not simply in terms of their structural variety but also in terms of their interrelationships and the resulting political and subjective effects over time. This is expressed well by Apple (1996, p 141): the 'difficult problem of simultaneously thinking about both the specificity of different practices, and the forms of articulated unity they constitute'.

The 'articulated unity' with which we are concerned is embedded in education and public sector services generally by a set of generic reform strategies that make use of a set of policy technologies that work to bring about *new values, new relationships and new subjectivities* in arenas of practice – schools, hospitals, universities, etc. However, these technologies do not totally displace previous forms of organisation or administration or previously important goals and purposes for education.

We can begin by considering an OECD report, *Governance in transition: Public management reforms in OECD countries* (1995). The OECD, with an odd but telling blend of description and imperative, summarises these reforms as a 'new paradigm for public management':

- a closer focus on results in terms of efficiency, effectiveness and quality of service;
- the replacement of highly centralised, hierarchical organisational structures by decentralised management environments where decisions on resources allocation and service delivery are made closer to the point of delivery, and which provide scope for feedback from clients and other interest groups;
- the flexibility to explore alternatives to direct public provision and regulation that might yield more cost-effective policy outcomes;
- a greater focus on efficiency in the services provided directly by the public sector, involving the establishment of productivity targets and

the creation of competitive environments within and among public sector organisations; and
- the strengthening of strategic capacities at the centre to guide the evolution of the state and allow it to respond to external changes and diverse interests automatically, flexibly, and at least cost. (OECD, 1995, p 8)

This is just one version of the generic global policy ensemble but the three policy technologies to which we return to shortly are embedded here. The reverberations of this 'new paradigm' can be traced very directly through the reforms of education undertaken in England over the past two decades (see Chapter Two) and they are very clearly embedded in *The UK government's approach to public sector reform* (Cabinet Office, 2006) (a document discussed in Chapter Three). But there is something else going on here. These public sector reforms reflect, respond to and reinforce changes in the forms and modalities of the modern state – how it goes about its business and achieves its goals, that is, changes in the policy process and new methods of governing society. In its simplest sense this is the shift from government to governance, that is, a shift from the government of a unitary state to governance in and by networks. What is emerging here is a new 'architecture of regulation' based on interlocking relationships between disparate sites in and beyond the state. It is a new mode of state control – a controlled decontrol, the use of contracts, targets and performance monitoring to 'steer' from a distance, rather than the use of traditional bureaucracies and administrative systems to deliver or micro-manage policy systems, such as education or health or social services. In general terms this is the move towards a more 'polycentric state' and 'a shift in the centre of gravity around which policy cycles move' (Jessop, 1998, p 32).

Policy technologies

Policy technologies involve the calculated deployment of forms of organisation and procedures, and disciplines or bodies of knowledge, to organise human forces and capabilities into functioning systems.

Various disparate elements are interrelated within these technologies: involving relationships, procedures of motivation, mechanisms of change and particular loyalties and responsibilities. Some of the key elements embedded in these technologies are presented in Table 1.1.

Table 1.1: The language of reform technologies

	Market	Management	Performance
Subject positions	Consumers Producers Entrepreneurs	Manager(s)/ leader(s) Managed/ workforce Teams	Appraisee Comparator
Discipline	Survival Income maximisation	Efficiency/ effectiveness Corporate culture	Productivity Targets Achievement Comparison
Values	Competition Institutional interests	'What works'	The performative worth of individuals Fabrication

The 'policy technologies' of education reform are generic in two senses: as part of a global convergence in reform strategies, as suggested already, and as deployed across the public sector as a whole. They constitute a 'one-size-fits-all' model for the 'transformation' and 'modernisation' of public sector organisations and systems. They interrelate and complement one another and work on individual practitioners, work groups and whole organisations to reconstitute social relations, forms of esteem and value, sense of purpose and notions of excellence and good practice. These technologies are devices for changing the meaning of practice and of social relationships. They provide a new language, a new set of incentives and disciplines and a new set of roles, positions and identities within which what it means to be a teacher, student/learner, parent and so on are all changed. Targets, accountability, competition and choice, leadership, entrepreneurism, performance-related pay and privatisation articulate new ways of thinking about what we do, what we value and what our purposes are. They work together to render education as like a 'commodity' rather than a public good (see Thrupp and Willmott, 2003, p 13). They bring into play new roles and relationships, those of client/consumer and competitor, manager/managed, contractor, appraiser/inspector/monitor, and they exclude or marginalise previous roles, loyalties and subjectivities. They change what is important and valuable and necessary.

The central figure in all of this is a relatively new actor on the stage of public sector organisations – the manager. The term 'educational management' began to be used in the 1970s, and brought with it a set of methods, ideals and concepts (objectives, resources, performance, monitoring, accountability) from the private sector. The manager became an agent of change and a cipher for policy (see Chapter Three on leadership). Significant education policy shifts from the 1980s on (see Chapter Two) gave managers devolved powers to control their organisational budgets, their workforce and internal decision making in innovative and creative ways to achieve new goals and purposes. The purpose of such devolution, as the OECD put it, 'is to encourage managers to focus on results by providing them with flexibility and autonomy in the use of both financial and human resources' (1995, p 8). This is 'the right to manage'. Throughout the installation of this new paradigm into public service organisations the use of new language is important, the new public management organisations are now 'peopled' by human resources that need to be managed, learning is re-rendered as a 'cost-effective policy outcome' and achievement is a set of 'productivity targets' and so on.

The scope and complexity of these reforms are breathtaking, extending from the ways in which teaching and learning is organised in classrooms, to new state modalities. However, crucially it is a mis-recognition to see these reform processes as simply a strategy of devolution and deregulation – they are processes of *reregulation*, not the abandonment by the state of its controls over public services but the establishment of a new form of control, what du Gay (1996) calls 'controlled decontrol', the use of devolution and autonomy as 'freedoms' set within the constraints and requirements of 'performance' and 'profitability'. As stressed by the OECD, a new relationship of the state to the public sector is envisaged, especially in 'exploring alternatives to direct public provision' and making service provision 'contestable and competitive': 'Corporatisation and privatisation are important policy options in this context' (OECD, 1995, p 9) (see Chapter Three). In England these options have been pursued with particular vigour. First under the Thatcher and Major Conservative governments and subsequently by Labour in the terms of the 'third way' through the use of surrogate or 'quasi-markets', contracting-out/outsourcing, privatisation and various forms of public–private partnership (PPP).

To reiterate, the new public service paradigm is a reform 'package'. This is important in several senses. First, because at certain times in different locations particular aspects of the package may be emphasised and others played down. Second, the processes of enactment of reform have to be viewed over time and in terms of the relationship of various elements. Again, as the OECD put it: 'A "selective radical" strategy for implementing reform may be the preferred solution ... complete re-design of governance structures is impossible' (1995, p 9). They go on to make the point that 'reform is a journey rather than a destination' (p 9) and that reform involves 'trade-offs'. These journeys and trade-offs will differ between countries and the extent or significance of them in any location is an empirical question. Third, these reform processes are not just a matter of introducing new structures and incentives but also require and bring about new relationships, cultures and values. The OECD note that 'This fundamental change in outlook has engaged all Member countries in a difficult process of cultural change' (1995, p 8), central to which is 'developing a performance-oriented culture' (p 8). Perhaps disingenuously the OECD note that concerns have been raised about 'an erosion' of 'traditional public service values' (1995, p 8). The new paradigm is set over and against, and is intended to replace or overlay, the older technologies of professionalism and bureaucracy, which have their own languages, identities and forms of social relations.

We will return to the issue of cultural change or 'reculturation' at several points in the book.

Now some of the specific ways in which these technologies work *to transform* and discipline public sector organisations and *to link* the processes and endeavours of such organisations to the political economy of global competition will be briefly outlined.

Market form

The creation of education markets rests on the introduction of the dynamics of competition into public sector systems with the effect of breaking them down into separate 'business' units, that is, competition between providers – schools, colleges and universities – to recruit students in order to maximise their 'income'. Competition as a device is only effective when market 'failure' impacts on the survival or well-being of individual organisations. In education the competitive dynamic is animated by parental and student choice – the removal or weakening of bureaucratic controls over school recruitment, together with support for and encouragement of choice and of movement around the system. However, education markets, or quasi-markets as they are called, are not in any simple sense 'free markets'. As Sayer (1995, p 104) points out, 'markets are social constructions whose birth is difficult and requires considerable regulation and involvement by the state'.

The new policy paradigm, and the market form in particular, constitutes a *new moral environment* for both consumers and producers, that is, a form of 'commercial civilisation'. Within this new moral environment schools, colleges and universities are being inducted into a *culture of self-interest*. Self-interest is manifest in terms of *survivalism* – an increased, often predominant, orientation towards the internal well-being of the institution and its members and a shift away from concern with more general social and educational issues within 'the community'. In 1995 Sharon Gewirtz, Richard Bowe and I (Gewirtz et al, 1995) noted several examples of such shifts of orientation. Three of the 14 schools that we studied abandoned or played down well-established work with students with special needs in order to recruit 'more able' students. Drawing on our subsequent research, Gewirtz (2002) outlines the 'values drift' evident in one school coming to grips with the 'demands' of the local market and, drawing on the same research, Reay (1998) gives an account of another school that abandoned its mixed-ability grouping in favour of streaming in anticipation of the perceptions and preferences of middle-class parents engaged in school choice. Within the 'opportunity structures' created by parental choice teachers are 'no longer *servants of* but ... *entrepreneurs for* an institution' (Scott, 1996, p 104; emphases in original). Here the rethinking of education in economic terms bites deep into institutional practices and values.

Within such arenas of competition Willmott (1993, p 522) suggests 'employees are simultaneously required, individually and collectively, to recognise and *take responsibility for* the relationship between the security of their employment and their contribution to the competitiveness of the goods and services they produce'. New administrative procedures are generated that 'make individuals "want" what the system needs in order to perform well' (Lyotard, 1984, p 62). We are encouraged to see our own 'development' as linked to and provided for by the 'growth' of our institution. Advocates of the market tend to approach the issues of values in one of two ways; either they see the market as simply value-neutral, as a mechanism for the delivery of education that is more efficient or responsive or effective, or present the market as possessing a set of positive moral values in its own right – effort, thrift, self-reliance, independence and risk taking, what is called 'virtuous self-interest'. Those taking the latter view clearly acknowledge, indeed proselytise, the market as a transformational force that carries and disseminates its own values.

The first nation to engage in a thoroughgoing market reform of education was New Zealand. A Labour Party government, several of whose key members had been educated within and influenced by the Chicago School of free market economics, introduced a new educational structure in 1988 based on the recommendations of the Picot Report (named after the businessman who chaired the

Taskforce to Review Educational Administration). The size of the central bureaucracy of educational administration was reduced, regional education boards were abolished, and each educational institution was given devolved powers over budgets, staffing, support services and staff development as self-managing units with elected boards of trustees. The state agencies, the Ministry, the Education Review Office and the Qualifications Authority, retained or indeed increased their control of national education policy – the state would 'steer' rather than 'row', another example of 'controlled decontrol'. There are both similarities and differences between these reforms and those following the 1988 Education Reform Act in England (see Chapter Two for details). The background to the reforms in New Zealand was primarily economic while in England they had strong political antecedents, relating to criticisms of teachers, the curriculum and progressive educational methods (see Chapters Two and Three). The New Zealand reforms did not have the 'neo-conservative' elements that underpinned important parts of the English 1988 Education Reform Act (for more on differences see Dale and Ozga, 1993).

Management

As noted already, management, or perhaps more accurately 'new public management' (NPM), has been the key mechanism in the political reform and cultural re-engineering of public sectors for the past 20 years. It has been the primary means 'through which the structure and culture of public services are recast. In doing so it seeks to introduce new orientations, remodels existing relations of power and affects how and where social policy choices are made' (Clarke et al, 1994, p 4). Management represents the insertion of a new mode of power into the public sector; it is a 'transformational force', and it plays a key role in the wearing away of professional-ethical regimes in schools and their replacement by entrepreneurial-competitive regimes – a process of 'de-professionalisation' (see Olssen et al, 2005, p 185).

The manager is the cultural hero of the new public service paradigm. The work of the manager involves instilling the attitude and culture within which workers feel themselves as accountable and committed or personally invested in the organisation (as indicated above). Such developments are deeply paradoxical. On the one hand, they are frequently presented as a move away from bureaucratic, centralised, forms of employee control. Managerial responsibilities are delegated, initiative and problem solving are highly valued. On the other hand, new forms of very immediate surveillance and self-monitoring are put in place, for example, appraisal systems, target setting, output comparisons. This is what management 'gurus' Peters and Waterman (1982) refer to as 'simultaneously loose and tight' – another version of 'controlled decontrol'. NPM is preoccupied with quality and accountability.

Clarke et al (2000, p 6) ascribe the following features to NPM:

- Attention to outputs and performance rather than inputs.
- Organisations being viewed as chains of low-trust relationships, linked by contracts or contractual type processes.
- The separation of purchaser and provider or client and contractor role within formerly integrated processes or organisations.
- Breaking down large scale organisations and using competition to enable 'exit' or 'choice' by service users.
- Decentralization of budgetary and personal authority to line managers.

Troman's (2000, p 349) case study work in UK primary schools found 'low trust' to be in the ascendant in most of those studied, creating a 'culture of distrust'. They noted a proliferation of formal 'security seeking' tactics, and resultant physical and emotional damage to teachers who displayed high levels of 'existential anxiety and dread'. In her 2002 Reith lectures, philosopher O'Neill (2002) discussed what she called 'a crisis of trust' in contemporary society, arguing that new and overbearing forms of accountability distort the proper aims of professional practice and rest on control rather than integrity.

The act of teaching and the subjectivity of the teacher are both profoundly changed within the new management emphases on performance, quality and excellence and the market imperatives of competition and choice. Through the cultivation of 'corporate culture' managers 'seek to delineate, normalise and instrumentalise the conduct of persons in order to achieve the ends they postulate as desirable' (du Gay, 1996, p 61). Through the micro-disciplines of management public sector organisations become part of a 'bigger picture', part of a larger ideological narrative and organisational strategy of the enterprise culture. In this and other ways educational institutions are now being expected to take on the qualities and characteristics of 'fast capitalism' (Gee and Lankshear, 1996). Gee and Lankshear specifically use the term 'fast capitalism' (or 'new capitalism') to describe an enterprise-oriented view that emphasises an enterprise's adaptability, dynamism, flattened hierarchy and continual reskilling/learning; the term applies to an entire enterprise, from manufacturing to service to management:

> The fast capitalist world is one that celebrates temporary and fast-changing networks, whether of co-workers or different businesses. The networks come together for a given project and disperse into other configurations as products, projects, and services change in the hypercompetitive and fast paced environment of the new capitalism. (Gee and Lankshear, 1996, p 40)

Performativity

Performativity is a culture or a system of 'terror'. It is a regime of accountability that employs judgements, comparisons and displays as means of control, attrition and change. The performances of individual subjects or organisations serve as measures of productivity or output, or displays of 'quality', or 'moments' of promotion or inspection. These performances stand for, encapsulate or represent the worth, quality or value of an individual or organisation within a field of judgement. Clearly, the issue of who controls the field of judgement and what is judged, what criteria of measurement are used or benchmarks or targets set, is crucial. The setting, monitoring and reviewing of performance, and the rewarding of performance achievements, are all critical and effective tools of management – hence 'performance management' as a method to achieve a constant state of 'activation' within organisations. One consequence of this is new kinds of 'professional dominance', that is, the logics of accountants, lawyers and managers, are made more powerful over and against the judgements of teachers, doctors and social workers, and so on.

The culture of performativity in practical terms rests on databases, appraisal meetings, annual reviews, report writing, quality assurance visits, the regular publication of results, inspections and peer reviews. The teacher, researcher and academic are subject to a myriad of judgements, measures, comparisons and targets. Information is collected continuously, recorded and published, often in the form of league tables, and performance is also monitored eventfully by peer reviews, site visits and inspections. Within all this, there is a sense of being constantly judged in different ways, by different means, according to different criteria, through different agents and agencies. There is a flow of changing demands, expectations and indicators that makes one continually accountable and constantly recorded. And yet it is not always very clear what is expected. Indeed, Shore and Wright (1999, p 569) argue, in relation to UK HE systems of accountability, that there is an undeclared policy 'to keep systems volatile, slippery and opaque'. Not infrequently, the requirements of such systems bring into being unhelpful or indeed damaging practices, which nonetheless satisfy performance requirements. Thus, performativity has the 'capacity to reshape in their own image the organizations they monitor' (Shore and Wright, 1999, p 570) and make individuals responsible for monitoring and disciplining themselves, to make them responsive and flexible:

> What is imposed is simultaneously limited and expansive. It is limited in the extent to which performance management focuses school leadership on to the core tasks of enhancing pupil progress against measurable criteria; but expansive in the extent to which the language and assumptions of

> performance management describe a cultural refocusing of schooling. (Husbands, 2001, p 10)

Crucially, all of this has social and interpersonal dimensions. The disciplines of performance are folded into complex institutional, team, group and communal relations (for example, the academic community, the school, the subject department, the university). But the consequences and effects have to be coped with by individuals, as ethical subjects find their values challenged or displaced by the terrors of performativity. The following quotations, taken from an article in the education section of *The Guardian* (9 January 2001), illustrate the struggles and dilemmas experienced by some teachers who find their professional commitments and personal well being at odds with the demands of performance:

> What happened to my creativity? What happened to my professional integrity? What happened to the fun in teaching and learning? What happened? (G.E. Johnson)

> I find myself thinking that the only way I can save my sanity, my health and my relationship with my future husband is to leave the profession. I don't know what else I could do, having wanted to teach all my life, but I feel I am being forced out, forced to choose between a life and teaching. (name supplied)

> I was a primary school teacher for 22 years but left in 1996 because I was not prepared to sacrifice the children for the glory of politicians and their business plans for education. (Christopher Draper)

However, the work of performativity also produces what Lyotard (1984) calls the 'law of contradiction'. This contradiction arises between intensification as an increase in the volume of first-order activities (direct engagement with students, research, curriculum development) required by the demands of performativity and the 'transaction costs' in terms of time and energy of second-order activities, that is, the work of collecting performance data, monitoring and reporting. Acquiring the performative information necessary for perfect control 'consumes so much energy that it drastically reduces the energy available for making improvement inputs' (Elliott, 1996, p 15).

Together, management, the market and performativity have effects of various sorts on interpersonal and role relationships (vertical and horizontal) within schools, colleges and universities:

a) increased emotional pressures and stress related to work;
b) the increased pace and intensification of work;
c) changed social relationships. There is evidence of increased, sometimes intentional, competition between teachers and departments. There is a concomitant decline in the sociability of school life. Professional relationships become increasingly individualised as opportunities for communities and professional discourse diminish and relationships are made amenable to and redefined as a 'contract' form or ones of 'contractual implication' within and between institutions;
d) an increase in paperwork, systems maintenance and report production and the use of these to generate performative and comparative information systems;
e) increased surveillance of teachers' work and outputs;
f) a developing gap, in values, purpose and perspective, between senior staff, with a primary concern with balancing the budget, recruitment, public relations and impression management, and teaching staff, with a primary concern with curriculum coverage, classroom control, students' needs and record keeping.

These technologies of public sector reform work in complex ways to bring about practical, cultural and discursive changes. They combine to rework organisational and state forms and practices into what Osborne and Gaebler (1992) call 'entrepreneurial government'. They change the ways in which we think about the public sector and its relationships, values and methods and embed a particular 'ethic of personhood'. In doing so, they reorient the public sector and education very specifically to requirements of the 'new' global economy, the knowledge economy, and thus to the demands and imperatives of globalisation. Bottery warns that 'nation states are in danger of becoming servants of global markets, their education systems providing the human resources to feed them' (2000, p vii).

What is argued in this chapter is that education policy is increasingly subordinated to and articulated in terms of economic policy and the necessities of international competition. The second part of the chapter sought to show how these necessities within policy are brought to bear directly within educational organisations through the technologies of the generic global policy ensemble.

The point has also been made several times that such global policies 'enter' very different national systems with particular cultural and political histories and are mediated by them. In the next chapter we will focus on one such system and its history – England – and see how the generic global policy ensemble has been played out within it.

Notes

[1] Transfer or borrowing of policies leads to diffusion but does not automatically lead to convergence (see Jakobi, 2005).

[2] See Novoa (2002). The idea of 'planetspeak discourses' refers to a way of reasoning that seems to have no structural roots, no social locations and no origin.

[3] Charles Leadbeater was a contributing author to this paper.

[4] A national ideology is 'a set of values and beliefs that frames the practical thinking and action of agents of the main institutions of a nation-state at a given point in time' (van Zanten, 1997).

[5] See Hampden-Turner and Trompenaars (1994), who conducted research on 15,000 business managers in seven different countries and identified distinct contrasts in the mindsets and ideologies of their respondents.

[6] 'Structural adjustment' is a term used to describe the policy changes implemented by the International Monetary Fund (IMF) and the World Bank (the Bretton Woods Institutions) in developing countries. These policy changes are conditions (conditionalities) for getting new loans from the IMF or World Bank, or for obtaining lower interest rates on existing loans. Conditionalities are implemented to ensure that the money lent will be spent in accordance with the overall goals of the loan. SAPs are created with the goal of reducing the borrowing country's fiscal imbalances.

[7] The Helsinki Department of Education now hosts 2,500 foreign visitors a year who come to see 'how Finland gets it right' (personal communication, Head of International Affairs).

[8] The most important of the EU institutions include the Council of the European Union, the European Commission, the European Court of Justice, the European Parliament, the European Council and the European Central Bank. The European Parliament dates back to the 1950s and the founding treaties, and since 1979 its members have been elected by EU citizens.

2

Class, comprehensives and continuities: a short history of English education policy

> From its late beginnings, public education was weakly developed in England, sapped by private and voluntary provision, fragmented, exclusionary and lacking in public support. (Johnson, 1991, p 32)

Policy is, by definition, restless and future-oriented and often works rhetorically by devaluing the present and making 'it ugly, abhorrent and unendurable' (Bauman, 1991, p 11). This arises in good part from 'the natural inclination of modern practice – intolerance' (p 8). Nonetheless, in practice most policy works by accretion and sedimentation, new policies add to and overlay old ones, with the effect that new principles and innovations are merged and conflated with older rationales and previous practices. There are rarely 'clean slates' for policy makers to work with and practitioners are as a result frequently left with inconsistencies and contradictions that they must solve, suffering criticism if they do not. Policy always has to be viewed in terms of both change and continuity – what changes and what stays the same.

To try to make sense of the present state of English education policy there is an emphasis here on both major changes and significant continuities – as Simon (1994) calls them, 'advances and retreats'. The particular lens through which policy history will be viewed is that of social class. The history is organised into four policy periods that are marked off from one another by *ruptures*, related to more general political and economic *shifts* (see Table 2.1). Each of these ruptures is also associated with changes in the *form and modalities of the state* (how it is organised and how it works). Attention shall also be drawn within each period to the role of 'policy intellectuals'.

It is important to recognise this way of presenting the history of policy as an heuristic device – a tool for thinking about the issues rather than an attempt at a comprehensive and detailed descriptive account of things. The periodisation of history always obscures as much as it reveals and the divisions between periods are often rough and ready and tend to exaggerate the extent of change. The other point to emphasise is that ruptures are particular points of struggle within the field of education policy 'between what are often opposing, or at least antagonistic social forces' (Simon, 1994, p 15). Most attention is given here to the last and most recent of these points of struggle.

1870-1944

State education emerged in the 19th century in response to the need to manage the new urban working classes and to accommodate the social and political aspirations of the new middle classes, a policy duality still relevant in contemporary educational politics.

The 1841 Census indicated that Britain had become the first urban society with more people living in towns and cities than in the countryside. London was the largest city in the world. Mass migration, internal and external, into the cities in the 19th century (first economic shift) produced enormous social and political problems that were responded to slowly and not without struggle by the development of a social state that began to provide education, public sanitation systems, health and social statistics and forms of social welfare and regulation through the work of the modern professions, such as teachers, social workers, health inspectors and probation officers. 'The urban' was then and is now a repository and magnifier of social problems. Forms of disorder that were regarded as threatening political stability were manifested in crime, juvenile delinquency, changing kinship structures and gender relations and 'race' immigration. These are still currently the focus of much of policy intervention. Concerns then about management of the empire and 'national efficiency' are paralleled

Table 2.1: Shifts, ruptures and the state

Shift	Rupture	State
1870-1944		
Political problems of management of urban working-class migrations and imperial industrial development and trade	Break with liberal resistance to state education and welfare	Modern (or interventionist) state
1944-76		
Postwar economic growth and the expansion of the middle class	Move to universalist welfare state education – national system locally administered	Welfare state
1976-97		
Economic crises, mass unemployment and shift from Fordist to post-Fordist regime of accumulation and the first stage of deindustrialisation	Break from emerging comprehensive national system and the end of professional autonomy for teachers and schools	Neoliberal state
1997-2007		
Assertion of the knowledge economy and new forms of work	End of a national system locally administered	Managerial or competition state

by those associated currently with globalisation and international competitiveness:

> The freedom of the casual labourer to live out his degenerate existence and reproduce his kind in filthy overcrowded slums was now seen as a lethal menace to 'national efficiency'. Draconic measures would be necessary if the empire was not to be dragged down by its unfit. Overcrowding and casual living conditions were not a misfortune but a crime. (Stedman Jones, 1984, p 331)

Alongside this politics of fearfulness focused on the urban working class, another specific class group were emerging as politically and socially significant in the 19th century, a 'new middle class' of industrialists, managers and professionals 'placed above the atmosphere of mingled suffering and recklessness which poverty creates, and below that of luxurious idleness and self-worship which surrounds great wealth' (Tod, 1874, p 3, quoted in Power et al, 2003, p 7):

> From the mid-late eighteenth century there took place, and strengthened, the industrial and commercial middle-class as a specific sector, one which rapidly became conscious of itself as a class in the early nineteenth century and which now articulated a specific education policy both for its own members and for the newly developing working class. (Simon, 1994, p 15)

In the 1830s education began to be recognised as an issue in which the state needed to take an interest – financial grants were made by a newly established education department within government to teacher training colleges being set up by Anglican and Nonconformist churches, although when the annual grant for the department was established parliament as a whole was barely interested. Until 1870 direct provision of elementary schooling was left almost entirely to 'dame schools',[1] church societies and voluntary organisations that were at that point supplemented by ('filling in the gaps'), then later incorporated into, the state school board system. 'Church schools' remain a significant factor and a focus of controversy within education policy to this day.

Timmins (2001, p 67) suggests that 'by opting to subsidise church schools rather than create secular state ones, Parliament invested in a problem Butler [see below] would still be grappling with more than a century later'.[2] The focus of state intervention prior to 1870 was on the training of teachers, encouraging the creation of teacher training colleges that were designed to ensure that the character of teachers would be appropriate as role models for their working-class students, and the expansion of Her Majesty's Inspectors (HMI) of schools. In 1862 a system of inspection based on 'payment by results'[3] (The Revised Code), as recommended by the Newcastle Commission, was introduced and remained in place until 1897. It constituted an essentially economic model of funding based on output measures – an early form of performativity (see Chapter One). Pupils were examined annually by an inspector, the amount of the governmental grant paid to individual schools largely depending on their performance.

As a 'system' of education began to emerge during the 19th century, in partial, halting and reluctant fashion, its form was modelled on the changing class structure. Elementary schooling provision rested primarily on the efforts of the Church of England (The National Society for Promoting the Education of the Poor in the Principles of the Established Church), Nonconformist (British and Foreign School Society) and Catholic schools societies and other voluntary and informal arrangements. In 1818 just 7% of children attended a day school and further growth was slow although faster than that of the population. By 1870 about 700,000 six- to ten-year-olds were in schools, while about one million were not (Timmins, 2001, p 68).

It is difficult to understand the slow progress towards a free, state-provided system in the 19th century until we grasp that education had long been regarded as a family decision, an issue of freedom from the state. Its provision by deeply antagonistic, powerful denominational groups ensured that state interference was resisted until regulation became a matter of urgent social control and economic improvement that philanthropy was failing to meet adequately. Best (1973, p 170) characterises 19th-century education policy as deliberately patterned to perpetuate class differences, magnifying 'its structure in detail', or putting 'education in a straightjacket of class' (Perkin, 1969, p 302). Indeed Hoppen (1998, p 101) notes 'the class tendency of much interventionist legislation' in the Victorian period and that 'many reforms had class-specific overtones and even intentions' (p 100), and R.H. Tawney wrote (1931, p 142) that 'the hereditary curse of English education has been its organization along the lines of social class'. This classed approach to education planning is clearly illustrated through the work and recommendations of the three great school commissions that were set up in the late 19th century to examine and make recommendations for the future of educational provision:

Newcastle Commission 1861: elementary schools
Clarendon Commission 1864: Royal Commission on Public Schools
Schools Inquiry Commission 1868 (Taunton Commission): grammar and endowed schools

The 1861 Newcastle Commission (The Report of the Commissioners appointed to Inquire into the State of Popular Education in England) found that education provision was limited and standards low. Only one in seven poor children attended school, often on a casual basis. By the age of 10, most had left to find work. Newcastle's chief monument to the 19th-century system was payment by results. The 1864 Clarendon Commission set out to report on and recommend reform and reinvigoration of the 'great' public schools (for example, Eton, Harrow), which were, at least formally, entirely independent of the state. According to the Commission, these schools were to follow a classical curriculum and science and technology were deliberately eschewed. They were to concern themselves with the reproduction of the culture and manners of the old and new 'upper classes'. The Schools Inquiry Commission (Taunton Commission) concerned itself with those grammar and 'endowed' schools that existed between the public and elementary schools; its investigations revealed the poor provision of secondary education, the uneven distribution of schools across the country and the misuse of endowments. It also showed that there were only 13 secondary schools for girls in the whole of England and Wales. The commissioners recommended the establishment of a national system of secondary education based on existing endowed schools, and the resulting 1869 Endowed Schools Act created the Endowed Schools Commission to draw up new schemes of government for them. Three grades of fee-paying school were outlined, excluding working-class students but matched to different fractions (lower, middle and upper) of the middle class, each with their own curriculum and leaving ages (14, 16 and 18 respectively). The basic assumption for education policy was, as Matthew Arnold, a member of the Newcastle Commission, put it: '[T]he education of each class in society has, or ought to have, its ideal, determined by the wants of that class, and by its destination' (Arnold, 1864/1969, p 112, quoted in McCulloch, 2006).

The work of the three Commissions formed the basis for what Simon (1991, p 12) calls 'the emergent system'. Three separate school systems developed (elementary for the working class, secondary for the middle class and private public schools for the ruling class), and a national system locally controlled and delivered for elementary, then secondary, schools was gradually put in place by a series of Acts in 1870, 1880, 1899 and 1902. (Welsh education began to diverge from the English system of provision at this point.) The 1870 Act was not a progressive reforming measure but rather was a political rearguard action, a compromise with voluntarism, going against the grain of 19th-century liberal political thought:

> The very complexity of the new social and economic environment and the comparative caution of the mid-Victorian elites meant that comprehensive and drastic solutions rarely seemed attractive let alone plausible. (Hoppen, 1998, p 91)

The 1870 Act left the administration of schooling and building of new state schools to local school boards who ran 3,692 schools by 1883, although in 1902 voluntary elementary schools still outnumbered state schools two-to-one. Compulsion was not introduced (for 5- to

10-year-olds) until 1881, while provision for 10- to 14-year-olds differed widely around the country. Fees were not abolished until 1891, a move viewed with alarm by many politicians and commentators. In introducing the 1870 Bill, W.E. Forster had argued that providing the full cost of elementary education would be 'not only be unnecessary but mischievous'. Nonetheless, the annual central education vote rose from £1.6 million in 1870, 4.1% of government expenditure, to £2.2 million in 1885, 8.6% of expenditure, in addition to local and voluntary funding.

The administration of education in the period 1870-1902 has been described as 'chaotic' (Archer, 1979). A fully universal, compulsory and free elementary education system was established only at the beginning of the 20th century. This kind of vacillation by the state and the processes of 'dissolution and conservation' (Brehony, 1985), embedded from the outset in its emergent system of education, will be evident again later. Nonetheless, things were gradually set in place, the infrastructure of a modern bureaucratic state system of education was established and continued to evolve between 1868 and 1902. Schooling became accepted as a social right, and it was within the field of education that a commitment to universalism first became embedded in state policy. The democratic and radical glimmerings that were represented by the directly elected but unwieldy system of 2,500 school boards were snuffed out by their abolition in 1902 and the responsibility for the provision and management of education was passed to local authorities as part of a unification of the central control of schooling. Finally, a board of education was also established by the 1902 Act.

Using a slightly different time frame, Hall and Schwarz (1985) describe the late 19th and early years of the 20th century as a period of 'profound crisis of the British state', a 'crisis of liberalism' representing a 'sharp historical discontinuity from the period which preceded it' (p 7), that is, a transition to a new 'collectivist' and 'interventionist' form of state organisation and social regulation, that eventually superseded the laissez-faire tendencies that had prevailed during most of the 19th century. In education the slow and reluctant move from non-interventionism is best represented by debates and tensions that surrounded the passing of the 1870 Education Act and the introduction of a system of school boards 'to fill in the gaps at least cost of public money' (W.E. Forster, who drafted the Act and had the responsibility of guiding it through parliament) left by existing provision of church and voluntary schools, 'sparing public money where it can be done without', as Forster put it. However, the passing of the Act also needs to be understood in relation to the newly significant extension of voting rights in 1867 and the political disturbances that had contributed to this extension. As Robert Lowe (Chancellor of the Exchequer) put it, despite his own ambivalences, the move to a state education system was 'a question of self preservation', the lower classes must be 'educated that they may appreciate and defer to a higher cultivation when they meet it' and 'to qualify them for the power that has passed ... into their hands' (Speech in House of Commons Debate on Education Bill). As Brehony (1985, p 270) suggests, the process of education reform and gradual centralisation of control was 'activated by a powerful fear of the working class'.

Part of this 'fear' that informed and stirred the process of reform came about, as noted already, from the problems of management of new urban populations. Internal migration from the countryside and from Ireland produced massive social problems in cities around housing, disease and political unrest. The form of the modern state and its 'positive disciplines', such as education, can be seen as a response to such problems and the making of a 'useful and docile' workforce. In elementary education considerable emphasis was given to both moral training and applicable skills. Indeed, the public activities of the state were gradually but slowly expanding and changing from the 1830s onward, and apparatuses of state practice in the social fields of poverty, health, sanitation and housing were being established and the legal framework of state controls were being extended. A key technology of emerging governance was 'state professionalism' with its 'expert' and esoteric knowledges ranging from social statistics to forms of psychology and eugenics. These state professionalisms (like teaching, social work, public health, and so on) were one of the important bases for the construction of the modern welfare state.

However, an important caveat needs to be entered here. As pointed out by Hall and Schwarz (1985), movement towards such a 'peculiarly British collectivism' did not mark total collapse of the classical liberalism that it usurped but, rather, 'neo-liberalism was coextensive with the formation of collectivist ideologies' and 'the project of neo-liberalism was systematically to contest and where possible uproot the political conditions in which collectivism flourished' (p 30). This remained particularly significant in the post-1976 period when, according to Green (1991, p 7), the liberal ideology of voluntarism 'continued in modified form into the modern period and has continued to undermine efforts to create a viable system of public education to this day'. Indeed, when I interviewed Keith Joseph (Conservative Secretary of State for Education, 1981-86) in 1989, he identified the major problems with the contemporary education system, in classical liberal terms, as being compulsion and state monopoly:

> We have a bloody state system, I wish we hadn't got. I wish we'd taken a different route in 1870. We got the ruddy state involved. I don't want it. I don't think we know how to do it. I certainly don't think Secretaries of State know anything about it. But we're landed with it. If we could move back to 1870 I would take a different route. We've got compulsory education, which is a responsibility of hideous importance, and we tyrannise children to do that which they don't want, and we don't produce results.

Versions of the 19th-century tiered and classed model of education continued up to the Second World War and in modified form for a period after until the system could no longer contain and satisfy the aspirations of the growing middle classes (second economic shift), nor be electorally defended either on economic grounds or in terms of fairness and equity. However, the relatively early and successful period of industrialisation in Britain pre-empted the sorts of economic pressures for educational expansion and technical education that were evident among Britain's major competitors, such as Germany. Both structure and content were resistant to change, although when W.E. Forster introduced the 1870 Bill to the House of Commons, sounding remarkably like the former Prime Minister Tony Blair (see Chapter One), he noted that:

> Civilized communities are massing themselves together, each mass being measured by its force: and if we are to hold our position among … the nations of the world we must make up the smallness of our numbers by increasing the intellectual force of the individual.

1944-76

By 1938 a total of 88% of children were attending 'all-age' schools up to the age of 14. Classes of 50 or more were not unusual and only one in 150 of these children ended up at university. A small, mainly lower middle-class group were selected at the age of 11 for 'special places' at local authority secondary schools where, overall, 45% of places were free. Still smaller middle- and upper-class groups attended independent grammar schools or public schools. Schooling reflected the gradations of society – only one in seven children remaining at school after the age of 13, the intake to grammar schools increasing only slightly from 90,000 in 1921 to 98,000 in 1938. Barnett (1986) called this a 'half-cock' education system where the figures for secondary participation compared poorly not only with Scotland and Wales but also Germany, France and the US.

The 1944 Education Act, drawing on the Norwood (1943) and Spens Reports (1938) reflected a strong sense within government that social and economic changes made the reform of post-war education an urgent necessity. However, while the Act may have established the principle of universal and free secondary education for all, the division into grammar, secondary modern and sometimes technical schools, different types of school for different 'types' of student with different 'types of mind', was clearly modelled on a class-divided vision of education, albeit a more porous one than previously. Rather than class per se and ability to pay it was 11 Plus attainment testing, which also included an element of intelligence testing, that was to provide the principle of allocation of students to grammar and other schools (see Table 2.2 below). The notion that these schools would be 'equal but different' clearly failed and what was referred to as 'parity of esteem' was never achieved. The Norwood Committee (Committee of the Secondary School Examination Council, 1943, p 4) argued that:

> In a wise economy of secondary education, pupils of a particular type of mind would receive the training best suited for them and that training would lead them to an occupation where their capacities would be suitably used.

Contemporary educationalist Fred Clarke was highly critical of the 1944 Act and deeply suspicious of what he described as its:

> … class prejudice, and it was fundamentally a social class project, in many ways the culmination of a project, the fulfilment of a vision which was basically that of Matthew Arnold, 80 years before. (cited in McCulloch, 2006, p 703)

The 1938 Spens Committee (on Secondary Education) had set aside a considerable amount of evidence that favoured a single, multilateral secondary school system. Despite the adoption in 1942 of a Labour Party Conference motion to establish 'multilateral' schools, experiments with them were discouraged by the post-war Labour government and 'tripartitism' prevailed, although only 52 LEAs ever established technical schools. But in reality tripartitism began to lose ground almost as soon as it was established even though the defence of grammar schools by the Conservative Party and vague and weak commitment to comprehensives by the Labour Party led to no clear alternative. As early as 1947 the London School Plan specifically rejected the idea of selection and planned for 64 comprehensive schools, 26 of which were open by 1958 (see below on growth of comprehensives). However, secondary school reorganisation on 'comprehensive' lines was local and patchy, driven by geography, as in Anglesey, the pattern and size of existing schools, as in West Riding, Leicestershire and Walthamstow, and a degree of aspiring working- and new middle-class discontent with selection processes in many areas.

The 1944 Act also grappled with the 'problem' of Church schools and embedded a further compromise over their position as part of the state system: 'The question of the future role of the churches in education proved more complex, more sensitive and more fiercely contested than any other in wartime education reform' (Barber, 1994, p 23). The Act allowed that Church schools could become 'controlled' or 'aided'. The former were fully funded and mostly run by LEAs, 6,000 of the 9,000 Anglican schools choosing this route, fewer than had been expected. 'Aided' schools retained responsibility for buildings, appointment of teachers and governors and provision of 'religious instruction' whereas controlled schools followed an 'agreed' religious education syllabus. Many of these 'aided' schools were among those most keen to take up the grant-maintained status offered in the 1988 Education Act (see below). However, Barber (1994, p 121), in his evaluation of the 1944 Act, argues that despite its shortcomings:

> … it was flexible. Radical or not in 1944, it provided the framework within which both the essentially conservative tripartite system flourished in the 1950s and the progressive comprehensive system developed in the late 1960s and 1970s. Such a framework is in strong contrast to the kind of rolling, detailed legislative programme which has characterized the late 1980s and early 1990s.

Nonetheless, the bi- or tripartite systems and the half-hearted comprehensive reforms that were to follow were the outcome of unstable compromises based on weak and reluctant central direction and a continuing political commitment to social division. As in the

19th century this period of education reform is characterised by both 'dissolution and conservation' rather than 'drastic' change.

During the 1950s and 1960s a series of government reports drew attention to the 'waste of talent' produced by the divided system. The Crowther Report (1959), for example, noted the need for a more educated, adaptable and skilled workforce for provision of which the grammar/secondary modern system was not functionally suited. The Early Leaving Report (Gurney-Dixon, 1954) found that even when attending the same school, working-class children left school before their middle-class counterparts and with fewer qualifications. The conclusion of the report noted the 'illogicality' of the system. Such reports and a considerable body of other research (for example, Glass, 1954; Floud et al, 1956) repeatedly demonstrated class divisions within the education system and reproduction of class differences in opportunity, performance and aspiration. Halsey et al (1980) found a fairly static picture of attendance at selective schools across four birth cohorts pre- and post-war (see Table 2.2).

The grammar schools remained predominantly middle-class institutions that still only 'assimilated' a small minority of highly selected working-class students, particularly in authorities where as few as 12% of the cohort 'passed' the 11 Plus, although in areas, such as parts of South and mid-Wales where 40% did so, their intakes were less inegalitarian. Olive Banks' authoritative and critical study of secondary

Table 2.2: Attendance at selective secondary schools (%)

Birth cohort					
Father's class	1913-22	1923-32	1933-42	1943-52	All
I, II (service)	69.5	76.7	79.3	66.4	71.9
III, IV, V (intermediate)	34.9	44.0	43.3	37.1	39.6
VI, VII, VIII (working)	20.2	26.1	27.1	21.6	23.7
All	29.6	37.0	38.8	34.8	35.0

Source: Halsey et al (1980, Table 4.9, p 63)

schools, *Parity and prestige in English secondary education* (1955), argued that grammar schools served to widen existing divisions of power and prestige in the social structure. Halsey et al (1980, p 71) concluded from their statistical cohort analysis of access to grammar schools that despite the faith put in intelligence testing as a device for meritocratic selection, 'it still turns out that meritocracy has been modified by class bias throughout the expansion of secondary opportunity'.[4]

The relatively small number of grammar school places available in some parts of the country was increasingly inadequate to respond to the educational aspirations of the burgeoning 'new' middle classes and aspiring working-class parents for whom secondary modern schools were clearly regarded as 'second best'. Indeed, until 1951 secondary moderns were unable to offer their leavers access to public examinations and even in 1960 still only one in eight secondary modern students recorded 'O'-level passes. In 1965 a separate, and again 'second-class', CSE examination was introduced, designed for less academically able students who were not capable of taking 'O'-levels.

However, slowly but steadily around the country comprehensive alternatives were created. By 1958 there were 26 such schools in London, by 1962 Wales had 22, as did Glasgow, and by 1960 there were 120 in England and Wales.

Box 2.1: Comprehensive factors

Simon and Rubenstein (1969) put forward five factors that underlay the move towards comprehensive schools:

- economic advance and technological change and the demand for new kinds of skilled and adaptable workers;
- changes in secondary modern schools that demonstrated the wastefulness and dubious validity of selection at the age of 11;
- changing parental aspirations;
- research findings on social class and opportunity;
- the growing criticisms of IQ testing and the negative effects of segregation. Research findings indicated that measured IQ scores of secondary modern pupils actually declined over time.

A Labour government was elected in 1964, and the following year Circular 10/65 requested LEAs to submit plans for comprehensive reorganisation and the 1976 Education Act made this a legal requirement (repealed in 1979 by the Conservatives). Between 1965 and 1976 it was left to LEAs to decide to move decisively, half-heartedly or not at all to local comprehensive systems and some submitted plans were more comprehensive in name than in structure or practice. Even at this time secondary modern schools were being defended. Senior Conservative politician Quentin Hogg, speaking in the House of Commons against comprehensive schooling, in a form of words that would not have sounded out of place either in 1870 or 1944, urged his fellow Members of Parliament (MPs) to visit secondary modern schools where 'these boys and girls were getting an education tailor-made to their desires, their bents and their requirements' (*Hansard*, vol 705, cols 421-3, January 1965).

Ironically, the largest number of comprehensives came into existence between 1970 and 1974 when Margaret Thatcher was Secretary of State for Education. Whereas in 1965 a total of 8.5% of the secondary age population was educated in 262 comprehensive schools, between 1966 and 1970 this rose from 12% to 40%, 50% by 1973, 80% by 1977 and 83% by 1981. While in 1960 there were 3,000 grammar schools in England and Wales and 130 comprehensives, by 1990 there were over 3,000 comprehensives and only 150 grammar schools. However, the term 'comprehensive school' remained slippery and such-named schools differed widely in their ability intakes, commitments and practices. Again this can be thought about in terms of a process of both 'dissolution and conservation'. The Labour Party's commitment to comprehensive education, such as it was, was always to a 'weak' definition of the school that saw it as a more effective and efficient institution for producing students with unequal qualifications. Johnson (1991, p 32) asserts that the failure to achieve a thoroughgoing comprehensive reform of education lies with 'Labour's failure to be a really educative movement … education was less an activity requiring its leadership, more an institution to be managed'.

Struggles over comprehensive education at every level, nationally, in local government, in schools and communities, were over matters of separation and hierarchy, forms of unequal access and provision (to schools, classes, courses and examinations and so on) and 'parity and prestige'. Change was slow and piecemeal and incoherent, with little evidence of what I have previously called 'drastic' reform. There was no national planning for the replacement of grammar and secondary modern schools with comprehensives, no set of articulated principles and little evidence of political will for thoroughgoing change. Furthermore, response to and critique of comprehensive schooling by the political Right (*Black Papers*, 1969-77) and what Johnson (1991, pp 35-41) calls the 'forming of the New Right educational tendency' was begun and started to gain ground at a time when few comprehensives were fully up and running, most had to compete with grammar schools for their intakes and hardly any had produced their first all-through graduates. It was the very idea of comprehensive education that was anathema to the critics. Struggles over education during the 1950s to 1970s continued to be played out on the terrain of social class laid out in the 19th century with a series of small advances and retreats on the sides of 'progress' and 'tradition'.

The *Black Papers* connected up campaigns, drew in activists and forged a 'New Right' political identity; they were not only a stout defence of selection and elite education but they also began to articulate a renewed vision of a liberal education system. The 1969 *Black Paper* argued for 'loans and grants' as a way of extending 'the possibility of private education to more and more people' (Cox and Dyson, 1969, p 14), which was realised in 1980 in the form of the Assisted Places Scheme by which children who could not afford to go to fee-paying independent schools were provided with free or subsidised places if they were able to pass the school's entrance examination. In 1975 Rhodes Boyson, a comprehensive school headteacher (later a Conservative Junior Education Minister), outlined the case for 'the educational voucher' (Cox and Boyson, 1975, pp 27-8) and the 1977 *Black Paper* argued that 'The possibilities for parental choice of secondary (and primary schools) should be improved via the introduction of the educational voucher or some other method' (Cox and Boyson, 1977, p 5). The *Black Papers*, together with a variety of linked and overlapping neoliberal or New Right think-tanks and advocacy groups (Centre for Policy Studies, National Council for Educational Standards, Social Affairs Unit, Institute of Economic Affairs and so on), clearly gained a considerable influence within Conservative education policy thinking during the 1970s and 1980s, and the 1988 Education Reform Act put into practice many of the ideas floated in these groups' publications. The *Black Papers* indeed signalled a new kind of 'think-tank' policy influence and form of policy making in education that played its part in moving and dispersing the articulation of policy ideas away from local government and the civil service. The writers and activists involved in these Conservative think-tanks also provided or rearticulated a set of ideas (or maybe more accurately two sets) that provided the basis for a renarration of the public sector in terms of neoliberalism (and neoconservatism). Arthur Seldon, Rhodes Boyson, Stuart Sexton and Denis O'Keeffe were to the forefront of the espousal of neoliberalism at this time, while Roger Scruton, a professor of philosophy and editor of *The Salisbury Review* (named after 19th-century Conservative Prime Minister Lord Salisbury), and Caroline Cox, a nurse educator, provided some substance to neoconservatism. But the most significant and substantial figure in Conservative social and economic policy and architect of Thatcherism was Keith Joseph (see below).

An educational 'settlement' was achieved in the period 1944-76 but it was a shaky, unstable settlement and also one that displayed a continuation of the entrenched, historic social divisions and class competition that had defined English education policy from the outset. This made thoroughgoing comprehensive reform difficult, if not impossible. Reynolds et al (1987, p 14), in their review of comprehensive education, describe the period 1965-87 as 'two decades of controversy' and sum up the end of that period by saying that 'it is the insecurity of the comprehensive enterprise which is now most striking' (p 15). And writing in 1991 on the 'peculiarities' of the English education system Green (1991, p 16), echoing one of the themes of this history of policy, suggests that:

> Weak commitment to a collective form of provision has led to a loosely integrated structure of state schooling. Indeed there is a sense in which England has never quite created a public system, and certainly not one which could win widespread confidence.

1976-97

Alongside the attacks of the *Black Papers* public confidence in comprehensive education was to suffer a further setback in 1976 when Prime Minister James Callaghan made his Ruskin College speech on education. It was unusual in itself at this time for a prime minister to devote a major speech to the topic of education. Whatever his intentions, the speech gave powerful encouragement to the 'discourse of derision' being aimed at schools and teachers by the *Black Papers*, some industrialists and sections of the media, in particular *The Daily Mail*. It raised questions about the value for money of educational spending and unsatisfactory standards of school performance: 'we cannot be satisfied with maintaining existing standards … and the challenge in education is to examine its priorities and to secure as high efficiency as possible'. It rearticulated the long-standing argument that school graduates were not being equipped with the sorts of skills needed by employers. Education should have two goals, Callaghan argued: to equip children for 'a lively, constructive place in society' and to fit them 'to do a job of work'. He also gave special emphasis to 'basic literacy and basic numeracy' and reiterated the need to mitigate 'as far as possible the disadvantages that may be suffered through poor home conditions or physical and mental handicap'. The speech also picked up *Black Paper* concerns about incompetent teachers, although Callaghan claimed that 'my remarks are not a clarion call to *Black Paper* prejudices'. However, he did challenge the monopoly of teacher education and educationalists over questions about the methods and purposes of education: 'I take it that no one claims exclusive rights in this field'. In particular, in a phrase that captured the media imagination at the time, it was argued that 'the secret garden of the curriculum' needed to be opened up. This indeed marked the beginning of the end of what Lawton (1980, p 22) called 'the Golden Age of teacher control (or non-control) of the curriculum'. Callaghan further announced a 'great debate' about education based around the themes of: curriculum, assessment of standards, education and training of teachers and school and working life (for a detailed account of the speech and the great debate and their reception see Chitty, 1989). In a number of ways the Ruskin speech anticipates and would not be out of place within the education 'policyspeak' of New Labour, and in a strategic sense it opened up a set of policy agendas that were vigorously pursued by the Conservative governments of 1979-97. Indeed, in a letter to MPs, published in the 1977 *Black Paper*, Cox and Boyson claimed that: 'In October 1976, Mr Callaghan, the Prime Minister, attempted to steal our clothes' (Cox and Boyson, 1977, p 5).

In the aftermath of the speech, despite a flurry of announcements, little of substance happened during the remainder of the Labour government's time in office. Brian Simon described this aftermath as a period of 'procrastination, indecision, delay at all costs – endless consultation' (1991, p 454). There were several ministerial references to the need to review the school curriculum and a reiteration of concerns about standards of teaching. At the North of England Conference in January 1977, Secretary of State Shirley Williams asserted that the problems of education lay with 'poor teachers, weak head-teachers and head-mistresses and modern teaching methods'. In part this absence of substantive activity stemmed from the fact that the Department for Education and Science (DES) did not know how to act and, more significantly, had no access to 'the levers' of reform, as Keith Joseph was to call them (see below). Nonetheless, what Ruskin did do was to further disrupt the existing settlement within education policy and begin to make what was to follow possible. It played a significant role in 'breaking' the existing paradigm of educational politics and policy. There was a discursive 'shift in the balance of power in policy making … and the real losers on this were the local authorities and teachers' (Lowe, 2004, p 137). Lowe goes on to suggest that 'there can be little doubt that Labour in office from 1974 to 1979 determined the politics of education to the end of the century and beyond' (p 138).

However, Callaghan's speech was also symptomatic of a more general unsettling of the post-war, welfare settlement. The government was beset with financial and economic problems and problems of 'ungovernability' that created opportunities for neoliberal criticisms of the welfare state to gain ground. The collectivist/interventionist consensus that seemed so firmly established in British politics suddenly began to seem fragile:

> The post war consensus finally collapsed under the Wilson-Callaghan Government of 1974-79, amid mounting inflation, swelling balance of payments deficits, unprecedented currency depreciation, rising unemployment, bitter industrial conflicts and what seemed to many to be ebbing governability. (Marquand, 1988, p 3)

In 1979 Margaret Thatcher's Conservative Party was elected to government. In hindsight, the resurgence of neoliberalism and the dominance of New Right education views between 1979-97 can be seen as a replay of struggles and tensions embedded in the crisis of the English state and the introduction of state education in the late 19th century that the compromises and vacillations around tripartitism and comprehensivism had done little to resolve. The New Right reasserted the social 'peculiarities' that mark English education, particularly exclusions around class and gender that had been basic to provision since the 19th century and, more recently, reproduction of 'colonial patterns around race and ethnicity' (Hall and Schwartz, 1985, p 30).

The New Right critique of the welfare state rested to an important extent on an attempt to deconstruct its collectivism and reinvent a form of Victorian laissez-faire individualism. This required policy makers to 'roll back the state' so as to eradicate 'institutional inefficiencies' produced by its bureaucracies, in their place reintroducing market forces as an antidote to regulation and intervention both within the public sector and in relation to the management of the economy. This was a reassertion of the twin pillars of individual liberty (the freedom to choose) and market freedom (the disciplines of competition). These were to be the basis of the relationship between Thatcherism and the public sector, an ideological return to Victorian political and economic thinking owing much to ideological work within the Conservative Party of Margaret Thatcher's mentor, Keith Joseph.

If the first legislative fruit of Thatcher's education policy was the 1980 Education Act introduced by Joseph's predecessor Mark Carlisle to give some degree of choice of schools to parents, including the Assisted Places Scheme, the first real beneficiary of the discursive space in education policy opened up by Ruskin was Keith Joseph himself, appointed Secretary of State for Education in 1981. His tenure was important not so much in terms of substantive policy but rather in establishing firm control over the 'levers' of education policy within the DES in the hands of the Secretary of State. One commentator described Joseph as 'nothing so much as some modernising and absolute monarch of the eighteenth century' (quoted in Denham and Garrett, 2001, p 397), which, given his ideological proclivities for neoliberalism, was more than a little paradoxical.

Keith Joseph was the 'first Conservative front-bench figure to offer a sustained and broad-ranging challenge to the direction of post-war British economic management' (Kavanagh, 1987, p 113); almost single-handedly he brought about a reorientation of the principles underpinning Conservative economic and social policy. In a series of speeches in 1974-75, and through the work of the Centre for Policy Studies, Joseph argued the case for a social market economy and for monetarism, and outlined an economic and social policy position that became known as New Right or, more broadly, neoliberalism (Joseph, 1975). This consisted of a rejection of extensive state regulation, high taxation, high levels of public spending, borrowing and subsidies, and the role of unions as monopoly suppliers of labour, and argued generally that the public sector was a drain on the wealth-creating private sector. What was needed was 'more market, less state', that is to say, deregulation, liberalisation and privatisation. During this period Joseph also began to influence the political ideas of Margaret

Thatcher and supplied the base for the decisive leap in her career to the leadership of the Conservative Party. His impact on Thatcher was to bring about what was in effect a reversal in post-war economic policy with its concerns with low unemployment, welfare state funding and economic intervention. Margaret Thatcher encapsulated this reversal in her first Party Conference speech as leader:

> Let me give you my vision: a man's right to work as he will, to spend what he earns, to own property, to have the state as servant and not as master: these are the British inheritance.

This signals a key facet of 'the neoliberal outlook', that is, its antagonism to the welfare state that is seen as the source of all evils and its antidote that is market-led economic growth. During Thatcher's three terms as Prime Minister the landscape of economic and political understandings of welfare changed irrevocably and a new discourse was established that expressed relationships between state, economy and public sector in new (or very old) ways. This meant that some public services could simply be sold off (water, gas, electricity, telecommunications and so on). Their special status as public services no longer applied. Other services that continued to be financed by the state were 'rethought' in terms of their conditions of operation, interrelationships and modes of planning and financing and made subject to competition and choice by the insertion of 'market proxies'. The market form (see Chapter One and below) and the logic, modes and visions of the private company, as a model, were to be the primary vehicle for internal reform of the public services. By changing relationships between users and providers and tying budgets much more closely to patterns of choice within these new relationships public sector organisations were required to act like businesses and in a businesslike way.

Arguably there were two phases to Conservative social and education policy. The period 1979-86 was dominated by efforts to cut public spending and liberalise labour markets that led to a gradual dismantling of parts of the welfare state through cuts and privatisation, deregulation and a new emphasis on individual choice and consumption. Spending constraint and privatisation were the central themes in policy debate during this period. The internal reform of the public sector, including social security, education, healthcare, housing and personal social services, began in 1986 and gained momentum after the 1987 election, continuing through John Major's period as Prime Minister even though, right up to 1997, he was continually beset by demands and challenges from Tory Right-wingers to return to policies of expenditure and tax reductions.

During the late 1980s and 1990s a framework of reform of state education based on private sector models was gradually enacted alongside a modest set of moves to 'privatise' aspects of public service provision through compulsory competitive tendering (CCT), City Technology Colleges (CTCs) and the National Nursery Voucher Scheme (NNVS), for example (see Box 2.2). The first two were taken up and developed further by New Labour. Such Conservative changes produced an infrastructure of possibilities within which business could establish a presence within state education services, while other policies, such as local management of schools (LMS), positioned schools as 'buyers' of services and began to displace LEA services. In 1992 the Office for Standards in Education (Ofsted or OHMCI, now Estyn, in Wales) was created through which privatised school inspections were to be undertaken for each school every three or four years. HMI was regarded with suspicion by the Conservatives as part of the old educational establishment. Kenneth Clarke (Secretary of State, 1990-92) announced that £75 million would be devolved from LEA budgets to allow schools to hire accredited inspection teams of their choice. In 1996 Ofsted was given powers to inspect LEAs.

In many ways the Conservatives' twin-track approach to reform, centralisation and devolution, coalesced around the weakening, and dismantling of LEA influence. At a Council of Local Education Authorities (CLEA) conference (18 July 1991) Howard Davies of the Audit Commission said that the government viewed LEAs as 'unloved and unwanted', although earlier, according to Denham and Garrett (2001, p 397), 'Joseph argued in Cabinet against the idea of removing local authorities from the education system', but the 1993 Education

Act displaced LEAs as sole providers of state education.[5] In practice, however, fewer schools than had been expected chose 'opting out' under the provisions of the 1988 Act and the Conservative government floated the idea of introducing legislation to make all schools grant-maintained or abolishing LEAs altogether.

Box 2.2: Conservative privatisations

CCT

Broke the LEA monopoly of service provision by requiring councils to contract services to lowest bidder and transferred workers to private providers (Hoggett, 1994). Replaced under Labour by 'Best Value', which shifted from an adversarial to partnership relationship between councils and the private sector and from cost reduction to quality.

CTCs

Encouraged businesses and business people to 'sponsor' and run state schools with a vocational orientation. Provided part of the model for academies.

LMS

Gave schools control of their budgets with a freedom to make spending decisions.

Parental choice

Encouraged schools to compete for recruitment and employ promotional techniques (see Gewirtz et al, 1995).

Ofsted

Inspections of schools and colleges contracted to private companies.

NNVS
A short-lived scheme intended to allow parents to 'spend' their voucher in state or private nurseries – abolished by New Labour.

School vouchers
A small pilot scheme initiated by Keith Joseph but deemed a failure by the civil service.

The main platform of Conservative education reforms was the 1988 Education Reform Act, which articulated six key elements of neoliberal and neoconservative advocacy around education policy:

- establishment of a 'national' curriculum that would entrench traditional subjects and British cultural heritage over and against 'misguided relativism' and multiculturalism;
- suspicion of teacher professionalism and the 'politics' of teachers and the need for systems of control and accountability;
- concomitant press for forms of 'teacher-proof' evaluation and assessment, alongside a distrust of public examinations, as a way of identifying 'poor' schools and 'failing' teachers as well as providing parents with 'market information' (see below);
- offering parents 'choice', that is, the right to express a preference, among state schools submitted to the disciplines of the market;
- devolution of control over budgets from LEAs to schools;
- enhancement of the roles and responsibilities of both governors and headteachers through LMS.

Aspects of almost all of these elements are taken up further in Chapter Three but it is important to note here how they tie together as a reform package that provides the infrastructure for an education market and a neoliberal vision of the education system. As John Major put it, somewhat disingenuously, but in words echoed in 2007 by Conservative Party leader David Cameron, he believed in 'trusting headmasters, teachers and governing bodies to run their schools and in trusting parents to make the right choice for their children' (*The Times*, 24 August 1995, p 5).

In other social policy fields markets were configured differently, for example, in health through what was called the purchaser–provider split (for an overview of social policy markets see Le Grand and Bartlett, 1993). In education the market form had six key elements, or seven if the national curriculum can be regarded as a common basis of 'trade':

- the 1980 and 1986 Education Acts had already made moves in the direction of choice for parents that were extended by the Education Reform Act in 1988. The 'Parents' Charter', published in 1991, gave parents the right to information about schools and their performance (it was updated in 1994);
- per capita funding meant that school 'income' was overwhelmingly driven by recruitment;
- diversity of provision was enhanced by both the creation of grant-maintained schools and CTCs;
- competition led to pressure on schools to promote and 'improve' themselves in order to attract parent choices;
- information gleaned from examination and test results, reported in the form of local league tables from 1992, was regarded as a form of market information for choosers, and the use of 'raw scores' as the basis of these tables was stoutly defended by education ministers. The first league tables were published for LEAs in response to a parliamentary question (18 January 1991) and showed that the percentage of students with 5 or more 'A'-'C' grades at GCSE ranged from 8.5% to 39.1%;
- new organisational ecologies, with much greater emphasis on forms of management modelled on business, with the intention of making schools more businesslike and market-sensitive, focused on 'efficient' use of resources and student recruitment as a means of budget maximisation (Chapter One).

In addition during this period a complex infrastructure of testing and assessment was put in place animating a continuing debate around rising and falling standards in schools (see Chapter Three). All of these elements are still significant within the current framework of education policy.

Underpinning the new diversities among and autonomies for schools was the national curriculum. During the 1970s and 1980s it had become widely accepted within the Conservative Party that the school curriculum was out of control and that 'real' knowledge was being replaced by an 'ideological curriculum' (see Knight, 1990). Anti-racist and anti-sexist initiatives were particular causes for concern. Thatcher addressed this in her speech to the 1987 Conservative Conference:

> Too often our children don't get the education they need – the education they deserve. And in the inner cities – where youngsters must have a decent education if they are to have a better future – that opportunity is all too often snatched from them by hard-Left educational authorities and extremist teachers. Children who need to be able to count and multiply are learning anti-racist mathematics – whatever that may be. Children who need to be able to express themselves in clear English are being taught political slogans. Children who need to be taught to respect traditional moral values are being taught that they have an inalienable right to be gay.

The implied relationships between curriculum, political order and citizenship are quite clear here. Once again inner cities are represented as a pathological 'other' in relation to certain fixed core values. The rearticulation of subjects such as history, geography, English and music for the national curriculum provided spaces for a 'restorationist' agenda. This took the form of a reiteration of assimilationism, nationalism and political consensus around a regressive reworking of past glories in a 'struggle over popular memory'. Thus, in restorationist history Britain is at the centre, a benign and progressive influence on the world, bearer of justice and civilisation, as part of a curriculum seeking to eschew relevance and the present, concentrating on 'heritage' and 'the canon'. It is a fantasy curriculum founded on Victorian myths about and inventions of ethnic Englishness and an assertion of tradition, of morality and literary history in the face of 'declining standards', cultural heterogeneity and a fragmented modernity.

Alongside the defence of the traditional academic curriculum and the introduction of a national curriculum the Conservatives also began to reinscribe some of the curricular divisions that had been embedded in tripartitism, in particular through the Technical and Vocational Education Initiative, and to reorient schools, at least to a small extent, more towards the needs and concerns of employers. The Initiative was a loose amalgam of programmes and initiatives intended to make schools and colleges more technically and vocationally oriented, to provide job-related training for 14- to 18-year-olds, and to steer young people to the boom spheres of business and industry. It was funded by the newly established Manpower Services Commission rather than the DES, although in 1995 the DES was renamed the Department for Education and Employment. In ways that anticipated New Labour policy (see below) the Manpower Services Commission contracted and funded local providers directly, including employers working in partnership with schools and colleges, and bids were judged both on their innovativeness and cost-effectiveness and the schemes were evaluated in terms of their outcomes. In terms of impact the significance of the Technical and Vocational Education Initiative is much more that of its style and method as policy than its effects on educational content and practice. Nonetheless, it is a further iteration of themes signalled in Prime Minister James Callaghan's Ruskin speech (speech at Ruskin College, Oxford, 18 October 1976).

In 1997 the Labour Party, as New Labour, returned to power under the leadership of Tony Blair after 18 years of Conservative government.

1997-2007: a third way?

Three further shifts and ruptures can be signalled at this point. Each of these are subtle but nonetheless distinct inflections of, or developments from, the period of Thatcherism or neoliberalism:

- a further move in political terms towards the economics of the knowledge economy (see Chapter One);
- a reassertion of the role and methods of the state, as what Jessop (2002) and Cerny (1990) call the 'competition state' (see Box 2.3) or more generally 'the third way';
- a rearticulation of Labour Party values and commitments in the move from 'Old' to 'New' Labour.

Movement from an industrial to informational and service economy placed education at the centre of the policy stage and New Labour indicated its intention to make Britain a country of 'innovative people'and the 'electronic capital of the world' (Speech by the Rt Hon Tony Blair MP, Leader of the Labour Party, at the Campaign for Freedom of Information's annual awards ceremony, 25 March 1996), combining 'dynamic markets with strong communities' (Tony Blair, 'Third Way, Phase Two', www.angelfire.com). In his biography of Tony Blair, Rentoul (1997, p 431) contrasts the role of education in Roy Hattersley's Old Labour thinking with Tony Blair's New Labour view:

> The issue of education is totemic for both Old and New Labour with the question of selection top of the pole. Hattersley's political experience was shaped by the 1944 Education Act's condemnation of the vast majority of the children of working people to second-rate schools. Many of his generation shared Anthony Crosland's profane desire to 'destroy every grammar school in the country'.... For New Labour, education plays a different role, but it is just as central.

> For Blair the social engineering function of education is much more to do with instilling discipline and responsibility than equality.

Roy Hattersley, sometimes seen as Blair's political mentor, wrote that 'It's no longer my party.... One by one the policies which define our philosophy have been rejected by the Prime Minister' (*The Observer*, 24 June 2001). Nonetheless, as far as education policy and comprehensive education were concerned, the support of Old Labour for reform was never unequivocal and the break here as far as education is concerned may not be as clear-cut as all that.

Box 2.3: New Labour and the fourth rupture

This is a political-economic shift from the Keynesian national welfare state to a competition state.

The competition state 'aims to secure economic growth within its borders and/or to secure competitive advantages for capitals based in its borders' (Jessop, 2002, p 96) by promoting the economic and extra-economic conditions necessary for competitive success (parts of which were explored in Chapter One). In effect Jessop's argument is that the changes that have taken place over the past 25 years in the UK's economy (as elsewhere) have made the Keynesian national welfare state increasingly redundant and indeed obstructive, undermining the conditions of capital accumulation. The Keynesian national welfare state became subject to mounting crises that could no longer be managed or deferred, that is, a conjunction of crises, financial, economic, social and political – including inflation, taxation costs, ungovernability, unemployment, demographic change, inequality, rigidity, changing national identities, family instability, movements of capital, ecological problems and so on – occurring across the society and the economic system. The form of the state–economy relationship, the 'spatio-temporal fix', as Jessop calls it, became untenable and a hindrance to international competitiveness. The state became 'overloaded' – trying ineffectively to manage a lumbering command economy. The Keynesian national welfare state has, as a result, become steadily delegitimated and subject to systematic but not total dismantling.

Whatever else you could say about Labour's education policies there is certainly no shortage of them. At the 1998 Labour Party Annual Conference a briefing paper for delegates (Labour Party Policy Unit, 1998) listed 47 education-related policies, initiatives and funding decisions that had been announced since the 1997 election victory. Many of these initial policy activities were aimed at remedying the perceived neglect and omission of previous Conservative administrations, such as protecting school playing fields from being sold off, cutting class sizes, additional funding for LEAs and £2 billion for school repairs. Another group clustered around issues of school improvement and raising educational 'achievement', including 'a new national literacy framework', 'national numeracy targets', 'improved teacher training', a 'Fresh Start' for 'failing schools', 'an expanded specialist school programme' (initially launched by the Conservatives in 1992), setting up 'Education Action Zones' (EAZs), and 'support projects to improve school attendance'. According to government figures, all of this amounted to a cash injection over three years of £19 billion.

Under Conservative governments of the 1980s and 1990s there had been a series of withering public spending cuts. However, under New Labour such cuts have not been a priority as much as new forms of financial control and financial allocation. These are important in two senses, first as a form of redistribution of funding within the public sector related to indicators of performance or competitive success and an increasing use of targeted funding and systems of programme bidding to achieve institutional refocusing and redesign. Second, a redistribution of funds has been achieved away from direct funding of public sector organisations and local authorities to contract funding of private, voluntary and quasi-public organisations for the delivery of public services and a concomitant process of making state agencies into free-standing, self-financing organisations.

Relatively little of previous Conservative policy, of which there was also a great deal, has been clearly dispensed with since 1997. Phasing out of the Assisted Places Scheme, compromise over grant-maintained school status (the schools were required to become either 'foundation' or 'community') closure of the Funding Agency for Schools and abandonment of the NNVS are exceptions. Furthermore, three key, non-governmental agency figures from the previous Conservative administration were retained: Chris Woodhead at Ofsted, Nick Tate at the QCA (Qualifications and Curriculum Authority) and Angela Millet at the TTA (Teacher Training Agency). It is hardly a startling conclusion then to suggest that despite the flurry of policy activity in and around education under Labour it is important to attend both to continuities and differences between Labour and the Conservatives. The significance of continuity was made explicit in the 1997 election manifesto: 'Some things the Conservatives got right. We will not change them' (Blair, Manifesto, p 3). This signalled something of the pragmatism of New Labour, a kind of post-political form of government, claimed to be based not an ideology but on 'what works', inducing Andrew Rawnsley (*The Observer*, 30 April 2006) to the view that 'New Labour has always emphasised managerialism over ideology. It has been a favoured mantra of Tony Blair that "what matters is what works"'.

The conventional academic wisdom on Labour Party educational policy is neatly summed up in a comment by Novak (quoted by Power and Whitty, 1999, p 545) in a pamphlet for the Institute of Economic Affairs, a New Right pressure group: 'the triumph of Tony Blair may in one sense be regarded as the triumph of Margaret Thatcher'. Giddens (1998b, p 25) also notes that critics of the third way, or at least Blair's version of it, see it 'as warmed-over neoliberalism'. John Major (1999, p 593) seemed in no doubt:

> I did not, at the time, appreciate the extent to which he would appropriate Conservative language and steal our policies. The attractive candidate was to turn out to be a political kleptomaniac.

This is reminiscent of Rhodes Boyson's comment on James Callaghan, quoted earlier. The continuities from Thatcherism/Majorism to New Labour cannot be ignored but they are not enough in themselves to 'explain' New Labour's education policies. There are significant differences between neoliberalism and the third way. While neoliberalism rests on a fairly unreflexive belief in markets and the private sector as the engine of national economic competitiveness, a 'free-market fundamentalism' (Eagle, 2003), which regards state intervention as almost always counterproductive, the third way rests more on adoption of a 'flexible repertoire' of state roles and responses. Neoliberalism and the third way involve different kinds of policy mixes but also have some important common elements. The third way draws 'selectively on fragments and components of the old' (Newman, 2001, p 46) but it is novel and distinctive. As Newman (2005, p 719) puts it, the third way signalled 'something different from the hierarchical governance of social democracy and market-based governance of the 1980s and 1990s … [but] the something different is hard to pin down'. It would not be possible without neoliberalism but differs in important ways in terms of the role of the state and its relationships with the public and private sectors, among other things. Paterson (2003) suggests three key elements to the third way repertoire:

- a version of progressive liberalism, with an inclination towards individualism, and a concomitant suspicion of the state;
- developmentalism, the explicit promotion of competitiveness by the state and a concomitant interventionism;
- New Social Democracy, with elements both of moral authoritarianism (made up of reciprocity, responsibility, strong values and community), new localism and a 'continuing insistence on the inadequacies of unregulated capitalism' (Paterson, 2003, p 166).

This latter element, Paterson suggests, is more evident in Wales and Scotland than in England. McCaig (2001, p 201) also argues that New Labour can be seen as a 'synthesis of three elements'. First, an 'older' plural ideology 'balancing egalitarians and meritocrats, authoritarians and libertarians in the familiar "broad church"', although these ideologies are not equally well represented at the level of practical policy. Second, a 'centralized policy making structure' with almost 'all power concentrated in the hands of senior parliamentarians' – under Tony Blair the Prime Minister's Office was very active in policy issues across the whole spectrum of government and particularly education. And third, electoral popularity, which in education 'has been reduced to a partially symbolic emphasis on standards and choice, with simple and clear messages for the electorate' (McCaig, 2001, p 201).

The third way does not look back to a pre-welfare market heyday – it is about moving on, and is centred on the project of modernisation: 'Modern government has a strategic role not to replace the market but to ensure that the market works properly' (Labour Party Manifesto, 1992, p 11). The state is positioned as a prime source and mediator of collective intelligence, in particular in relation to the 'necessities' of globalisation (Chapter One). As noted in Chapter One, this does not mean that the state is less active or less intrusive but it acts differently. Indeed, the total amount of state intervention will tend to increase as it itself involves the promotion, support and maintenance of an ever-widening range of social and economic activities.

Following the Conservative neoliberal experiment the limits of market mechanisms had to be 'relearned' and other forms of coordination to supplement, complement or compensate for the inadequacies of the market had to be reinvented albeit 'disguised behind changed names, innovative discourses, policy churning and institutional turnover' (Jessop, 2002, pp 244-5).

In education policy we can discern various aspects of third way thinking and policies, some of which will be traced later (Chapter Three). As already indicated education was to be a key policy area for New Labour and it was clear that the Prime Minister himself would take a keen and ongoing interest in the 'modernisation' of education (see Chapter Four). All indications are that the current Prime Minister Gordon Brown will maintain a focus on education as economic policy, to create what he called in his final Mansion House speech (2007) 'world class schools', to meet the challenge of globalisation.

'New Labour'/new policies

Almost all of the key themes of New Labour education were signalled in the White Paper *Excellence in schools* (DfEE, 1997) published just 67 days after taking office. The White Paper developed ideas from the 1995 policy document *Diversity and excellence: A new partnership for schools* (Labour Party, 1995) and election manifesto promises. The 1997 Election Manifesto committed the government to:

- a reduction in class sizes to 30 for all five- to seven-year-olds
- nursery places for all four-year-olds
- an attack on low standards in schools
- access for all to computer technology
- set up a University for Industry (Ufi) as a focus for lifelong learning
- increased spending on education.

The White Paper announced that:

- education would be at the heart of government
- policies would be designed to benefit the many, not just the few
- standards would matter more than structures
- intervention would be in inverse proportion to success
- there would be zero tolerance of underperformance
- the government would work in partnership with all those committed to raising standards.

In specific terms, the 'standards' involved giving priority to literacy and numeracy in primary schools; performance tables amended to show student progress; every school inspected every six years;

'under-performing schools' 'causing concern' (later 'failing schools') would be 'warned' and might be closed and replaced by a 'Fresh Start' school or taken over by a more successful one; a Standards and Effectiveness Unit (headed by Michael Barber) would be established along with a Standards Taskforce; 'setting' by ability would become the 'new' norm in schools; baseline assessments would be made at entry to primary school; and national targets reset in English and maths (80% of 11-year-olds in English and 75% in maths to achieve levels of performance expected for their age by 2002). There was also a pilot of 25 EAZs in areas of social disadvantage involving representatives of 'local business and the social community' and an expansion of the specialist school programme. National guidelines were laid down on school admissions and home–school contracts were introduced; the fate of grammar schools was to be decided by a vote by parents. Following the abolition of grant-maintained status, schools were redesignated as one of three types: aided, community or foundation.

Almost all of the key themes of education policy for the next 10 years were signalled here, as was a new style of policy (see Box 2.4) whose textures, texts, form, culture, architecture and geography were all changing. Policy was becoming increasingly diverse, complex and dynamic (Kooiman, 2003). As outlined in Chapter One, the underlying principle of education under New Labour was made very clear: 'We are talking about investing in human capital in an age of knowledge. To compete in the global economy' (DfEE, 1997, p 3). 'Above all the [White] paper signalled the economic imperative that lay behind raised educational standards' (Tomlinson, 2003, pp 196-7).

Box 2.4: New Labour texts

As a textual example of the 'newness' of New Labour, the dissemination of *Excellence in schools* (DfEE, 1997) incorporated a very modern approach. The document was widely circulated (and was available at supermarket checkouts). The summary document was available in six world languages. The document was accompanied by a video (copyright restrictions lifted) and was published on the department's website – called, interestingly enough, open.gov.uk/dfee. The paper is carefully colour-coded; each chapter has its own colour (blue for the chapter on teachers); each chapter contains coloured summary boxes; snappy summaries of the key questions for consultation are highlighted in the chapters' colour code; lively colour photographs taken in schools are interspersed throughout; mini-case studies of good practice are contained in colour-coded bordered boxes. In its wide-ranging sweep (from preschool to secondary provision, including the role of the local education authority and the professional development of teachers, heads of schools and new community partnerships) this is a broad agenda for raising standards; 'our top priority'. Again, in the foreword, Blunkett sets the tone for what is to follow:

> To succeed we need the commitment, imagination and drive of all those working in our schools and colleges, if we are to set aside the doubts of the cynics and the corrosion of the perpetual sceptics. We must replace the culture of complacency with commitment to success.

Source: Maguire (2004, pp 3, 11)

These initiatives are itemised for several reasons. We can see here both echoes of the Ruskin speech and a framework and principles for further policy developments up to the present time that were established. Continuities and breaks from the Conservative period are evident and, in passing, we can note yet again an unwillingness to abolish remaining grammar schools. 'The basics' remain central (John Major had pronounced the need for 'a return to the basics'), standards and targets and performance monitoring are given a sharper edge, further reforms of the teaching profession are indicated and the intention to involve business and the voluntary sector in service delivery and school 'improvement' is signalled. More weakly we can recognise movement towards greater diversity of types of schools. What is not much in evidence here is New Labour's difficult relation with parental choice, although the concomitant issue of schools admissions is present. Nonetheless, emphasis given to 'standards not structures' and diversity and, later, to differentiation and personalisation (see Chapter Three) indicates New Labour's pursuit of the recreation of a system 'friendly' to the interests, fears and social skills of the middle class (see Ball, 2003). Indeed, journalist Nick Davies (*The Guardian Unlimited*, 12 July 2000) argued that education policy since 1944 is: 'a triumph for class politics, for the power of the British middle-class to corner what is best for its children, much of it disguised as the exercise of parental choice'.

Charles Clarke, Secretary of State for Education (2002-04), explained to Michael White and Rebecca Smithers (*The Guardian*, 9 July 2004), as he launched Labour's five-year plan: 'There is a significant chunk of them who go private because they feel despairing about the quality of education. They are the people we are after'. The journalists commented that the 'government's plans to revitalize secondary education are designed to give working-class families a fair deal and to lure middle-class families who "go private" out of "despair" back into the state sector'.

Some of the trajectories of these policies are traced in later chapters. Also in the 1997 White Paper, the last of nine bullet points on 'Standards and accountability' asserted that:

- schools would be taking practical steps to raise minority ethnic pupils' achievements and promote racial harmony.

This is significant in two ways, both in its modesty and insignificance within the document as a whole, only a further 280 words being devoted to the 'problem' of the 'under-performance' of minority ethnic children, and because it did 'at least put the issues on the agenda', especially as:

> Conservative education reforms of the 1980s and 1990s came increasingly to be characterized by a 'de-racialised' discourse that effectively removed ethnic diversity from the agenda and glossed many discriminatory processes. (Gillborn, 1998, p 718)

It might be said that this account of education policy is also guilty of 'deracialising' policy, with its primary focus on class, although class and ethnicity are interpenetrating and compounding oppressions. Gender has thus far been neglected. And these omissions are also not properly remedied by their inclusion in Chapter Four as policy issues, but this is in part a reflection of the marginal role that they have in the discourses and practice of education policy. Education policies construct the 'problems' they address and, thus, the solutions they propose, typically within a form of language and set of social concepts that are colour- and gender-blind and apparently neutral. 'Race' and gender only become the focus of policy at points of crisis (see Chapter Four). 'The daily banalities of discrimination and exclusion are ignored, as is the fact that many young people from working-class and minority ethnic backgrounds – despite their own commitment to education – experience schooling as unjust' (Gillborn, 1998, p 731). In particular the effects of policies and practices, such as those on 'ability' grouping, selection, the curriculum in terms of opportunities for minority ethnic students, are all systematically ignored. As a result, as David (1993, p 207) points out, 'despite both the gender-neutral and race-neutral language, reforms and research have been constructed around gender and racial divisions'. It is suggested in Chapter Four that 'race and education policies' are exhortative rather than directive and are typically deflected into reports and inquiries rather than related to action.

It would take a great deal of space to outline all the subsequent policy developments and Education Acts generated by New Labour. The amount of legislation and policy activity has been astonishing, as noted in the Introduction. But one or two points are worth noting as iterations and elaborations of the New Labour reform agenda.

The 2001 White Paper *Schools: Achieving success* (DfES, 2001) dealt with: the need for greater diversity and flexibility; delivery of high minimum standards; supporting teachers and schools to deliver change; and encouraging innovation with the best schools leading the system. Through such policy language education is being rearticulated in terms of modernisation and dynamism (see Chapter One), echoing the pace of globalisation and speed of contemporary capitalism. Education is no longer 'extra-economic'. What might be called the welfare model of schooling and its 'structures' and what Blair's communication director Alastair Campbell called 'bog standard comprehensive schooling' (archive.thisiswiltshire.co.uk) are being 'disarticulated' (Scott, 1997). Throughout the reform agenda there is an ambivalence or even downright hostility on the part of Labour Party leadership even to the weak idea of 'the comprehensive school'. In 2002 the Secretary of State for Education Estelle Morris (2001-02) said in a speech, significantly to the Social Market Foundation:

> Comprehensive schools don't cherish their differences. Equality of opportunity will never be achieved by giving all children the same education … we have to get away from the perception that 'one size fits all schools' and the concept of 'ready-to-wear, off-the-shelf' comprehensives. (Morris, 2002)

> Comprehensive education was formed out of the injustice of rigid selection on grounds of ability through the 11-Plus, but with it came another injustice. Because there was insufficient focus on educational standards and on high attainment, there seeped into parts of the system a deadening uniformity. The goal was to make the system comprehensive, whereas in reality the goal should have been, through abandoning selection, to bring high quality education to all. (Blair, 2005a)

This is part of a process of what Whitfield (2001, p 69) calls *destabilisation*: an 'unrelenting criticism of public services, often by generalising individual failures' that began with the *Black Papers* and the Ruskin speech. It forms a 'discourse of derision' that deploys exaggeration and 'ludicrous images, ridicule, and stereotypification … a caricature has been developed and presented to the public as an accurate depiction of the real' (Kenway, 1990, p 201). The deployment of derision is a way of creating rhetorical spaces within which to articulate reform.

In the 2002 Education Act 'faith schools' were promoted as a way of creating 'a truly diverse secondary system' and school governing bodies were enabled to set themselves up as companies and to invest in other companies. The Act also gave the Secretary of State new powers to form companies for involvement in any area of school or LEA life (Kelly, 2002). Finally, around 1,000 schools were given freedom to vary the curriculum and change teachers' pay and conditions.

Conclusion

This very selective history of education policy has focused on a set of relationships between the state, economy and social class. The chapter began by sketching some of the ambivalences around state intervention into and provision of education and suggested that contemporary policy, first via Conservative neoliberalism and latterly through the politics of the third way, reworked and revived these ambivalences. Philanthropy, voluntarism and faith schooling are all very much back on the education policy agenda and policy initiatives such as the academies programme and trust schools (see Chapter Four) and the concomitant sidelining of LEAs may, arguably, signal the break-up of the 'national system of education locally administered', alongside a steady increase in powers held and used centrally.

In terms of the other major theme of this history I would suggest that New Labour policies address a very similar social agenda to that which underlay the development of state education in the 19th century. This relates to the dual and contradictory policy imperatives that derive from the aspirations and fears of the middle classes, on the one hand,

and the limited participation and underachievement of various sections of the working class, on the other.

Moreover, this chapter has tried to show that policy is now being done in particular ways, some different from those previously. Policies have to be looked at over time as incremental, experimental and tactical and, under New Labour, integrated into a strategic project of modernisation and transformation of the public sector (see Chapter Three). I am not suggesting that all policies fit together into a neat and 'joined-up' whole; there are contradictions, outliers and 'knee-jerk' reactions to crises. In policy analysis both sorts of policy making have to be borne in mind. Nonetheless, changes in education and social policy since 1988 can be understood as having had a 'ratchet effect' on changing practical and discursive possibilities (see Ball, 1990), which has continued under New Labour. This involves step-by-step processes of breaking up established modes of operation and taken-for-granted practices, introducing new 'freedoms' and new forms of intervention and regulation, new players and new kinds of relationships. Sometimes these are modest, sometimes bold. 'If anything we have not pushed fast enough and hard enough' (Blair, 2005c). Each move makes the next thinkable, feasible and acceptable. In this way the process of 'modernisation' or transformation involved here is both creative and destructive, a process of attrition and reinvention and 'although the transformation process may sometimes appear to be disjointed or uncoordinated' (Whitfield, 2001, p 69), it has an internal logic, a set of discernible, if not necessarily planned, facets.

Finally, let us return to the question of the continuities and differences between Conservative and New Labour education policy. Although it is easier to point to similarities and consistencies – the use of market forms, disarticulation of the state system, use of private companies for delivery of state services and the role of private sponsorship – than it is to pin down differences, nonetheless, I have tried to indicate that there is something distinctive about the third way and the role of the state as a 'competition state' under New Labour. The Labour approach to investment in education through PFI and BSF (Building Schools for the Future) schemes is also very different from the Conservative neglect of buildings and infrastructure. Labour has mobilised the private sector to these ends in a much more thoroughgoing way than the Conservatives ever did. New Labour's 'moral authoritarianism' and its emphasis on responsibility, community and social capital (see Chapter Four) are also different from the narrower view 'that there is no such thing as society', which was a hallmark of Thatcherism. Some of these issues of continuity and difference are taken up again in the following chapters. I shall also seek to supplement the emphasis on New Labour's modernisation programme in this chapter with an argument (in the concluding chapter) that suggests that current education policy is marked by circularities or reinventions of the past – for example, class and segregation, privatisation, voluntarism and philanthropy, IQism (talented and gifted) and the role of faith schools.

Notes

[1] 'Dame schools' was a common term used to describe small private schools that provided an education for working-class children before they were old enough to work. These schools were usually run by an elderly woman who taught children to read and write and other useful skills, such as sewing. Fees were about 3d a week and the quality of education that the children received varied enormously, some schools and teachers providing a good education, others no more than childminders.

[2] The 1944 Education Act changed the education system for primary and secondary schools in England and Wales. This Act, commonly named after the Conservative politician R.A.B. Butler, replaced elementary schools up to the age of 14 with primary and secondary education, transfer between which was mainly at the age of 11. Working out the detail of how to provide the new, free secondary schools led many LEAs, under advice given by the Department of Education in 1947, to allocate pupils to grammar and secondary modern schools as well as, in a minority of areas, to technical schools. This became rather inaccurately known as the 'tripartite system' of secondary education

although most pupils were never offered the chance of technical education, and a substantial minority of LEAs opted for one of several versions of 'middle schools' followed by 'high schools'.

[3]The same term ('payment by results') is now used to refer to the rules-based system for paying National Health Service (NHS) trusts for their work. It is intended to reward efficiency, support patient choice and diversity and encourage activity for sustainable waiting time reductions. However, it does not entail hospital inspectors checking on patients' and doctors' progress at bedsides or in surgeries.

[4] During the whole of the period 1950-80 HE remained as a class 'backwater', changing little apart from the spurt of expansion in the 1960s, again arguably an 'adjustment' response to the expansion of the middle class. More recent expansion in the overall HE participation rate has actually increased class differences. Around half of the population describe themselves as working in occupations that are classified as skilled (manual), partly skilled or unskilled. Yet, in 2000, just 18% of young people from these backgrounds were benefiting from HE. While this was an increase of 8 percentage points on the position in 1990, the increase in participation by people from families with professional and non-manual occupations was 11 percentage points (from 37% to 48%). In other words, the gap in participation between those in higher and lower social classes has grown. Indeed, if one turned the clock back to 1960 when there were just 200,000 full-time students, the gap between the two groups was actually less than it is now (see www.dfes.gov.uk/hegateway/uploads/EWParticipation.pdf).

[5]The 1992 Further and Higher Education Act removed FE and sixth form colleges from LEA control and established the Further Education Funding Councils (FEFCs).

3

Current policy models and *The UK government's approach to public service reform*

One of the key points reiterated in this book is that education policy is now almost entirely subsumed within an overall strategy of public services reform, and that many of the specific initiatives in the organisation and delivery of education have more or less direct parallels in other parts of the public sector. This may be already clear from the previous chapter. The strategy is made up of a package of technologies – mechanisms of change – which are generic and not only being deployed across the public sector in England, but, as suggested in Chapter One, also being used within a variety of different nation-states around the world. I have also tried to stress the incremental or additive nature of the reform process, ideas and tactics that once seemed radical or even unthinkable as policies have become established as possibilities or have been made to appear obvious or even necessary over time. In practice, the impetus or direction of policy is made up of a continuous series of small 'moves', which, in themselves, may seem insignificant or marginal, punctuated by occasional grand flourishes, like the 1988 Education Reform Act. These moves involve both changes in the infrastructure and what Keith Joseph called the 'levers' of policy (see Chapter Two), along with the development of new policy languages (see the Introduction to this book). The expectations and assumptions embedded in the language of policy, the way it is thought about and talked about, are reworked over time. New (or indeed old) vocabularies of description and identification of policy problems and their solutions are brought into play. In other words, policies have trajectories over time and the 'family relationships' they accumulate or evolve are presented and accounted for within evolving policy narratives. As we shall see, these form the objects about which they speak – for example, 'failing schools'.

In this chapter, first a recent version of New Labour's generic reform package, *The UK government's approach to public service reform* (Cabinet Office, 2006), will be presented, and its application to education discussed. Second, in doing so, the genealogies of some of the key elements within New Labour education policy and their continuities with and differences from Conservative policy will be explored. This will allow us to home in on some of the specific concepts and models that now influence, inform and animate education policy.

As indicated in the previous two chapters a considerable amount of discursive work has gone into making the case for the need for public sector reform, creating a context of 'reform-readiness'. The Cabinet Office document succinctly states that 'Public services face major challenges from social, economic and technological changes and from major changes in public attitudes and expectations' (p 3), and that 'Reform is needed to ensure efficiency and effectiveness' (p 4). These are presented as the problems whose solution necessitates the reforms outlined. Lister (2000) argues that 'this is a discourse that brooks no opposition, for who wants to appear as old-fashioned and backward-looking?'. The 'approach' to reform that is summarised in the Cabinet Office document (2006) consists of four fairly simple mechanisms that should be recognisable as versions of the policy technologies discussed in Chapter One:

- top-down performance management (pressure from government);
- the introduction of greater competition and contestability in the provision of public services;
- the introduction of greater pressure from citizens including through choice and voice; and
- measures to strengthen the capability of civil and public servants and of central and local government to deliver improved public services.

In its full form the model, 'a self-improving system', looks like this:

Figure 3.1: The UK government's model of public service reform: a self-improving system

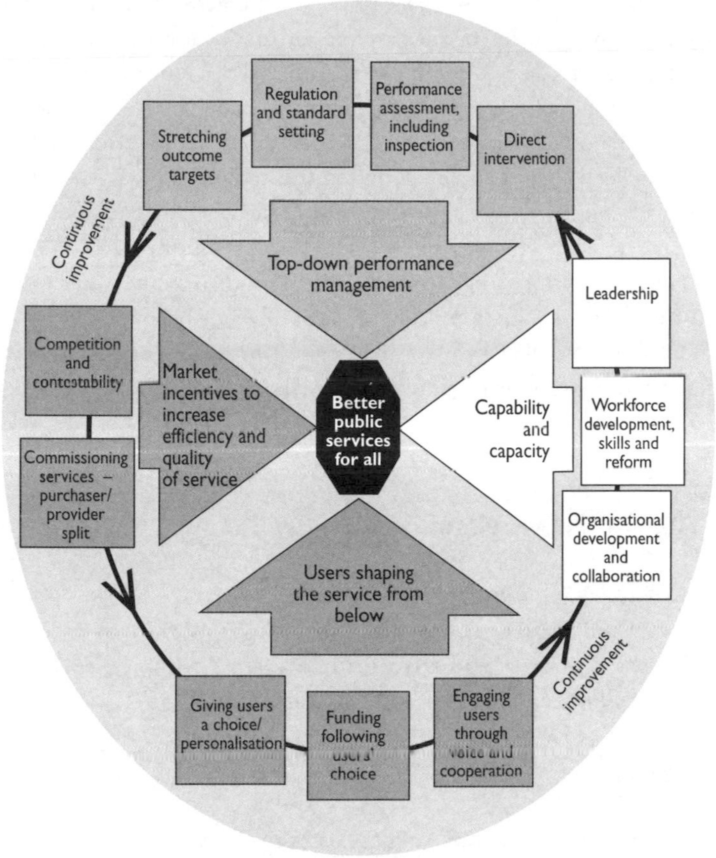

The model is in some ways a post hoc construction but also represents an analytic and 'research-based' and formative version of New Labour's 'approach' to policy. 'Approach' is an appropriately loose term here that signals the importance of variations in its application in different sectors of public service.

The policy genealogies that are rehearsed below indicate that a number of the components of the model had their beginnings in the period of Conservative reform, although a 'simple' linear relationship is not being suggested in every case. As noted already, however, the Conservative reforms opened up opportunities for further reform, 'softening up' or weakening the embedded assumptions of the welfare model of education and public service. These initial moves, and several others that were stalled at the time, can be traced back to the 'intellectuals' of neoliberalism and the neoliberal think-tanks that were advising or influencing ministers, some of whom were noted in the previous chapter (Joseph, Seldon, Hayek, Institute of Economic Affairs, Centre for Policy Studies, Adam Smith Institute and so on). In the same way the 'footprints' of a number of Labour's third way intellectuals are evident here (see below) in the deployment of key reform ideas, as are again, more generally, the activities of various think-tanks – Institute for Public Policy Research, Demos, Social Market Foundation and so on.

Box 3.1: The intellectuals of New Labour

Anthony Giddens/the third way

Now Lord Giddens, primary intellectual of the 'third way', once described as Tony Blair's favourite academic, author of *Beyond Left and Right: The future of radical politics* (1994), 'After the Left's paralysis' (1998a) and *The third way: The renewal of social democracy* (1998b):

> Giddens' impact upon politics has been profound. His advice has been sought by political leaders from Asia, Latin America and Australia, as well as from the US and Europe. He has had a major impact upon the evolution of New Labour in the UK. He took part in the original Blair–Clinton dialogues from 1997 onwards. (www.lse.ac.uk)

Michael Barber/world-class education

Michael Barber joined McKinsey (a management consultancy company) on 1 September 2005 as the expert partner in its

Global Public Sector Practice. Prior to joining McKinsey he was (from 2001) Chief Adviser on delivery to the Prime Minister. As Head of the Prime Minister's Delivery Unit he was responsible for the oversight of implementation of the priority programmes in health, education, transport, policing, the criminal justice system and asylum/immigration. He worked closely with ministers and top officials to ensure the policies, systems and processes put in place would deliver promised outcomes.

Between 1997 and 2001, Barber was Chief Adviser to the Secretary of State for Education on school standards. In this role he was responsible for the implementation of the government's school reform programme including the literacy and numeracy strategies at primary level, tackling 'school failure' at all levels and the contracting out of 'failing' LEAs. Publications include *The learning game: Arguments for an education revolution* (1997a), *How to do the impossible: A guide for politicians with a passion for education* (1997b) and *The virtue of accountability* (2005). He has acted as adviser to the governments of Australia, the US, Russia, Estonia and Hong Kong, and to the OECD, the World Bank and the IMF. In 2007 at the invitation of Gordon Brown he joined the National Council for Excellence in Education.

Tom Bentley/creativity
Executive Director for Policy and Cabinet for the Premier of Victoria, Australia from September 2006. He was Director of Demos from 1999-2006 (referred to in policy circles as the 'do-tank'). Prior to that he was a special adviser to David Blunkett MP, then Secretary of State for Education and Employment, where he worked on issues including school curriculum reform, social inclusion and creativity. His publications include *Learning beyond the classroom: Education for a changing world* (1998) and *The creative age: Knowledge and skills for a new economy* (1999).

David Hargreaves/epidemic/networks
Associate Director for Development and Research, Specialist Schools and Academies Trust, Demos author, author of *About learning* (2005), *Creative professionalism* (1998) and *Education epidemic* (2003a).

Charles Leadbeater/personalisation
'A new organising logic for public provision' (2004) (and see Chapter One for references to *Living on thin air*, 2000a). Leadbeater is a Demos author and a 'senior adviser to governments over the past decade, advising the 10 Downing St policy unit, the Department for Trade and Industry and the European Commission on the rise of the knowledge driven economy and the Internet, as well as the government of Shanghai. He is an advisor to the Department for Education's Innovation Unit on future strategies for more networked and personalised approaches to learning and education' (www.charlesleadbeater.net).

Andrew Adonis/academies/selection
Now Lord Adonis, co-author with Stephen Pollard of the book *A class act* (1997), which argues strongly for selection in schools and the need for education reform as a means of retaining middle-class commitment to the public sector. Associated with the think-tank Demos he became an adviser to the Number 10 Policy Unit on education in 1998 and is generally regarded as the key influence in Labour's education policies. In 2005 he was elevated to the peerage and appointed as Junior Education Minister. He is particularly associated with the academies programme.

David Halpern/social capital
Member of the Prime Minister's Strategy Unit (PMSU), which focuses on the development of long-term, cross-cutting policy. Has previously held positions at the University of Cambridge, Nuffield College, Oxford, and the Policy Studies Institute, London. He has authored PMSU discussion papers on social capital, life

satisfaction, and personal responsibility and behaviour change (see also Halpern and Misokz, 1998); he is author of *Social capital* (2005).

Michael Fullan/reculturing
He is the Dean of the Ontario Institute for Studies in Education of the University of Toronto. A 'change guru' and policy entrepreneur, he has developed a number of partnerships designed to bring about school improvement and educational reform. Fullan led the evaluation team that conducted a four-year assessment of the National Literacy and Numeracy Strategy in England. He is author of *Leading in a culture of change* (2001).

It is worth noting here some of the biases that arise from this kind of 'think-tank' policy making. One that is often referred to is the London base of the main 'think-tanks' and policy entrepreneurs that have sought or had influence in education policy making. The Institute of Economic Affairs, Social Affairs Unit, Centre for Policy Studies, Social Market Foundation, Adam Smith Institute and Institute for Public Policy Research all have their offices in London. This is not surprising, as they seek to be close to the 'centres of power', but it does tend to give a particular inflection to education policy making. It could be said that the North London family (with the Blairs as the archetype; see Chapter Four) is the dominant species in the social world of education reform. Rentoul (1997, p 433) presents this as indicative of the 'metropolitan, middle-class assumptions of "New Labour"'. On the other hand, this is also an urban bias as, like in the 19th century, a great deal of social and education policy is driven by the problematics of 'the urban'. The concentration of influence also reflects a more general literal and metaphorical redrawing of the 'map' of education policy and policy 'spaces' (see Chapter Five). The erosion of LEA powers and the paraphernalia of the national curriculum and other policy moves has meant that sources of innovation and fresh thinking outside of London have been cut off – although Birmingham may be a recent exception for the Labour Party from which a number of examples of 'good practice' have been taken. There is certainly little evidence at the school level of a 'counter-flow' of influence and ideas from other parts of the UK or the English regions – while in the 1960s and 1970s comprehensive education reforms and a great deal of curriculum innovation were initiated by schools and LEAs. The flow of policy and policy ideas in England has become increasingly from the centre outward; although 'successful' headteachers are recruited to run or participate in government programmes. But there are paradoxes here. While education and local government policy has generally, since the early 1980s, steadily and dramatically withdrawn regional and local powers, the 1988 and 1993 Education Acts granted considerable autonomy (perhaps more apparent than real) to individual institutions. Furthermore, there is also an emphasis within the New Labour reforms on the identification and dissemination of 'good practice' in and between schools through partnerships and federations and an impetus given generally to innovation, creativity and entrepreneurship. Nonetheless, the possibilities of innovation are tightly framed within the reform narratives of enterprise and performance. Innovations have to make sense within the terms of these narratives of reform.

We will now work through each of the four main components of the 'Cabinet Office approach' using short genealogical accounts of some of the main education policy initiatives and moves that are related to them. These accounts will of necessity be indicative rather than definitive given their massive volume, especially after 1988. As in previous chapters some extracts from policy documents will be quoted as illustrations of the new ways in which education is being conceived within policy and the concepts that are in play. Neither the accounts nor the use of the Cabinet Office model are intended to suggest that all and every piece of policy fits neatly together within a rational framework. There is a great deal of ad hocery, short-termism and bluster in the recent history of education reform.

Top-down performance management

Concern with performance and accountability, as a mechanism of policy, arguably has it origins in Callaghan's Ruskin speech and the creation in 1974 of the DES Assessment of Performance Unit (APU). The APU's remit was: 'To promote the development of methods of assessing and monitoring the achievement of children at school, and to seek to identify the incidence of underachievement'. Its specific tasks were:

- to identify and appraise existing instruments and methods of assessment that may be relevant for these purposes;
- to sponsor the creation of new instruments and methods of assessment, having due regard to statistical and sampling methods;
- to promote the conduct of assessments in cooperation with LEAs and teachers;
- to identify significant differences related to the circumstances in which children learn, including the incidence of underachievement, and to make the findings available to all of those concerned with resource allocation within the Department, local authorities and schools.

The proposals for the work of the APU now sound modest and benign. However, as with other policy 'moves' in the 1970s and 1980s, its importance was strategic and symbolic. It was indicative of a shift in the loci of power in education beginning at this time away from classrooms and schools and LEAs towards the centre, the DES and HMI. It announced a different kind of relationship between central government and the education service, articulated through the setting, monitoring and publication of performance outcomes that provided a lever of judgement and bases for critique. At the time it provoked considerable 'hostility and resentment ... in some quarters of the teaching profession' (Chitty, 1989, p 80). In Maclure's view, it was related in a number of ways to a further much more decisive shift in power relations that was being mooted and discussed at the same point in time, a national curriculum: 'It would be another ten years before ministers would talk quite openly of their desire for a national curriculum, but the process of achieving one began at Ruskin' (Maclure, 1987, p 11). These moves of accountability and specification were also indicative of the sense that the form of the education system and its 'outputs', in a general sense, were viewed as no longer 'fit for purpose'. In other words, that education was to take the blame for at least some of the country's economic and industrial difficulties, inasmuch as the needs of industry were not being well served. However, this has to be counterposed with the *Black Paper*/neoconservative critique that was that education had changed too much and changed inappropriately, that it was too radical and too progressive and that tradition and national culture and heritage had to be reasserted. The 1988 national curriculum was the primary vehicle for that reassertion. In both respects teachers were increasingly regarded with suspicion, as not to be trusted, as both too conservative and resistant to change and as dangerously progressive (Ball, 1990). Indeed, throughout the processes of reform and transformation Conservative education policy and to a lesser extent New Labour policy have tried to mix and match tradition and modernisation in their reforms. The other reference in the Ruskin speech noted already was to 'incompetent teachers' and the need for teacher accountability, again indicative of the beginnings of a changing relationship between government and teachers, and again not unconnected with the derision aimed at teachers by the *Black Papers* and fed by the cause célèbre of a 'progressive' primary school – William Tyndale school (Davis, 2004) – and media attacks on and 'exposés' of 'bad' teachers led by *The Daily Mail*. As Levin (2004) argues, media coverage of education is primarily about 'blaming' or more generally, Lingard and Rawolle (2004, p 361) suggest, that there has been a 'mediatisation of policy' in education, that the media are a major player in the field of policy influence. We will return to the trajectory of 'teacher reform' below but I do want to make the point that these two reform genealogies, performance and teachers, are closely linked in terms of their effects within contexts of practice – schools and classrooms – not least in the sense that the construction within policy and public discourses of the 'untrustworthy teacher' creates the basis for the assertion of more accountability and more control over their education and their certification and performance (for a very good account see Furlong, 2001) and legitimates the withdrawal of aspects of their professional autonomies.

The 1979 Conservative Party Manifesto (p 24) proposed more 'effective use' of the APU in setting 'national standards in reading, writing and arithmetic, monitored by tests worked out with teachers and others and applied locally by education authorities'. While still set within a teacher–LEA–DES framework of cooperation we can see here the seeds of both the system of national testing that was introduced in the 1988 Education Reform Act and New Labour's national targets for education. A whole new lexicon of policy is being adumbrated here to 'apply' to education, as a way of rethinking it in terms of accountability, benchmarks, performance monitoring, national standards and school failure and so on.

From this point on there were further incremental moves. In 1984 a scheme of pupils' records of achievement (RoAs) was launched and the term 'attainment targets' was first used in the White Paper *Better schools* (DfES, 1985), although the White Paper stated that the government had no intention to introduce legislation redefining responsibility for the curriculum. However, the 1988 Education Reform Act did introduce a national curriculum and put in place a system of national testing measured as 10 levels of attainment at four Key Stages (7, 11, 14 and 16) based on the programmes of study for each national curriculum subject. The task of providing the initial specification of the testing system was given to the Task Group on Assessment and Testing (TGAT), chaired by Professor Paul Black; his appointment served to mollify the concerns of many sceptical teachers. It was recommended that a combination of standard assessment tasks (SATs) and teacher assessments (TAs) be used to generate individual test scores and that these should be used as formative, diagnostic instruments based on a close interdependence between curriculum, teaching and assessment. However, the government response to TGAT gave much greater emphasis to the summative role of the testing to inform parents about their child's progress and the publication of test results. As reported in *The Observer* (22 October 1989, p 4), 'Mrs Thatcher's determination to downgrade teachers' views and force schools to rely more on banks of national tests now appears to have won the day'. Here again we have a prime minister taking a close, hands-on interest in educational matters. Furthermore, over time the role of TAs in the tests, as part of normal classroom activity, was reduced and finally replaced by complete reliance on formal 'pen and paper' testing. In July 1989 contracts worth £14 million were awarded for the development of SATs in the core curriculum subjects. The examination and assessment system was now made the responsibility of the Secondary Examinations and Assessment Council (SEAC) working alongside the National Curriculum Council (NCC).

The establishment of the scheme of national testing was also another moment in the process of shifting powers between teachers and the centre. The crucial value added in policy terms of the national testing regime was that the results could provide attainment data not only to compare individual students in their classrooms but also schools and LEAs in the form of league tables. Such tables were introduced in 1992, with the avowed purpose as noted previously of providing market information to parents in their choice making. They were quickly taken up by the national and local press and continue to provide news stories annually about 'the worst school in England'. Coverage of test and examination performance is now extensive and 'predictable, simplistic, ritualistic' (Warmington and Murphy, 2004, p 290). They are extensively used in the various commercial 'guides' to 'good schools' that are now available to parents, and are quoted by schools themselves in promotional literature. Again the public discourse around such tables and the test results brought the notions of 'good schools' and 'bad schools', as defined by performance, into common parlance, making them a vehicle for further policy. The 1993 Education Act, which was at that point the largest piece of legislation in the history of education, included new measures on intervention into 'failing' schools. The league tables also made it possible to compare between types of school. Thus, in 1996 the DfEE was able to announce that the 'opted-out' grant-maintained schools (created by the 1988 Education Reform Act) 'achieve better results than LEA schools' (DfEE, 1996, p 21). The 1993 Education Act also abolished the NCC and SEAC, replacing them with the School Curriculum and Assessment Authority (SCAA). This was replaced in turn by the QCA in 1997.

All of this then provided an infrastructure of policy possibilities that were taken up and taken much further by New Labour, as signalled by Tony Blair's commitment to an educational reform process that was to be about 'standards not structures' (Labour Party, 1997). The *Times Educational Supplement* report on 'The buzzwords of 1998' noted that 'standards' occurred 2,272 times, more than twice as frequently as the word next most used, appearing in one quarter of all articles, and 'achievement' received 782 mentions and 'inspection' 627. 'Under New Labour "standards" has replaced "curriculum" as the discursive hub of educational policy-making' (Davies and Edwards, 1999, p 262).

In 1997 Stephen Byers was appointed Standards Minister and the government announced the successful achievement of its national education targets as a key test of its performance. The government was applying a version of its performance management device to itself. Ministers staked their reputation on targets that demanded that 80% of 11-year-olds reach the expected literacy standard, and 75% the numeracy standard, by 2002. In January 1998 Byers claimed that 57% of 11-year-olds attaining the literacy standard in 1996 'will not do – that is why we have set a target of 80% by 2002' ('Councils get tough new English test targets – Byers', 7 January 1998, at www.ginfo.pl/more). The Secretary of State at the time, David Blunkett (1997-2001), also staked his job on achieving such targets, and his successor as Secretary of State, Estelle Morris, party to the original claim, resigned in 2002, at least in part because the target was not reached. At the end of 2002 the government admitted that many of its earlier targets had also been missed.

The setting of national targets is also indicative of the reconceptualisation of the education system as a single entity and as a fundamental component of national economic competitiveness, as suggested in Chapter One. The ways in which reform objectives, particularly the 'raising of standards', were tied to the economic necessities of international competition were evident in a speech given by Tony Blair to the National Association of Headteachers' (NAHT's) annual conference in 1999, the first time a British prime minister had addressed a teacher union conference:

> Average standards have been far too low. Variation between the best and worst has been far too great. And a long tail of poor achievers, a large proportion not even reaching basic competence in literacy and numeracy after eleven years of compulsory schooling, has consistently marked us out from our leading economic competitors.... If we fail to seize this opportunity to create a world-class system, we betray our generation and those that follow. That means schools with standards that match or exceed the best internationally. It means eliminating the tail of non-achievers, so that all young people leave the education system with the skills to find a good job and a capacity for lifelong learning. It means schools which develop in young people not just academic success, but care, compassion and confidence.

Again, all of this should be understood as part of a generic device, the use of indicators, benchmarks and targets to drive reform. During the 1990s targets were in increasing use in education settings around the world. The use of 'learning targets' was, for example, central to the United Nations Educational, Scientific and Cultural Organization's (UNESCO's) Education for All (EFA) initiative (www.unesco.org). Goldstein argues that:

> The obsession of EFA with achieving specific learning targets seems to reflect a similar set of concerns within certain national education systems, as has been indicated with examples from England and the United States. Within such systems the imposition of targets for institutions or school authorities can be viewed as an effective means of centralized

> control ... even within the rhetoric of diversity and local decision making. At the international level, even if unintended, the eventual outcome of pursuing EFA targets may well be an increasing control of individual systems by institutions such as the World Bank or aid agencies, supported by global testing corporations. (www.aea-europe.net/userfiles/Harvey%20Goldstein%20Discussion%20Group%202.pdf)

Generated by and interwoven with the standards agenda particular policy attention was given to 'failure' and 'failing schools' – a term of use shared with the US (see Box 3.2). Indeed, throughout Labour's time in office 'failing schools' have been a recurrent subject of policy and popular media attention.

Box 3.2: Failing schools under-reported

> Many states and local school districts are underreporting the number of schools failing to teach children to read and do mathematics at their grade level as required by the 2-year-old No Child Left Behind Act, fearful of ultimately losing control over poorly performing schools. Education Secretary Rod Paige says the problem of districts and states 'playing games' to avoid accountability for poor teaching and learning in their schools is not yet 'under control' and is anticipated with 'any big change like this'. (George Archibald, *The Washington Times*, 2004, www.washingtontimes.com/)

Schools that do not achieve targets for improvement – 'failing schools' – can be made subject to further inspection and intervention, and indeed closure, followed in some cases by a 'fresh start'. Under the Fresh Start scheme, failing schools were closed and reopened with a new name, new management and often new staff and new 'superheads', as they came to be called. In March 2000, Education Secretary David

Blunkett called on education authorities in England to set up Fresh Start secondary schools where less than 15% of pupils achieve five or more good GCSEs (grades A*-C) for three years. This led to a list of 86 schools under threat being published by *The Times*. Failure, in other words, allows the government to 'act tough', to demonstrate seriousness of purpose and an unwillingness to tolerate poor performance:

> Tough intervention to tackle failure – identified by the school inspectors Ofsted – has helped turn around 1500 schools, and has reduced the total number of failing schools from over 500 to barely 200.... There are now just over 60 schools where fewer than a quarter of youngsters gains five good GCSEs compared with over 600 in 1997. And the number of non-selective schools where more than 70 per cent of pupils reach that standard has risen from 83 to over 580. (Press release, No 10 Downing Street, 2007, www.number10.gov.uk/output/Page10502.asp)

Apart from providing a continuous stream of newspaper headlines the language of 'failing schools' is both an opportunity and, like national targets, a risk for government – an opportunity in the sense of driving the necessity of reform, making it unstoppable – failure cannot be defended – and a risk to the extent that continuing failure opens up the reform agenda to political criticism. In January 2006 a National Audit Office (NAO) report claimed to show that at least 980,000 children were being taught in 1,557 primary and secondary schools officially classified as 'poorly performing', although the auditors also warned that the true figure could be much higher, arguing that the DfES had yet to identify all sub-standard primary schools:

> **Our failing schools: one in eight children gets sub-standard education.**
>
> More than a million children are receiving a sub-standard education because they are forced to attend poorly performing

> schools, the National Audit Office warns today. About one in eight pupils in England is being denied a decent education despite £1bn spent by ministers on attempts to improve struggling schools last year. (*The Independent*, 11 January 2006, Sarah Cassidy, education correspondent)

The standards agenda as a performance management device also articulates with other very different aspects of New Labour's reform programme. For example, while gradual reduction in LEA powers and responsibilities, with greater autonomies given to schools and the involvement of other kinds of 'providers' (see below), was being pursued, specific attempts to address underachievement in schools located in areas of social and economic deprivation were also being made. In March 1999 the then School Standards Minister, Estelle Morris, was given special responsibility for education in the inner cities and to oversee an acceleration in inspections of local authorities in deprived areas. Extra checks were announced on 'the worst-performing schools', with the lowest 5% in performance tables being subjected to monitoring every six months.

Competition and contestability

There were two related aspects to the changes and pressures involved here and they can be represented fairly straightforwardly in terms of what Hatcher (2000) calls *endogenous* and *exogenous* privatisation. The first was the main emphasis within the Conservative governments of 1979-97 and involved making public sector organisations, like schools and colleges and universities, act in more businesslike ways and more like businesses by creating 'quasi-market' systems (or market-like mechanisms) that brought competition to bear on the relationships between providers (see Chapter Two) by shifting the opportunity structures within which they operated. This was achieved mainly by linking funding to recruitment and thus to consumer choice (see below), but also involved giving greater managerial and budgetary autonomy to institutions (LMS) so that they were able to achieve internal 'cost savings' and generate new income streams by acting entrepreneurially, as well as giving greater attention to their promotion and marketing activities (see Maguire, 1996). A further aspect of the pressures of competition is the use of market information such as league tables and performance indicators, discussed above. Working together they were intended to bring about the 'enterprising up' of public sector organisations.

Such terms of competition can lead to forms of 'cream-skimming behaviour' on the part of providers seeking market advantage, which may require the development of regulatory responses. However, both Conservatives and Labour have also built into their 'new' schools initiatives the possibility of selection, which, in itself, dampens and distorts competitive effects.[1] It is important to recognise that these education markets (and the same is true of many commercial markets) are highly regulated. They work in ways allowed for and necessitated by the policies that form them but they also tend to generate unanticipated consequences. For example, one issue that has exercised both Conservative and Labour governments, which is an unintended side-effect of competition and performance maximisation, is the exclusion of students. Publication of league tables in 1992 led to a massive increase in permanent exclusions; excluded students did not count at that point in performance figures. The government responded by the setting up of a network of Pupil Referral Units (PRUs).[2] Labour has addressed the problem of exclusions, within the logic of its 'approach', by setting exclusion targets. Figures, published in May 2001, showed that exclusions had fallen from 10,400 in 1998/99 to an estimated 8,600 in 1999/2000, very close to the national target of 8,400 by 2002, at which point the targets were abandoned, with David Blunkett stating that 'I am satisfied the level we have reached is sustainable' (4 May 2001, news.bbc.co.uk). However, government attention quickly switched from exclusion, as a policy problem and a school problem, to truancy, as a problem of parenting (see Chapter Four).

There are three main aspects to the 'drivers' embedded in the 'theory' of 'quasi-market competition'. One is the efficiency effects of competition itself, the idea that performance levels will improve across the system as a whole as institutions become more focused on the achievement of performance outputs. This assumes that the outputs are appropriate and well chosen and that the providers do not engage in 'opportunistic behaviours' in achieving their improvements or significantly increase the effort and expenditure being devoted to presentation and promotion. A second is market failure, that is, that unpopular providers will be driven out of business – what Keith Joseph, quoted in Chapter Two, talked about as importing the notion of 'bankruptcy'. In practice the closure of 'failing' schools is not always straightforward (see also Fresh Start discussed above and academies considered in Chapter Four). Third, in bringing choice into play as a competitive force it is expected that institutions become more responsive to the interests, needs and concerns of clients (see below). But again this is far from straightforward and does not necessarily sit easily with a top-down system of performance indicators that has the potential to lead to a differential valuing of clients by institutions – the development of 'local economies of pupil worth'. In this economy, some children (white and middle-class, first language speakers) are of high value, are 'value-adding' and much sought after; others are of low value (immigrant children, those with disabilities, those with social and behavioural difficulties, and some fractions of the working class), they 'add negative value' (Kenway and Bullen, 2001, p 140) and are, where possible, avoided. Students and their parents are, in effect, producers of the exchange value of the institution. The parent 'is expected to work hard at making their children work hard' (Kenway and Bullen, 2001, p 138).

While the Conservatives primarily focused on endogenous competition, Labour have given much more impetus to exogenous contestability, that is, allowing for the possibility of new providers from outside the state sector to deliver public services of various kinds either when public sector providers have been judged to have 'failed', in the provision of new services or as a way of replacing permanent provision with 'flexible' contracting – what is known as 'outsourcing'. There are a myriad of examples of such contestability and outsourcing in education currently (see Ball, 2007), including three schools in Surrey and one in Enfield that are or have been managed by private companies, and a series of high-profile 'privatisations' of LEA services. In the case of 'failing' LEAs, the contracts for some of which have now come to an end (Swindon, Haringey), private providers take over the whole or parts of these services on a for-profit basis and have to seek to meet performance targets that are set in their contracts. Some government programmes – such as the National Strategies and Connexions (careers advice services) – are also run by private companies.

Interestingly, in the run-up to the 1988 Education Reform Act, Under-Secretary of State for Education Bob Dunn floated the idea of crown schools and company schools – the former, a version of grant-maintained schools; the latter, groups of schools tendered to private companies, as packages, with attendant tax relief. Their performance would be compared with LEA schools after a five-year period. Teachers' salaries would be set by the companies and related directly to performance. This was not taken up within policy but versions of all of this were to appear in policy later, as we shall see below.

In this form of contestability the private sector serves as a kind of discipline, held to be an alternative to the public sector if modernisation is resisted or fudged: 'If you are unwilling or unable to work to the modern agenda, then government will have to look to other partners to take on your role' (Tony Blair's 1998 address to public agencies, cited in Newman, 2001, p 51). The private sector is also a model to be emulated: 'we need to make sure that government services are brought forward using the best and most modern techniques, to match the best of the private sector' (Cabinet Office, 1999, p 5). Again this was a recurring theme of Tony Blair's rhetoric of reform:

> Prime Minister Tony Blair used his monthly press conference to make clear his determination to use private-sector practice to push through public-sector reform. It would be a mistake of 'fundamental historic importance' to change course now, he said. (J. Slater, *Guardian*, 20 May 2003)

The idea here is to create a diversity of providers, public, private and voluntary, breaking the public sector monopoly and bringing new 'energy' and 'creativity' into the system.

Figure 3.2: A genealogy of competition and contestability

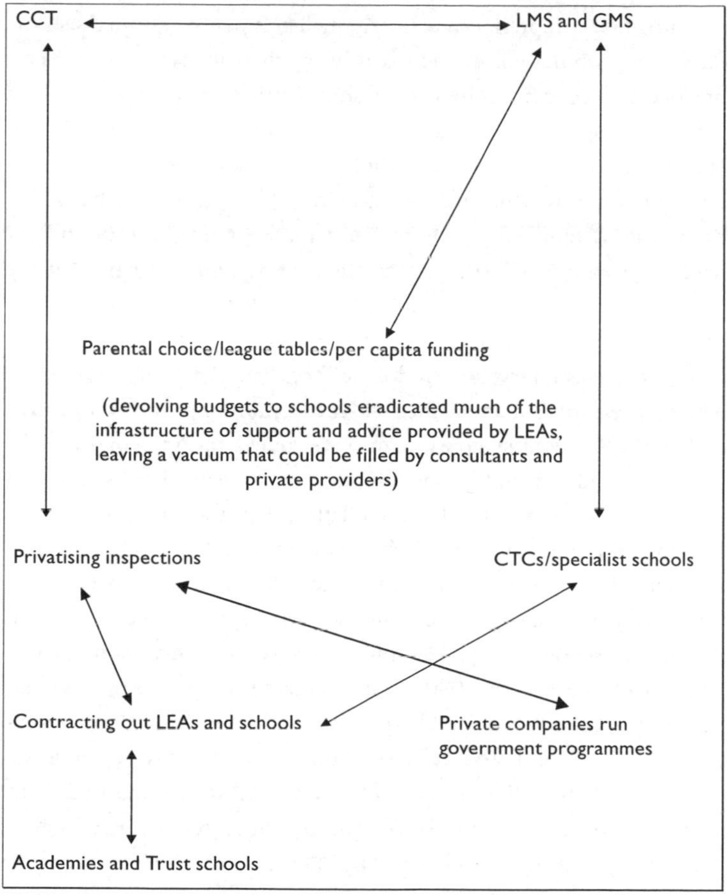

Note: GMS = grant-maintained school

The other dimension to competition and 'choice' policies, which has been pursued by both Conservative and Labour governments, is 'diversity' within the state sector. In terms of the simplicities of market theory, competition and choice only work if there are a variety of types of provision and of providers. The baseline to this is that the English education system has always included a considerable degree of such diversity, although unevenly distributed through the system. Despite the inroads of comprehensivisation a small number of grammar schools remain, and some 'comprehensives' were such in name rather than practice; indeed, comprehensives fashioned themselves in a variety of forms ranging from progressive to very traditional, and, in addition, 'aided' faith schools (Roman Catholic, Church of England and Jewish and more recently Muslim, Sikh and Greek Orthodox) are a basic part of the state system. Even so, both Conservative and Labour politicians have in recent years characterised the state system in terms of what Secretary of State John Patten (1992-94) called the 'dull uniformity of comprehensive education' or what Alastair Campbell (Tony Blair's former press secretary) referred to as 'bog standard comprehensives'. The Conservatives made a decisive intervention into this uniformity, and at the same time considerably weakened the role of LEAs in educational administration, by allowing grant-maintained schools to 'opt out' of LEA control, to be funded directly by the DfES, and to have additional autonomies, particularly over the use of their budgets. Grant-maintained schools were also entitled to apply to central government for capital grants for essential building works. Skegness Grammar School was the first school to apply for, and to receive, grant-maintained status and by 1996 there were 1,090 grant-maintained schools, 60% of which were secondary schools. The legislative conditions that created grant-maintained schools lasted from 1988 until 1998. They were abolished by the 1998 School Standards and Framework Act that required them to choose to become foundation schools[3] or to rejoin their LEA as maintained community schools. The Blairs had themselves exercised the possibilities of parental choice in not sending their son Euan to a local secondary school but rather to a Catholic grant-maintained school, The London Oratory, and were the butt of considerable press and public criticism; other New Labour ministers, including Harriet

Harman, Ruth Kelly and Lord Adonis have been subject to similar criticisms of their choices of schools for their children.

The two other Conservative contributions to greater diversity were CTCs and specialist schools. CTCs are 'independent state schools' that charge no fees as their recurrent costs are borne by the DfES and private business sponsors and they specialise in teaching mainly technology-based subjects such as technology, science and mathematics. CTCs also forge close links with businesses and industry (mainly through their sponsors, for example, ADT, Dixons, Djanogly), and often their governors are directors of local or national businesses that are supporting the colleges. The CTC programme was originally intended to be much larger but the Conservative government found it difficult to attract sponsorship from businesses. The legislative framework for CTCs was used to establish academies. The government is currently encouraging CTCs to convert into academies, although the differences between the two types of school are relatively small (the main one being that CTCs are allowed to select pupils while academies are not).

The Specialist Schools Programme was launched in 1994, when a small number of grant-maintained and voluntary-aided schools began operating as technology colleges. In the following year, all maintained secondary schools in England were given the opportunity to apply for specialist status. By January 2004, more than half of them (54%) had gained specialist status and 2006 began with the proportion at 75%. The programme enables schools, in partnership with private sector sponsors and supported by additional government funding, to pursue distinctive identities through their chosen specialisms and to achieve their targets to raise standards. Specialist schools have a special focus on their chosen subject area but must meet the national curriculum requirements and deliver a broad and balanced education to all pupils. Up to 1999, all schools wishing to apply for specialist status were required to raise £100,000 in sponsorship from business, charitable or other private sector sponsors. This was then reduced to £50,000 and there are funds available to help schools that have difficulties in raising sponsorship. Any maintained secondary school in England can apply to be designated as a specialist school in one of 10 specialist areas: arts, business and enterprise, engineering, humanities, language, mathematics and computing, music, science, sports and technology. Schools can also combine any two specialisms. (For more on specialist schools see www.risetrust.org.uk/specialist.html.) The *Five-Year Strategy for Children and Learners* (DfES, 2004) envisaged specialist schools as the universal model for secondary education. The strategy also provided for any school to become a foundation school by a vote of their governing body, further residualising LEAs.

The other main growth area in terms of new sorts of schools has been 'faith schools'. In 2001 there were 7,000 state faith schools – 589 secondary and 6,384 primary in England, out of a total of nearly 25,000. In total 40 were non-Christian, 32 of them being Jewish. Between 1997 and 2005, 103 new faith schools were created (from 112 applications) including the first Sikh, Greek Orthodox and Muslim state schools. The Church of England, which has 4,700 schools, educating 940,000 children, is about halfway through a programme of establishing 100 more secondary schools. The Catholic Education Service is responsible for about 2,200 schools and sixth form colleges, with a total of 720,000 pupils.

Tony Blair, as a committed Christian, gave his personal backing to the role of faith schools on a number of occasions as well as arguing for a more prominent role for faith-based organisations in policy and public debate (see, for example, *The Observer*, 3 March 2003; *The Guardian*, 23 March 2003). Faith organisations and individual Christian sponsors are prominent within the academies programme. The argument for 'faith' schools as part of a diverse system is based on 'effectiveness' in terms of their relative performance advantage over non-faith schools and their so-called 'ethos'. However, there are social differences in their intake – faith schools recruit a smaller proportion of students in receipt of free school meals compared with community schools (approximately 12% as opposed to 20%). The increase in the number of such schools is justified on both grounds in terms of responsiveness to parental preferences:

> Faith schools consistently achieve better results than other state schools, and the Government believes this is in part due to a stronger ethos being laid down in the classrooms. Recent surveys show that 45 per cent of the population of England has no religious belief while nearly a third do not believe in God, but perversely for every place in a Church of England classroom there are 160 applications from parents. (*The Observer*, 'Faith schools spark fears of "apartheid"', 30 September 2001)

The other two New Labour contributions to school diversity are academies – 'independent schools within the state system' – and trust

Figure 3.3: A genealogy of diversity and contestability (schools)

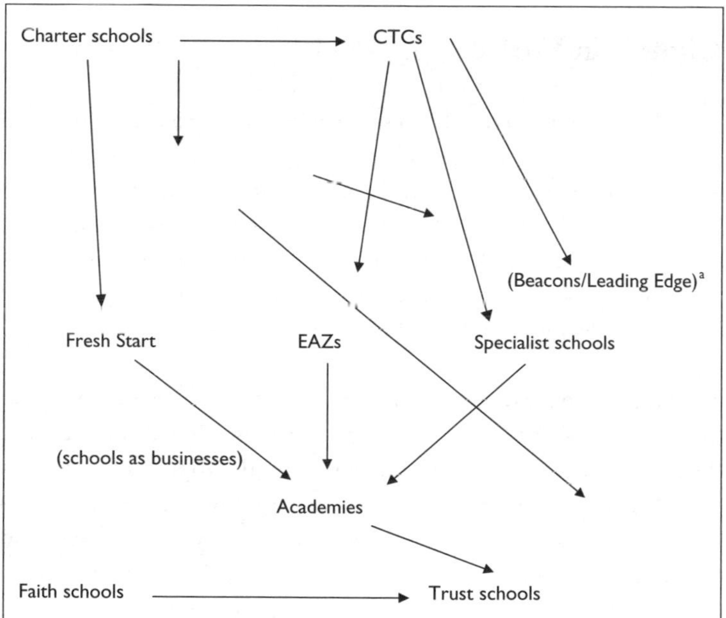

Note: [a] Collaborations/federations

schools (created by the 2006 Education and Inspections Act), both of which are also discussed in Chapter Four.

In all the respects outlined above competition and contestability are part of a dismantling of an only partly realised universal and uniform welfare model of comprehensive education. They are also part of the recalibration of the education system to the necessities of international economic competition. Moreover, they provide a particular kind of response to middle-class educational aspirations at a time of uncertainty. They also work to replace bureaucratic and professional forms of control over education services with more entrepreneurial and arguably more responsive forms, and play a part in reworking the sense and meaning of education from being a public good to an economic good and a commodity. They are also directly connected in policy terms with the mechanisms of choice and voice.

Choice and voice

> The purpose of the reforms is to create a modern education system and a modern NHS where within levels of investment at last coming up to the average of our competitors, real power is put in the hands of those who use the service – the patient and the parent; where the changes becoming self-sustaining; the system, open, diverse, flexible able to adjust and adapt to the changing world. (Blair, 2005d)

In education policy research and in the field of policy advocacy, parental choice is one of the most contested and most difficult of concepts. There is now a massive global literature on the topic and it remains a central issue in education politics, in the US in particular. Choice and voice are also slippery notions that are often used loosely and elusively by advocates, policy makers and critics. According to Clarke et al (2006), choice is an indeterminate concept, and:

> In a submission to the recent Public Administration Select Committee on Choice and Voice in Public Services, Ministers of State argued that choice must be central because:
>
> - it's what users want;
> - it provides incentives for driving up quality, responsiveness and efficiency;
> - it promotes equality;
> - it facilitates personalisation (Ministers of State, 2004, p 4).

Clarke et al go on to say, 'Each of these claims is, as the Select Committee indicated in its report (2005), contestable' (2006, p 1).

Parental choice in education was introduced by the Conservatives in the 1980s and has been strongly endorsed by New Labour, but there are arguably differences between the Conservative and Labour versions of choice. At face value the Conservative version was a neoliberal choice model that included two experiments with vouchers (see below). However, in practice there was a fairly quick recognition that 'choice' was easy to offer politically but more difficult to operationalise in practice. The Conservatives also attempted, in a fairly limited way, to enhance the role of school governors as a form of lay 'voice', by requiring parental and business representatives to be appointed and involving parents through the requirement for a public meeting to discuss the annual report of every school – these have turned out to be notoriously poorly attended. Both choice and voice are part of a more general shift from producer to consumer power, and the creation of 'citizen-consumers' (Clarke et al, 2007), although again offset against other developments like the increased possibilities for selection and for schools to control their own admissions.

Vouchers, as the most radical form of parental choice, are a keynote of neoliberal education policy and are used on a small scale in some US school districts (Milwaukee is the best known example – see Witte, 2001) and across the school system in Chile (Carnoy, 2000). The introduction of vouchers involves, as Keith Joseph put it, 'imposing freedom' (interview, Ball, 1990). Voucher schemes pass the funding mechanism for schools directly to parents, who may, in some versions, 'top up' the value to exchange the voucher in the private sector, as is the case in Chile. As neoliberal Conservative adviser Arthur Seldon argued, 'The voucher would restore the [market] link by giving the parent purchasing power.... The education voucher would be a halfway house to the eventual policy of leaving income with tax payers to use for education' (Seldon, Editorial Director of Institute of Economic Affairs, 1977/86). In other words, it would be a move towards the disassembly of state monopoly education. However, the small-scale experiment with vouchers conducted in Kent, during Keith Joseph's time as Secretary of State, was inconclusive and he was forced to accept that 'largely for political reasons, it wouldn't be practical' (interview). Reflecting back on the 1988 Education Reform Act, Kenneth Baker claims that his aim was 'to achieve the results of a voucher scheme, namely real choice for parents and schools that responded to that choice by improving themselves' (Baker, 1993, p 212).

The other Conservative voucher scheme, for nursery schooling, was also short-lived. It was intended as a means to expand nursery provision and increase choice and began in four pilot areas managed by private services company Capita. The scheme was linked to a set of guidelines for pre-statutory settings: *Desirable outcomes for children's learning on entering compulsory education* (SCAA, 1996). Since its introduction early childhood education has become a major issue on the national policy agenda, and there have been significant changes in policy and practices (see Vincent and Ball, 2006). The voucher scheme allowed parents to use vouchers worth up to £1,100 per child for up to three terms of part-time education for their four-year-old children, in any form of preschool provision. In order to register for the receipt of vouchers, preschool providers had to show that they were moving towards the *Desirable outcomes* – 'learning goals' – that children should achieve before entering compulsory education. These emphasised early literacy, numeracy and the development of personal and social skills, and were designed to contribute to children's knowledge, understanding and skills in other areas. Labour abolished the voucher scheme in 1997 before it was extended nationwide, on a mixture of ideological and practical grounds and because the transaction costs of the scheme were deemed excessive. Labour's approach to preschool provision has been very different, resting on the development of a mixed economy of private fee-paying and state-funded Sure Start nurseries and Children's Centres, backed with a system of child tax credits for low-income families (see Box 3.3).

Box 3.3: Sure Start

Sure Start was launched in 1999 to provide parenting, health, education and childcare services under one roof for the under-threes with £3 billion of funding from the Treasury and is the cornerstone of the government's drive to tackle child poverty and social exclusion, initially targeted at the most deprived areas in the country. The government promised 3,500 centres by 2010 and in October 2006, Children's Minister Beverley Hughes announced that the government's roll-out of Sure Start Children's Centres had reached the 1,000 milestone early, catering for 800,000 children.

In various ways Labour has moved both to increase parental choice and, if sometimes reluctantly, to more closely regulate it, and they have also gestured towards collective choice and parental voice and what is called 'co-production'. For example, the 2006 Education and Inspections Act gave new and greater powers and new 'voice' to parents in relation to schools. Describing the provisions of the initial Bill, some of which were altered in the process through parliament, the Labour Party website asserted that:

> Labour will give parents a real say in how schools are run;
>
> Labour will tailor tuition to the needs of each individual child;

Labour will reform schools to give them the freedoms and flexibilities to deliver tailored learning and offer parental choice to all; Labour will give teachers a positive right to discipline and hold parents accountable for the behaviour of their children; and Labour will give Local Authorities a strong new role as the champion of parents and pupils.

In our first two terms, Labour pushed higher standards from the centre: for those standards to be maintained and built upon, they must now become self-sustaining within schools, owned and driven by teachers and parents.

Labour plans parent power • Parents will be able to set up new schools supported by a dedicated capital funding; • Parents will have access to better and clearer information about local schools, and dedicated advisers to help the least well-off parents to choose the best school; • Poorer families (on free school meals or maximum Working Families Tax Credit) will have new rights to free school transport so their children have the option of attending the three nearest secondary schools in a six mile radius; • It will be easier for schools to introduce fair banding admissions policies, so that they can keep a proportion of places for students who live outside a school's traditional catchment area to provide a genuinely comprehensive intake; • Parents will receive regular, meaningful reports during the school year about how their child is doing, with more opportunities to discuss their child's progress at school; • Parents will be able to form elected parents' councils to influence school decisions on issues such as school meals, uniform and discipline; and • Parents will have better local complaints procedures and access to a new national complaints service from Ofsted – who will be able to call a school meeting to hear parents' complaints

> or call an immediate inspection of the school. (www.labour.org.uk/)

Here parents are offered the prospect of new opportunities and responsibilities as consumers of education provision and the possibility of 'personalisation through participation', part of the process Leadbeater (2004, p 37) describes as rewriting 'the scripts for public services'. This is further linked by him to 'consumerised services' (p 49) and 'citizen-led services' (p 53) as a means of 'giving users a right to a voice in the design of the services they use' (p 90). These new 'scripts' are also intended to work to achieve changes inside schools and classrooms, through 'personalised learning', part of an 'agenda' of government to 'reconfigure the environment for learning' within new spaces, new timeframes (within and outside of the school day) and through access to technologies and new processes. In October 2004, David Miliband, the then School Standards Minister, launched a 'national conversation about personalised learning' (DfES press release, 2004/0171). Lesley Saunders (GTC [General Teaching Council] Policy Adviser for Research) describes 'personalised learning' as 'not a government initiative but a big idea that goes across all government departments' (Seminar, Institute of Education, 27 February 2007). In July 2007 Secretary of State for Schools, Children and Families Ed Balls announced an extra £150 million for personalisation in schools. Hulme and Hulme (2005, p 40) suggest that this involves 'a reworking of equality of opportunity as an individual right to be addressed at an interpersonal level rather than a social level'. This articulates directly with the New Labour emphasis on 'meritocracy' (see Chapter Four) and Johnson (2004, p 18) argues that: 'Talk of personalised learning increases the perception of schooling as a commodity, but centre-left governments should stress its vital contribution to society as a whole'. In 2006 the DfES announced a review of teaching and learning for the year 2020 (DfES, 2006):

> The next steps were taken today in the Government's commitment to reshape the education system around the

> individual pupil and to ensure that no school adopts a 'one size fits all' approach to teaching, as a new review group starts work on developing practical steps to help schools cater for every child's talents and needs. (DfES press release, 13 March 2006)

The remit of the review committee included looking at:

- improving parental engagement;
- how personalised learning can close the achievement gap and boost social mobility;
- addressing the needs of gifted and talented children;
- use of ICT and pupil data to personalise learning;
- the potential for workforce reform to support personalisation.

A number of themes of education reform reappear here and these elements of personalisation constitute a further decomposition of a common and universal system of education.

Alongside the enabling of parental voice, but at the very margins of policy, there are a series of small moves towards greater student voice and participation and in 1998 the government commissioned a report on education for citizenship (QCA, 1998). The 2002 Education Act requires schools to consult with pupils, and Ofsted guidance notes indicate that part of any inspection should involve assessing the degree to which schools give pupils a say (Fielding and Bragg, 2003). Student councils and other forms of participation form part of the agenda of citizenship education.

Overall within education the use of choice and voice mechanisms both under the Conservatives and New Labour have been confusing and contradictory and difficult to translate into practice. In a system where many schools now control their own admissions procedures, where there are various, if marginal, forms of selection, and where many 'good schools' have the effect of driving up house prices in their locality, choice making and getting your choice of school are different. There is also a considerable body of evidence that choice systems in themselves promote inequality in as much as 'choice policies' create social spaces within which class strategies and 'opportunistic behaviours' can flourish and within which the middle classes can use their social and cultural skills and capitals advantages to good effect (see Ball, 2003). The possibilities of choice available to parents and to schools are taken advantage of differently by different social groups, who are able to bring different resources and skills to bear, or have different sorts of priorities, or face different sorts of challenges in supporting their children's schooling. As a way of addressing some of these problems in 2007 Brighton Council announced that it would be introducing a lottery to assign students to secondary school places in the town. There was real opposition to the plan by some parents.

Drawing on their research, which uses the national PLASC (Pupil Level Annual School Census) database, which covers all pupils in primary and secondary state schools in England, can be linked to each pupil's test score history and contains a number of personal and school characteristics, Burgess and his colleagues (2006) report on the social outcomes of choice (see below). Their results indicate that more choice leads to more segregation in class and ethnic terms.

Box 3.4: Choice and equity

Affluent families whose nearest secondary school is of poor quality are much more likely to 'bus' their children out to schools further away than are poorer families. They have the resources to either live near better schools in the first place, or to transport them to better schools if not. Poorer families follow this strategy too, and go to other schools if the local one is weak. But they achieve this outcome to a much lesser extent. Policy should be aimed at redressing this imbalance. Of course, the school choice agenda is broader than this, the idea being that the competitive pressure applied to schools vulnerable to losing more mobile pupils will lever up standards everywhere. But the aim of increasing practical choice for poorer pupils seems a reasonable place to start. The two important practical issues in the reform of school choice are transport and access. The average secondary school commute is 1.7km, lower in urban areas, higher in rural. A quarter of pupils travel over 3.3km, and 10% travel over 6.6km. One key fact is that only around half of all secondary school pupils in England attend their nearest school. But it is important to see that not all of this movement away from the local school is 'choice' in the sense of consumer choice, in the sense of a desired outcome. The school system has been more-or-less a closed system – that is, roughly speaking there are as many school places as children, and each school can neither expand nor contract very rapidly. This is not of course exactly the case – there are excess places in some areas, and schools can change size. But one useful analogy for the system is a modified game of musical chairs – there are enough chairs for everyone, but some are more desirable than others. The point is that one person's choice of chair has implications for the places available to others. Unlike in most consumer choice contexts, choice by one person has spill-over effects on others. The issue for policies around transport and access is how things look when the game finishes – which pupils are going to which schools. The facts show that the present system does not work well for pupils from poor families. We have analyzed our data on which pupils go to their nearest school, looking in particular at the quality of that local school, and whether the pupil comes from a poor family or not. Quality is measured by the previous league table score of the school in terms of the percentage of its pupils awarded at least 5 A* to C grades at GCSE. We measure the pupil's family background in terms of eligibility for free school meals. The findings show that as the quality of the local school is lower, children from affluent families are less likely to go there. If we focus on schools in the bottom quarter of the national league table, a pupil eligible for free school meals is 30% more likely to attend their low-scoring local school than an otherwise-identical pupil from a better-off family. The present system, which can be characterized as a mixture of neighborhood schooling (where pupils simply attend their local school) and choice-based schooling, leads to the sorting of pupils. Pupils are not evenly spread across a group of schools in terms of their key stage test scores, their eligibility for free school meals, or their ethnicity. This sorting is higher where there is more choice. The interplay of the decisions of schools, parents and LEAs produces an outcome in which there is clustering together of pupils scoring well in the key stage tests, and a clustering together of pupils from poorer backgrounds. This is unlikely to be to the advantage of the latter pupils. It is important to point out, however, that this sorting is much lower in comprehensive LEAs, even those with high choice, than it is in the few LEAs retaining elements of ability selection. Choice is feasible for most secondary school pupils in England, in the straightforward sense that they have more than one school near to where they live. In fact, 36% have at least three schools within 2km of their home, and over 80% have at least three schools within 5km. Obviously, this varies over the country. In rural areas, the numbers are lower (only 42% have at least three schools within 5km) and in London almost all students have at least three schools within 5km. Put another way, three quarters of secondary school pupils in England have at least three schools within 4km from their home. The policies have to make a reality of this choice in principle. Components of the policy include continuing the programme of creating more schools close to where poorer families live; supporting decision-making by poorer families by providing information;

and subsidizing the transport costs of poorer families. The school choice reforms face a number of difficulties in achieving their aims.
Source: Burgess et al (2006)

In one respect all of this makes good policy sense given that New Labour's political agenda involves making the public sector more middle-class-friendly. Stephen Pollard, co-author with Andrew (now Baron) Adonis of *A class act* (1997), makes this link very clear:

> When Labour took office in 1997, Andrew Adonis and I wrote a book which argued that the flight of the middle classes from the state system was depriving it of those very people who could make a real difference in helping to lift standards across the board. To help redress this, we argued for reforms which would give parents more control, and schools more independence. (www.stephenpollard.net/002397.html)

Figure 3.4: A genealogy of choice and voice

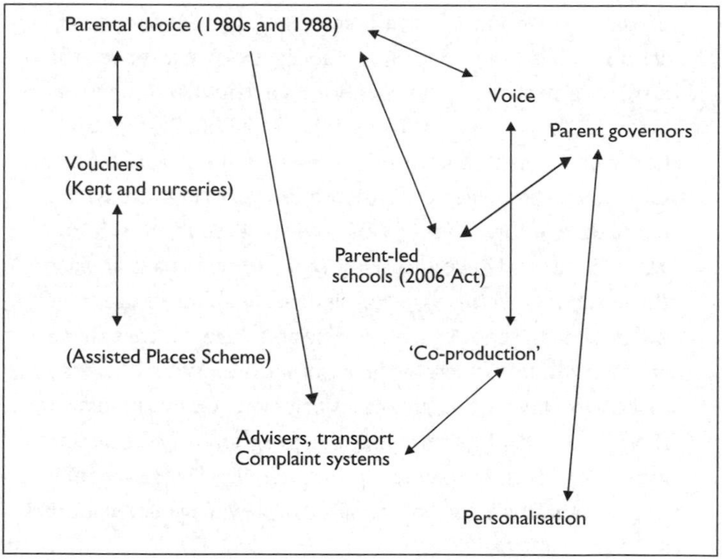

As McCaig (2001, p 201) suggests, 'New Labour have reconceptualized a comprehensive education system designed to meet the needs of its new individualistic voter base'. However, this may work against the commitment in education policy to improve the achievements of pupils in schools in deprived areas and to fight social exclusion that are also part of the New Labour policy portfolio (see Chapter Four). Some sort of resolution of the conundrum of choice, selection and exclusion is presented by the particular vision of equity in education that is embedded in New Labour 'thinking' – that is, meritocracy. This and other aspects of equity and education are discussed in the following chapter.

Capability and capacity

The fourth and final component of the reform model again contains a dual element of intervention and devolution. It involves a further set of moves, through a new discourse of leadership, which enhance the roles of public sector managers, crucial agents of change in the reform process (see Chapter One). At the same time it requires the 'remodelling' of the teaching workforce as part of a more general strategy of 'flexibilisation' and 'skill mix' across the public services. Within all this, there is also a dual process of reprofessionalisation (the construction of a new cadre of qualified and trained school leaders) and aspects of deprofessionalisation (a much closer specification of the work of school practitioners, particularly in primary schools, and the introduction of new kinds of workers – like classroom assistants – into schools). Flexibilisation of teachers' labour also involves changes in their pay and conditions of work. On the one hand, Labour has improved the pay of teachers considerably and introduced a GTC, but, on the other hand, it has attempted to tie pay scales more closely to performance. Alongside this, various 'policy experiments', like EAZs and academies, have allowed for the non-application of national agreements on pay and conditions, including in the case of academies the employment of non-registered, non-qualified teachers. In 2007 a report by PricewaterhouseCoopers

(PWC), commissioned by the DfES, recommended that 'Schools should be led by chief executives who may not necessarily be teachers' (PWC website). A further duality or tension can be identified in the role of capability and capacity within the 'approach' as a whole. Alongside the competitive relations that have been discussed above, this component of the model emphasises cooperation and collaboration in order to achieve organisational development. This is one iteration of the notion of 'partnership' that is again a generic policy tactic for innovation and change across the whole of the public services (see Cardini, 2006). Again the genealogy of the policy 'moves' involved here can be traced back to the Conservative reforms. These moves are outlined here along three interrelated dimensions: leadership, collaboration/partnership and 'remodelling' teachers.

Leadership

The LMS and grant-maintained schools initiatives both involved the considerable devolution of management responsibilities to schools and the concomitant development of the role of headteachers and their co-optation to the cause of institutional reform. The Conservative rhetoric of school reform cast headteachers as new kinds of hybrid actors. As David Hart (NAHT General Secretary) explained to me in an interview, 'The secretary of state certainly needs heads. They are the lynchpins of the system, and he can't deliver the reforms without the heads' (Ball, 1990, p 67). In the DES-commissioned report on LMS from management consultants Coopers & Lybrand (1988), the point was made that LMS would require 'a new culture and philosophy of school organisation' (p 2). The headteacher was given the role and the powers to bring about this 'reculturing' of school organisation:

> We're talking about a change in the culture of schools and a change in the culture of teaching. We know that when we think about change we have to get ownership, participation, and a sense of meaning on the part of the vast majority of teachers. Reculturing is the main work of leadership,

> and it requires an underlying conceptualization of the key elements that feed it.... Moral purpose is more than passionate teachers trying to make a difference in their classrooms. It's also the context of the school and district in which they work. That means principals have to be almost as concerned about the success of other schools in the district as they are about their own schools. (Interview with Michael Fuller,[4] in Sparks, 2003)

The particular emphasis on culture within leadership reflects the 'cultural turn' in the 1990s within management theory. Davies and Ellison (1997, p 5) see leadership as part of the 'second wave' of education reform and as about 'hearts and minds' rather than structures: 'we consider it equally important to reengineer mindsets as well as processes within schools'. In Fullan's words (see Sparks, 2003), the three aspects of capability and capacity identified are reiterated – the work of leadership, changing teachers and working collaboratively. Each of these have been pursued and developed in policy 'moves' across the three post-1997 Labour governments.

In 2000 the National College for School Leadership (NCSL) was launched; the College has since developed a national training and development framework structure for heads, deputies and others in leadership positions in schools. This Leadership Framework provides a single national focus for school leadership development and research together with professional development and support for school leaders throughout their careers. Since 1 April 2004 it is mandatory for all first-time heads to hold National Professional Qualifications for Headship (NPQH), or to be working towards it. Once in post, they must gain the NPQH qualification within four years of their appointment. The Leadership Programme for Serving Headteachers (LPSH) provides experienced heads with an opportunity to focus on how their leadership influences standards in schools. Launched in September 2003, Leading from the Middle is a professional development programme for middle-level leaders in schools and aims to develop their leadership skills. A 'fast-track' procedure has also been introduced to identify 'high-fliers' who might move more rapidly through the career stages of teaching and into leadership. In effect leadership has become a generic mechanism for change as well as a new kind of subject position within policy (see Busher, 2006).

In a sense the new school leader embodies policy within the institution and enacts the processes of reform. The self-managing school must surveil and regulate itself. The leader becomes, among other things, the manager of institutional performances. Bell and Stevenson (2006, p 90) argue that: 'In essence, headteachers are in danger of ceasing to be senior peers located within professional groups and are becoming distinctive actors in a managerialist system'. This is consonant with the PWC recommendation. Leaders, as opposed to managers (on this distinction see Thrupp and Willmott, 2003), are the key agents in the reculturing and re-engineering of the school. New Labour's 'transformational leaders' are expected to instil responsiveness, efficiency and performance improvement into the public sector but also to be dynamic, visionary, risk-taking, entrepreneurial individuals who can 'turn around' histories of 'failure'[5] deploying their personal qualities in so doing. As Newman (2005, p 721) notes, 'this idea is entirely consonant with the style of Blair himself' and in the words of Barber and Phillips (2000, p 11), two of Labour's key education advisers, 'The driving force at this critical juncture is leadership.... It is the vocation of leaders to take people where they have never been before and show them a new world from which they do not want to return'. The literature and discourse of school leadership draws explicitly on business writing and the ideas of business gurus.

Collaboration/partnership

> Transformation requires schools to be willing to give away their innovations for free, in the hope of some return but with no guarantee. A paramount value is freedom – to create, to appropriate, and to redistribute knowledge. We need to engineer an educational epidemic which would truly qualify as a transformation. (Hargreaves, 2003b, p 10)

Conservative Secretary of State Kenneth Baker initially viewed grant-maintained schools as being few in number but centres of innovation piloting educational ideas that could, if they proved successful, be disseminated more widely. Margaret Thatcher took the view that grant-maintained schools should work as free-standing and competitive education businesses (indicating tensions between state-managed and neoliberal reform in Conservative Party politics). The former idea was taken up by New Labour in the form of Beacon and Leading Edge schools as part of its collaboration and cooperation strategy (see Box 3.5). This has been taken up further through the idea of federations.

Box 3.5: The Beacon schools programme

The Beacon schools programme was established in 1998 and phased out by 2005 and all types and phases of state-maintained schools were included. It identified high-performing schools across England and was designed to build partnerships between these schools and represent examples of successful practice, with a view to sharing and spreading that effective practice to other schools to raise standards in pupil attainment.

For secondary schools the Leading Edge Partnership programme builds on the success and knowledge about collaborative practice gained from the Beacon schools programme. Schools within these partnerships are committed to working collaboratively to design, develop, test and share innovative ideas to raise standards of teaching and learning where improvement is most urgently needed.

At the primary level, Primary Strategy Learning Networks (PSLNs) are being established to help schools work together to raise further the standards their pupils attain in literacy and maths and to increase schools' capacity to deliver a broad and rich curriculum. Groups of primary schools establish themselves as a network with a particular learning focus to help to raise standards of attainment. The long-term aim is that all primary schools should be part of an effective learning network; the vast majority should be in that position by 2008.

Source: Taken from the DfES website (www.dfes.gov.uk/).

The 2002 Education Act that allowed for the creation of a single governing body or a joint governing body committee across two or more schools from September 2003 onwards defines federations as:

> A group of schools with a formal (ie written) agreement to work together to raise standards, promote inclusion, find new ways of approaching teaching and learning and build capacity between schools in a coherent manner. There is a £50m Targeted Capital Fund for Federations of schools with shared governance and Fresh Start Schools to develop joint facilities (buildings and ICT), which would be used across a partnership of schools to enhance collaborative activity. (DfES website, www.dfes.gov.uk/)

Collaboration and partnership are policy buzzwords; partnership is 'a favourite word in the lexicon of New Labour' (Falconer and Mclaughlin, 2000, p 121), although its meaning in relation to practice is often vague and slippery and carries dangers of being made meaningless by overuse. Partnerships constantly recur in New Labour discourse and policies where almost any relationship between organisations or social agents is described as a partnership. It is a classic third way trope that dissolves important differences between public sector, private sector and voluntary sector modes of working and obscures the role of financial relationships and power imbalances between 'partners'. Partnerships are everywhere – 'partnershipitis', Huxham and Vangen (2000, p 303) call it. There are a number of agencies and animateurs, both public and private, which foster, support and facilitate PPPs. The term encompasses a wide range of relationships stretching from PFIs, which have been reconceptualised as a form of partnership by New Labour and commercial joint ventures between public and private at one end, to school collaborations like networks and federations at the other: 'Here the practitioner is viewed as facing outwards, building partnerships and engaging communities for the purpose of delivering "joined-up" and sustainable policy outcomes' (Newman, 2005, p 720). Collaboration, partnership and the dissemination of 'what works' is intended to enhance system capability.

Remodelling teachers

The other major dimension of the 'capability' project is that of the 'remodelling' or the 'disciplining' and 'flexibilisation' of the teaching profession. This involves:

- the reconstitution of teachers from an obstacle to reform – 'Teachers too often seem afraid of change and thereby resist it.... Many seem to believe they are unique victims of constant change ... [who hold a] fatalistic view ... that nothing can be done to change [things]' (DfEE, 1998a, p 16, para 24) – to an instrument of reform – as 'new professionals' (p 14);
- the establishing of a relationship between pay and performance;
- the devolution of contract negotiations to the institutional level;
- the deregulation of the work of teaching to allow 'non-teaching' staff to undertake classroom activities.

Again aspects of such 'flexibilisation' processes have their beginnings within Conservative policy although the principle of the curriculum as the teachers' 'secret garden' was initially breached by the Ruskin speech. Teachers were very much objects of criticism by the Conservatives (see Chapter Two) and were 'blamed' for many of the supposed 'failures' of the education system. Conservative neoliberals saw them as dangerously self-interested, a producer lobby resistant to change and risk-averse, while for neoconservatives they were dangerously radical and progressive, responsible for too much change and politically motivated, not to be trusted, one of the reasons why a national curriculum was deemed necessary. Such 'blaming' was tied to a supposed 'lack of accountability' and provided the legitimation for greater oversight, control of and intervention into teachers' work.

Furthermore, the 'failure' of several years of teachers' industrial action in the mid-1980s to achieve its aims left the profession politically weakened and ripe for reform. In 1987 the government abolished the system of national pay negotiations and set up the School Teachers' Review Body, an independent group to advise on teachers' salaries, and during the 1990s the Conservative government introduced a series of further measures to 'regulate' teachers. This included Initial Teacher Education 'competency-based assessments' – now 'standards' (Circular 9/92 [secondary] and 14/93 [primary]). The 1994 Education Act created the TTA that symbolically reverted from teacher education to teacher training. During this period CTCs, like academies, were exempted from national pay agreements and the Conservatives experimented with several schemes to speed up and loosen up entry into qualified teacher status (QTS), including 'school-based training' alternatives to college and university courses. Once again these various moves put in place an infrastructure that would enable New Labour's remodelling agenda: 'The status quo is not an option. After decades of drift, decisive action is required to raise teaching to the front rank of professions. Only by modernisation can we equip our nation for the new century' (Blair, 1998b).

However, in contrast to their Conservative predecessors, New Labour governments have tempered their criticisms of teachers with a more positive vision of teachers: 'Success in the 21st century will depend crucially on having an ambitious, forward-looking, outward-facing teaching profession in which success is recognised and rewarded' (Blunkett, DfES New Centre, 23 September 1999, p 10 [www.dfes.gov.uk]). *Excellence in schools* (DfEE, 1997) announced the scheme of training for headship (see above) and a new grade of advanced skills teacher (AST), the setting up of the GTC to 'speak for the professionals', and steps to 'improve appraisal'. However, this was immediately followed by Circular (4/98), 'Teaching high status high standards', which introduced a still more prescriptive 'national curriculum for teacher training', finally eradicating the intellectual and disciplinary foundations of teacher education, which were replaced by a skills and classroom management curriculum. *Teachers meeting the challenge of change* (DfEE, 1998b) introduced the intention to reward 'our leading professionals ... to recruit, retain and motivate high quality classroom teachers by paying them more' (p 6) through performance-related pay systems tied to career progression and movement through a *threshold* (see below). Again this was part of a general strategy for the public services as a whole. The White Paper *Modernising government* (Cabinet Office, 1999) argued that:

> Pay must be flexible and put service needs first. This means reforming outdated systems by tackling aspects which make insufficient contribution to performance. It means challenging outdated assumptions, for example the idea that 'fair pay' means that everybody should get the same increase. (Cabinet Office, 1999, p 8, para 28, cited in Mahony and Hextall, 1999, p 2)

The Green Paper *Schools: Building on success* (DfEE, 2001) brought further reforms to initial teacher training (ITT), and floated the idea of sabbaticals and time for research. Increasingly the language of these documents was one of valuing rather than deriding teachers, capturing them in the discourse of modernisation (see Maguire, 2004): 'The key themes … leadership, rewards, training, support … will remain at the centre of our thinking' (p 53); 'We are clear that teaching must be, and feel, a manageable job as well as a valued and important profession' (p 55).

The *threshold* is the point at which after five years teachers submit themselves to an assessment process that involves providing evidence that they have met eight performance standards. If they pass the threshold they move onto a new pay scale and receive an extra £3,000 per annum. Performance points are awarded by school governors on the advice of headteachers, placing teachers and teachers' work at the heart of a regime of performance management and constituting teacher professionalism in new ways, within which, Mahony et al (2004) argue, teachers 'are presented as units of labour to be distributed and managed' (p 136). The threshold scheme was designed and implemented by six private companies: Hay McBeer was contracted to develop standards; CfBT to train assessors; Cambridge Educational Associates to verify judgements; TLO and QAA (Quality Assurance Associates) were subcontracted to write training materials; and Ernst and Young was brought in to design and monitor the implementation of the programme.

As Bell and Stevenson (2006, pp 88-9) note, performance-related pay schemes for teachers are currently being deployed in the US, Hong Kong, New Zealand, Israel and Japan, and there is also now an Australian scheme. This is again a transnational phenomenon and not just a particularity of the English education reforms. Indeed, Smyth et al (2000, p 175), and others, see the remaking of teaching as a global project and argue that 'to make sense of what is happening to teachers' work with practical and emancipatory intent requires a critical theory capable of connecting globalization to the everyday life of the classroom'.

In England, *Schools: Achieving success* (DfES, 2001b) recognised that teachers' workloads were high and that there were teacher shortages. It suggested that greater 'flexibility' was needed and that teachers could delegate some of their responsibilities to others in school, promising 10,000 more teachers and 20,000 more support staff, together with the opening up of 'alternative routes to qualification' (p 54). In the same year, a report commissioned from PWC, the 'Teacher Workload Study' (see Teachernet document bank), found that 'in terms of volume of work, teachers' and headteachers' working weeks are often more intensive than most other occupations, with fifty to sixty hours being the norm' (internet interim report, www.teachers.org.uk/resources/word/exec_summary.doc). Government also signalled its intention to take powers to override the School Teachers' Review Body. The reorganisation of teachers' work was taken further by the National

Workload Agreement (NWA) (DfES, 2003), which was the outcome of an industrial dispute over rising workloads following which agreement was reached between the employers and trade unions representing teaching and non-teaching staff, with the exception of the NUT, which refused to sign; the NAHT also later withdrew its support. The NWA included a number of measures to reduce teacher workloads in exchange for removal of regulations requiring qualified teachers to have responsibility for whole classes and the introduction of the role of a higher-level teaching assistant (HLTA), with their own national professional standards.

Over time, as the effect of this concatenation of policy moves, teachers have been remade within policy, and their work and the meaning of teaching have been discursively rearticulated. This has been brought about by the introduction of new forms of preparation, new work practices and new workers into the classroom and the use of a new language through which teachers talk about what they do and are talked about, think about themselves and judge themselves and one another and are measured and appraised, and paid, in relation to their performance.[6] In effect they are incorporated into the project of public sector modernisation and the political economy of globalisation. Part of this project, as noted earlier, involves breaking down bureaucratic and professional structures, and their systems of control over qualifications, pay and entry into work, to create more 'flexible' and 'efficient' and 'enterprising' forms of organisation. As is the case with leadership, and collaboration (and competition), the relationships among teachers, with their managers and leaders, and indirectly with pupils and parents, are all changed.

This brief run-through of the key policy moves related to teachers and their work also illustrates important aspects of the 'policy process' and the work that is done within policy texts, as Maguire (2004, p 137) explains:

> ... in marking out, setting and justifying new policy agendas. Where one document asserts a need and suggests an intervention, a successive document asserts its success

Figure 3.5: A genealogy of teacher 'modernisation' and flexibilisation

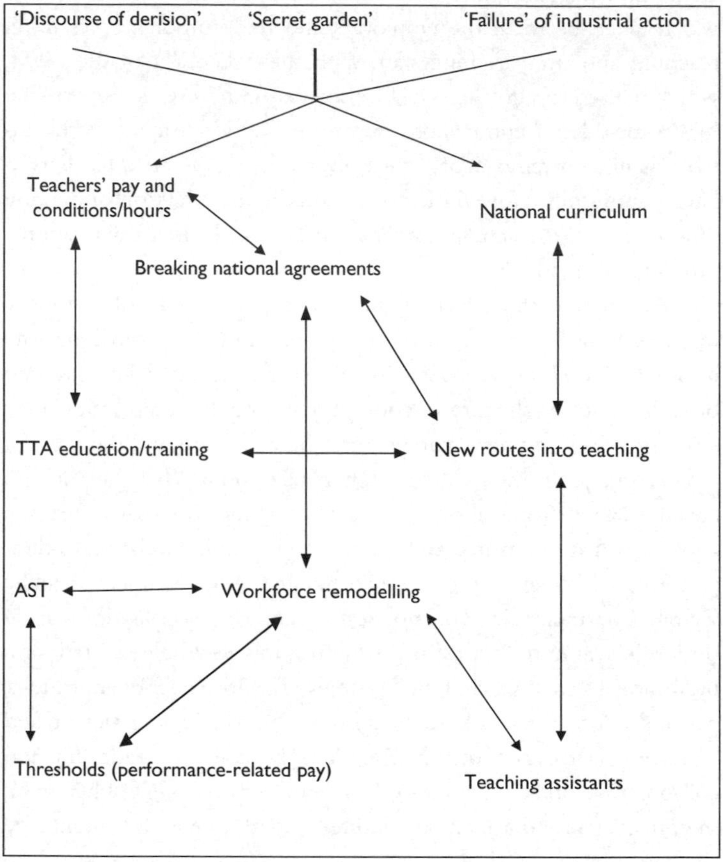

and bolsters up the policy work. Thus, a cycle of problem, solution, success and new problems is articulated across the documents.

Conclusion

What is happening within this ensemble of policies, laid out in the 'approach' document, is a modelling of the internal and external relations of schooling and public service provision on those of commercial market institutions. In the process 'the structure and culture of public services are recast' (Cabinet Office, 2006, p 10). These policies introduce 'new orientations, remodel existing relations of power and affect how and where social policy choices are made' (Clarke et al, 1994, p 4). They play a key role in wearing away professional-ethical regimes and their value systems, and their replacement by entrepreneurial-competitive regimes and new value systems. They are also involved in the increasing subordination of education to 'the economic', and rendering of education itself into the commodity form. By such means 'education systems have been made objects of micro-economic reform with educational activities being turned into saleable or corporatised market products as part of a national efficiency drive' (Taylor et al, 1997, p 77). Educational provision is itself increasingly made susceptible to profit and educational processes play their part in the creation of the enterprise culture and the cultivation of enterprising subjects. Parents and pupils are repositioned as consumers and entreated to compare schools in terms of published performance indicators and are offered 'personalised' learning experiences. Competition between schools for market share is encouraged. However, at the same time, schools are expected to cooperate with one another and share and disseminate good practice and form partnerships among themselves and with other organisations.

The general orientation of Labour education policy to economic global competitiveness is very clear and recurs constantly in policy texts of various kinds. This orientation is itself part of a global flow of policy concepts related to fairly abstract conceptions about the shift towards 'knowledge-based', 'high-skills' economies and a consequential realignment of education policies. In effect, social and educational policies are collapsed into economic and industrial policy. Such collapses are often indicated in policy condensates like 'The Learning

Society' (in the UK) or 'The Clever Country' (Australia). As David Blunkett explained in his 1998 Labour Party Conference speech:

> We recognise the very real challenge facing manufacturing industry in this country and the way in which we need to support and work with them for skilling and re-skilling for what Tony Blair has described as the best economic policy we have – 'education'. (p 5)

Inside classrooms teachers are caught between the imperatives of prescription and the disciplines of performance. Their practice is both 'steered' *and* 'rowed'. It is still the case that teachers are not trusted.

One of the key elements in the new policy ensemble is the use of highly prescriptive systems of accountability – performance indicators, inspections, league tables and achievement targets. Schools are rated and compared in terms of 'achievements' measured by tests and examinations, for which students are carefully prepared. Institutional and national increases or reductions in test scores are then taken to be indicators of rising or failing standards of schooling. But the question that is avoided here is whether these indicators actually 'stand for' and thus 'represent' valid, worthwhile or meaningful outputs. Does increased emphasis on preparation for the tests and the adaptation of pedagogy and curriculum to the requirements of test performance constitute worthwhile effects of 'improvement'? In terms of economic competitiveness, is what is measured here what is needed?

In all of this social justice issues seem peripheral. Concerns about equity continue to be tagged on to the list of Labour's priorities rather than being central to their content or planning decisions about education (see Chapter Four). Further, the 'what works' ideology of the third way, which is presented as 'beyond' politics, obscures the class politics embedded within current education policies.

Labour's policy stance in education has a paradigmatic similarity to education policies in many other developed nations. To reiterate, I am not intending to suggest that we need not attend to the specificities of Labour's local educational concerns and projects; rather, quite the opposite. The third way in particular needs careful examination, but I do want to underline the need to see these policies, in part at least, as embedded in powerful, coherent global *policyscapes*.

Notes

[1] The 1998 School Standards and Framework Act:

> rules out any new selection by ability, except for sixth forms and banding arrangements and allows grammar schools to continue with their selective admission arrangements. These arrangements can only be changed by parental ballot or by proposals from the school's governing body.

[2] A Pupil Referral Unit (PRU) is a school specially organised to offer short-term alternative provision for children who are out of school or who are not gaining qualifications.

[3] Unlike community schools, foundation schools employ their staff directly and control their own admissions arrangements, and their buildings and land are owned by the governors or a charitable foundation.

[4] Michael Fullan was also contracted to be evaluator of the National Literacy and Numeracy Strategies, and draws on ideas arising from the evaluation in this interview.

[5] In 2007 the government announced an extension of its Future Leaders initiative, which aims to place 'outstanding leaders' in inner-city schools.

[6] One of the side-effects of this, together with other pressures on teachers, had been that almost twice as many teachers retired early in 2006 compared to seven years previously. A total of 10,270 teaching staff took retirement in 2006, with 5,580 doing so in the 1998-99 academic

year, according to figures released by the government following a Conservative question in the House of Commons. In addition, the percentage of secondary school teachers taking early retirement has increased by 93% since the Labour Party took office in 1997.

4

Current key issues: forms of policy and forms of equity

This chapter addresses those aspects of current policy that relate, directly or indirectly, to issues of social equity in education. While a commitment to *forms of equity* are a part of New Labour's agenda for education, equity is rarely presented as a primary goal of policy in itself and is tied to the achievement of other ends and purposes, usually economic. As Bell and Stevenson (2006, p 120) put it in their discussion of EAZs, New Labour education policy often involves 'reconciling equity and economy'. However, the logic of New Labour's policy strategy in education is that 'good' policies will produce fairer outcomes by raising the achievement of all pupils. Indeed, the focus on standards and attention given to entrenched patterns of underachievement and to 'failing schools', particularly in inner-city areas, is a mainstay of the New Labour approach to social justice. In addition, specific initiatives like EAZs and Excellence in Cities (EiC) have been targeted at areas of social disadvantage. In turn these initiatives are part of a broader social policy strategy of tackling 'social exclusion'[1] (see Box 4.1), with its particular emphases on bringing excluded groups back into employment, through the development of 'social capital' (see Box 4.2) and early 'interventions' into 'failing' families. The National Childcare Strategy (1998) and Sure Start (see Chapter Three) are examples of policies where both social and economic goals are represented. Within this approach exclusion is constructed and addressed as primarily a social problem of community and family inadequacies rather than an economic problem of structural inequality. Families and circumstances, and cultures, are to blame and where appropriate the state will intervene to 'interrupt' the reproduction of deficit and disadvantage:

> I am saying that where it is clear, as it very often is, at a young age, that children are at risk of being brought up in a dysfunctional home where there are multiple problems, say of drug abuse or offending, then instead of waiting until the child goes off the rails, we should act early enough, with the right help, support and disciplined framework for the family, to prevent it. This is not stigmatizing the child or the family. It may be the only way to save them and the wider community from the consequences of inaction. (Blair, 2006b)

Box 4.1: Social exclusion

> The Government has defined social exclusion as 'a shorthand term for what can happen when people or areas suffer from a combination of linked problems such as unemployment, poor skills, low incomes, poor housing, high crime environments, bad health and family breakdown'. Educational differences are crucial in generating and sustaining social exclusion. We define social exclusion as the capacity to be involved in work, in the everyday consumption patterns enjoyed by most people, in social and political life. (Centre for the Analysis of Social Exclusion Brief 12, London School of Economics and Political Science, November 1999)

Inclusion refers to a condition in society where all citizens feel themselves to be stakeholders able to enjoy the benefits that it brings and to participate in shared social and political processes. Exclusion, on the other hand, is about loss of this sense of stakeholding, denial of common benefits and non-participation in shared processes (see, for instance, Giddens, 1998b).

As we shall see, the interventionary dimension of policy is also invested with aspects of 'moralisation' and the importance within New Labour or third way thinking given to civic 'responsibilities'.

Box 4.2: Social capital

> The extent to which people feel part of strong, social and community networks can best be encapsulated in the term 'social capital'. This has been defined as 'features of social life, networks, norms, and trust that enable participants to act together more effectively to pursue shared objectives.... Social capital, in short, refers to social connections and the attendant norms and trust'. (Putnam, 1995)

Putnam suggests that there are three types of social capital:

- Bonding: characterised by strong bonds, for example, among family members or among members of an ethnic group.
- Bridging: characterised by weaker, less dense, but more cross-cutting ties, for example, with business associates, acquaintances.
- Linking: characterised by connections between those with differing levels of power or social status, for example, links between the political elite and the general public or between individuals from different social classes.

Social capital research finds education to be associated with higher levels of social capital. It would appear that with every extra year in education individuals appear to have additional, larger and more diverse networks (see also Halpern, 2005).

The education and childcare initiatives noted above and others, like EAZs and academies, are new ways of dealing with old social and educational problems. They are third way solutions that differ in important ways from the statist and welfarist policy paths of 'Old' Labour:

> The old monolithic structures won't do. We can't engineer change and improvement through bureaucratic edict. (Blair, 2001)

> There's nothing wrong with the old principles but if the old ways worked, they'd have worked by now. (Blair, 2002)

New Labour policies involve multiagency working, business participation, attempts to engage local people in decision making and 'the use of EAZs as laboratories for the promotion of greater service diversity, particularly in terms of curricular provision' (Bell and Stevenson, 2006, p 123). These new approaches also emphasise aspects of the 'citizen-led' services discussed in the previous chapter and involvement of new policy actors from business and the voluntary sector.

> Doing things to people will no longer do. Doing things with them is the key – whether to improving health, fighting crime, regenerating neighbourhoods or protecting the environment. And to those who say this is conceding too much to citizens' rights, I say bringing the public inside the decision-making tent is the only way of getting people to accept their responsibilities. (Milburn, 2006)

These new policy communities bring new kinds of actors into the policy process, validate new policy discourses and enable new forms of policy influence and enactment and, in some respects, disable or disenfranchise established actors and agencies, like LEAs. All of this rests on a contrast between *governance* that is accomplished through the 'informal authority' of networks and *government* that is done through the hierarchies of specifically public sector bureaucracy. Governance, then, involves a 'catalyzing [of] all sectors – public, private and voluntary

– into action to solve their community's problems' (Osborne and Gaebler, 1992, p 20) and 'explores the changing boundary between state and civil society' (Bevir and Rhodes, 2003, p 42). Networks also serve as a policy device, as a way of trying things out, getting things done quickly, disembedding entrenched practices, and avoiding established public sector lobbies and interests. They are (1) a means of interjecting practical innovations and new sensibilities into areas of education policy that are seen as change-resistant and risk-averse; and (2) in general terms, they 'pilot' moves towards a form of 'post-welfare' education system in which the state contracts and monitors but does not necessarily deliver education services itself.

The analysis of current policies requires attention both to their substance (what they are about, what problems they address) and to their form (how they work, who is involved) and in particular the new modes of state action that they signal. The policy work of New Labour has reconstructed the nature of educational problems and redistributed blame, producing new kinds of policy solutions and methods of policy. These aspects of policy change are, in other words, 'joined up' in two senses. First, solutions to educational problems are sought in part through changes in forms of governance. Second, educational problems are linked both with the needs of the economy and to social problems, for example, through 'failing' parents and 'dysfunctional families' to disaffection, truancy, school and social exclusion and crime and anti social behaviour.

Four arenas of policy that engage the issues introduced above will now be briefly considered in different ways: *participation and performance* (with a particular focus on issues of 'race' and gender), *parenting*, *meritocracy* and finally *academies, trusts and privatisation*.

Participation and performance

The two main and very simple organising principles for New Labour's approach to issues of social equality in education are levels of performance or achievement, as discussed in the previous chapter, and rates of participation in education, which primarily concern participation in post-compulsory education and training and in HE but also encompass issues of school exclusion and truancy. Questions of patterns of social inequality in terms of 'race', gender and class are addressed primarily in these terms and the 'successes' and 'failures' of policy, long and short term, are often judged in relation to these indicators – a further extension of the use of performance management as a policy device. However, the drive to increase levels of participation and performance is seen in policy terms not only as an equity issue but also as a means of maximising the stock of skills and qualifications possessed by the UK workforce on which economic performance is seen to strongly depend.

Participation in post-compulsory education in England increased from 45% in 1988 to 70% in 1993 and has remained at roughly that level ever since. The participation rate for the 2.4 million 16-year-olds and over continuing in post-compulsory education and training in 2004/05 was 73% in the UK as a whole, 78% of whom were females and 68% males. However, there are high rates of drop-out from post-compulsory courses, especially those of lower academic status that usually recruit students who have performed poorly at school level. In terms of western European and OECD comparators England performs poorly in respect to retention post-16 (OECD, 2004). The Labour government is addressing this relatively poor retention record in one particular way – announcing in November 2006 its intention to explore ways of raising the school leaving age to 18 and an 'aspiration' to increase post-compulsory participation to 90% by 2015.

Participation rates in HE have also increased dramatically in recent years and the Labour government has set itself the target of achieving a 50% rate for 18- to 25-year-olds by 2010. However, rates continue to vary considerably by social class: 'Through all this expansion there has been a persistent, consistent and continuing tendency to recruit students from the middle class' (Archer et al, 2003, p 73). In 2004 44% of 18-year-olds in England whose parents were in higher professional occupations were studying for a degree or equivalent compared with 13% whose parents were in routine occupations and only 1% who came from social class 5 (unskilled) (see Table 4.1).

Table 4.1: HE achievement

Social class	% with at least 'A' or AS levels at age 21	% of 21- to 30-year-olds who have achieved HE qualifications	% of those with entry qualifications at age 21 who obtain HE qualifications by age 30
I Professional	69	63.7	92.3
II Intermediate*			
IIInm Skilled non-manual	65	23.6	36.3
IIIm Skilled manual	46	8.4	18.2
IV Partly skilled	39	10.7	27.4
V Unskilled	33	6.1	18.5

Note: * Missing from original
Source: Adapted from Archer et al (2003, pp 79-80)

Minority ethnic students are more likely to continue in post-compulsory education (71% in 2001) and overall get better results than White students. Minority ethnic students are also over-represented in university courses, making up 9% of all 18- to 24-year-olds in 2002 but 13% of those at university, although they tend to be concentrated in the 'new' post-1992 universities, and particularly those where 'drop-out' rates are highest. Their over-representation is even more marked in certain subjects like law and medicine although we do not know completion rates for these courses. However, while recognising that the minority ethnic category is far from homogeneous, generally graduate unemployment is much higher among minority ethnic than other groups.

This is not the place to pursue all of the issues raised by these various figures and indicators but they do signal some basic questions about achievement and participation of different social groups in education in terms of 'race', class and gender and it is to the policies that have been deployed to address these differences that we now turn.

Gender

Arguably it is only in the past 40 years that gender and education has become a problem for policy, or regarded as a problem at all. Until the 1960s differences in educational provision, opportunities and achievements between boys and girls were accepted, for the most part, as the playing out of natural, inherent differences between the sexes and as appropriate in terms of future roles within work or the family. As Tomlinson (2001, p 148) notes, 'in the 1950s middle class boys were twenty one times more likely to attend university than working class girls'. The passing of the Equal Pay Act (1970) and Sex Discrimination Act (1975) and the setting up of the Equal Opportunities Commission were all indicators of a change in policy awareness and policy climate. However, as many commentators have argued, important changes brought about in the educational experiences of girls, and, indeed, those of minority ethnic students, from the 1970s onwards are to be explained not so much in terms of national policies with a big P but, rather, those with a small p, that is, work done in communities and institutions and struggles by local communities and pressure groups. Gender represents a fascinating example of grass-roots policy change and policy effects with some schools and some LEAs developing programmes and strategies to address the poor performance of girls at secondary level. The ILEA (Inner London Education Authority) in particular was active in the development of anti-racist and anti-sexist strategies in its schools but, for the most part, these were dismantled after its abolition by the Conservative government in 1992. Also we have to note that where gender and education policies began with the problem of the underachievement of girls they are currently more focused on the problem of the underachievement of boys.

Throughout the UK during the late 1980s and 1990s equal opportunities programmes were moving from the grass roots into the centre of the policy arena and were exerting some influence on the national scene. Stemming from the political impact of the second-wave women's movement in the 1970s, these equal opportunities initiatives were bottom-up rather than top-down, with minimal central state involvement, although, interestingly, given the increasing importance noted earlier of multilateral policy making: 'To the extent that equal opportunities initiatives received any formal legitimation from the centre, this tended to come from Europe' (Riddell and Salisbury, 2000, p 3).

Changes in curriculum, teaching and learning and assessment and targeted equal opportunities programmes had dramatic consequences. In 1989 29.8% of boys and 35.8% of girls attained five or more A-C GCSE grades, a 6% gap, which by 1999 had increased to 10% (42.3% boys and 53.4% girls). In 2005 51% of 11-year-old boys reached the expected level 4 in reading, writing and maths, compared with 63% of girls (see Chapter Three). There was a one percentage point drop in boys' scores compared with 2004 and a one percentage point rise for girls. In thinking about this we need to bear in mind that girls are doing well and boys are only falling behind relatively; that is to say, improvements in performance for all is a different issue from that of gaps in performance between groups. It should also be remembered that patterns of achievement vary between subjects. There are enduring patterns of sex-stereotyping in subject entry and although girls have 'caught up' in science and maths, in vocational subjects boys, on the whole, still perform better. And importantly, despite the considerable attention given to the relative achievements of boys and girls, '[t]he gender gap is considerably smaller than the inequalities of attainment associated with ethnic origin and social class background' (Gillborn and Mirza, 2000, p 23). We will return to this later.

The picture is different, however, when educational qualifications are translated into jobs. As Arnot and Phipps (2003, p 18) put it, 'there is no guarantee that such academic capital could be converted and indeed would be converted into academic and economic privilege'. Whatever class of degree female graduates achieve, males with the same level of qualification earn more. This is particularly the case in the private sector and in law and engineering jobs. Indeed, this gap is evident across the workforce as a whole. In November 2006 the Equal Opportunities Commission reported that:

> Annual statistics from the Office for National Statistics (ONS) were published this month, showing the full-time pay gap remains at 17.2%. We calculated that this means the average woman working full time will lose out on around £330,000 over the course of her working life. (www.eoc.org.uk/Default.aspx?page=19726)

Female graduates are also more likely to be employed in routine work positions than men although they do gain a greater premium in terms of earning than men, relative to women without degrees. Minority ethnic women also find it more difficult to turn their educational qualifications to equal advantage compared with men and, indeed, compared with their White female peers.

> The reality these young Pakistani, Bangladeshi and Black Caribbean women are likely to face in the workplace is very different to that of White girls. The latest statistics show that women from these groups are more likely than White women to be unemployed, less likely to be in senior roles and are even more concentrated than White women in a narrow range of jobs and sectors. Pakistani and Bangladeshi women also face a bigger gender pay gap than White women. (www.eoc.org.uk/Default.aspx?page=19421)

Despite this, during the 1990s the underachievement of boys became something of a 'moral panic' spurred by media attention, and New Labour responded in 1998 with a 'coordinated plan of action' to tackle 'the problem', to which it would be very difficult to find any earlier parallel for girls. The DfES Standards website (www.standards.dfes.gov.uk/) currently includes a list of 54 academic books and papers on boys' underachievement, together with reports from a four-year (2000-04) Raising Boys' Achievement Project focused on issues associated with academic achievement differentials of boys and girls at Key Stages 2 and 4 in schools in England. Moreover, the DfES gender and achievement website (www.standards.dfes.gov.uk/genderandachievement) provides research and resources in terms of case studies, statistics and guidance for schools on how to set up a strategy to tackle boys' underachievement. It invites news and feedback and features a Raising Boys' Achievement toolkit, while noting that:

> While gender is one of the key factors affecting educational performance, it affects different sub-groups of boys and girls in different ways. Social class, ethnic origin and local context are all factors that are strongly linked to performance. The crucial point is in ensuring that policies designed to improve boys' results do not do so at the expense of girls.

To a great extent the problem of boys' underachievement is a working-class one, and one for those from some minority ethnic groups, but this is often lost sight of in both the media and policy initiatives. Class, 'race' and gender are complexly interrelated in patterns of educational performance and participation.

Similar concerns about the underachievement of boys have entered into policy in the US and Australia but are played out in somewhat different ways and the question of 'which boys' underperform is also dealt with differently. In Australia the Federal Parliament established a national enquiry to establish the reasons for boys' underachievement, which led to the funding of two national programmes: the Boys Lighthouse Project ($7 million) and Success for Boys ($19.4 million). These projects focus on changing schools to better meet boys' needs through the use of male mentors, a more masculinised curriculum and the development of positive relations with boys.

In its current iteration in the UK, the 'moral panic' about boys' underachievement has been focused on Black boys in particular and a flurry of reports and policy ideas have generated a number of related controversies. In March 2005 the Commission for Racial Equality (CRE) Chairman Trevor Phillips sparked controversy by appearing to recommend a US scheme of segregated teaching for Black boys. Aspects of the ensuing debate mirrored the 'cultural turn' noted earlier in relation to social exclusion. For example, responding to the furore, a CRE spokesperson noted that '[h]e [Trevor Phillips] also feels that Black children need role models and ideally parents, especially fathers, should play a more active role in their children's education'. Rather than focusing on 'hard', structural issues, '[w]e find instead a "soft" approach focusing on culture, behaviour and the home' (Mirza, 2005b, p 16). Again, in 2007 in a 'seminar of experts' held at No 10 Downing Street, among other things, it 'emerged' [sic] that 'parental involvement is far more critical than social class or ethnic identity in determining how children do at school' (report in *The Guardian*, 14 January 2007). In contrast, Mayor Ken Livingstone, in his foreword to *The educational experiences and achievements of Black boys in London schools 2000-2003*, a report by the Education Commission of the London Development Agency, which made 72 recommendations, stated that:

> It has been clear for some years that Britain's education system is failing to give Black boys the start in life which they, and their parents, are entitled to expect. As this report shows, African Caribbean boys, in particular, start their schooling at broadly the same level as other pupils, but in the course of their education they fall further and further behind so that in 2003, for example, roughly 70% of African Caribbean pupils left school with less than five higher grade GCSEs or their equivalents. This represents the lowest level of achievement for any ethnic group of school children.

Perhaps what we see here is some traces of Old Labour–New Labour differences in the framing and definition of policy problems.

'Race'

The most recent government research on the attainment and participation of minority ethnic pupils (DfES, The Statistical First Release, National Curriculum Assessment, GCSE and equivalent attainment and Post-16 attainment by pupil characteristics, in England, 2005, available at www.dfes.gov.uk/rsgateway/DB/SFR/s000640/index.shtml) indicates a complex and diverse pattern. The number of minority ethnic students has grown much more than the school population as a whole and by 2004 made up 17% of the maintained school population, ranging from 1.5% in East Riding of Yorkshire LEA to 84% in Hackney LEA. In terms of GCSE performance (5+ A-Cs), Indian (70% girls/60% boys), Chinese (79%/71%), the so-called 'model minorities' (Mirza, 2005a, p 15), White–Asian dual heritage (69%/61%) and Irish students (62%/58%) were the highest achievers, while Gypsy/Roma (23%/24%), Irish Travellers (39%/43%), Black Caribbean (40%/25%) and White–Black Caribbean dual heritage students (47%/32%) were the lowest. The last two groups also have the largest gender gap. A recent Equal Opportunities Commission report noted that:

> Pakistani and Bangladeshi girls are catching up with White girls in terms of GCSE results, and have already overtaken White boys. Black Caribbean girls showed the biggest increase of all groups between 2003 and 2005. Ethnic minority women from all these groups, aged 16-22, are slightly more likely than White British women to be in full-time education. (www.eoc.org.uk/)

White British students come in the middle of the achievement range (57%/46%). Overall, the national average for girls is 56% and for boys 46%.

However, the 'attainment gap' between Key Stages 1 and 4 is wider for Black Caribbean students and students from other Black backgrounds. Furthermore, Black Caribbean and 'Black other' boys are twice as likely to have been categorised as having behavioural, emotional or social difficulty as White British boys and they have, with Irish Traveller, Gypsy/Roma and White–Black Caribbean students, higher than average rates of permanent exclusion. Within the EiC initiative Black Caribbean and Black African students were more likely than other groups to have reported seeing a learning mentor and were less likely than White students to be identified for gifted and talented programmes. The report also notes that minority ethnic children are more likely to live in low-income households (38%) compared with White students (18%), and for Pakistani/Bangladeshi households this figure rises to 65% and is reflected in higher rates of eligibility for free school meals. However, among a representative sample, a higher proportion of parents/carers of minority ethnic students (53%) reported feeling involved overall with their child's education than across the sample as a whole (38%). Finally, in England as a whole 9% of teachers are from a minority ethnic group; in London 31%.

Box 4.3: Black pupils close GCSE grade gap

Black schoolchildren have started to close the gap in educational performance on their White classmates by doing better than ever in tests for 14-year-olds and GCSE exams. Black boys, whose underachievement at school has particularly alarmed ministers and community leaders, have recorded significant improvements in the last few years, according to an independent analysis of Government initiatives to improve pass rates.

An evaluation of the Aiming High programme, aimed at Black pupils, has found that many of those who received extra help recorded dramatic increases in their attainment. The report says that the percentage of Black Caribbean boys achieving at least Level 5 in tests for 14-year-olds had gone up by 13% in mathematics, 12% in English and 3.5% in science. These rates were higher than the average for all pupils at the 100 schools in England which are now part of Aiming High and above the national average for Black Caribbean boys in general. (Campbell, 2006)

Overall, the data suggest that experience of and engagement with school is very often different for students of different ethnicities. In particular, for Black Caribbean students and, more especially, Black Caribbean boys, historic patterns of underachievement, exclusion and labelling remain entrenched despite some recent improvements in participation and performance. As Mirza puts it:

> The more things change, the more they stay the same and while racist treatment of our children may not be so blatant as 35 years ago we are still plagued by the problem of racial differentiation in educational treatment and outcome for Black Caribbean young people. (Mirza, 2005b, p 117)

Gillborn and Youdell (2000) highlight the way that decision making and selection processes about access to course and qualification routes in schools still work against the interests of Black students and Hunte (2004) indicates four factors that may be involved at school level in the production of underachievement:

- discriminatory school practices
- eurocentric curriculum
- under-representation of Black staff at senior level
- pupil identity and peer influence.

The national curriculum, despite several updates, does little to address racism or reflect cultural diversity, although in 2007 the Secretary of State asked the QCA to ensure that all children would be taught about slavery. Generally, post-1997 Labour governments have been resistant to 'race'-specific education policies and setting targets for minority ethnic achievement. In contrast to the flood of interventionary, enabling and constraining policies in other areas of educational practice national policies for 'race' and gender equality and for equal opportunities have been few. The DfES (see Aiming High, www.standards.dfes.gov.uk/) estimates that between 2005 and 2006 the government committed

£168.6 million to measures aimed specifically at raising achievement among minority groups.

Despite a number of more recent initiatives, education policy in relation to 'race' and racism is to a great extent only brought to the forefront at moments of 'race crisis' and, even then, typically displaced into enquires and reports and 'enacted' through exhortation and good intentions rather than practical actions and often subsumed within other standards-raising moves. This is a form of 'non-performative' policy making – it looks like action is being taken but nothing much really happens or indeed the announcement of 'a response' – like an enquiry – blocks or avoids other policy activity, that is 'the investment in saying as if saying was doing can actually extend rather that challenge racism' (Ahmed, 2004). Aside from moments of crisis, the 'normal' practice is, as Gillborn (1997) suggests, to 'deracialise' policy.

Five moments of crisis and response could be said to 'mark' the history of 'policy' on education and 'race'. Rampton and Swann (see Box 4.4) were responses to community concerns about dramatic educational underachievement of minority ethnic students. Burnage was an inquiry into the murder of pupil Ahmed Iqbal Ullah at Burnage High School in 1986; Macpherson an inquiry into the racist murder of Stephen Lawrence in 1993; and Cantle an inquiry into interracial riots in three north of England 'mill towns' in 2001. Gillborn (2005, p 486) argues forcefully that:

> … virtually every major public policy meant to improve race equity has arisen *directly* from resistance and protest by Black and other minoritized communities. Indeed, some of the most significant changes have come about as the result of blood shed.

Box 4.4: 'Race' reports

Rampton Report (1981) *West Indian children in our schools*

Swann Report (1985) DES, *Education for All*, report of the Committee of Inquiry into the Children from Ethnic Minority Groups

Burnage Report (1988) *Murder in the Playground*, Report of the Macdonald Inquiry into Racism

Macpherson Report (1999) *The Stephen Lawrence Inquiry*, Cm 4262-I

Cantle Report (2001) *The Inquiry by the Community Cohesion Review Team into the riots in Bradford, Burnley and Oldham 2001*

In 1977 a government select committee recommended that statistics on West Indian [sic] pupils, students and teachers should be collected and analysed. The government accepted its recommendation but four years later the Rampton Report observed that little progress had been made in its implementation. Rampton expanded the recommendation to refer to all students, including those in HE and FE, and data on attainment, strongly urging immediate implementation, although preceded by consultation with, among others, local authorities and teacher unions. Again nothing was done and it was another 21 years before Aiming High (see above) provided reliable national statistics cross-tabulating attainment and ethnicity.[2] The Rampton Report (1981) found significant underachievement among West Indian pupils, and similar figures were indicated by the Swann Report (1985), which, in both cases, was attributed to the existence of racism and prejudice in schools. Swann's extensive documentation of racism in education received a hostile reception from the Right-wing press and New Right lobby groups when the findings were published. Mirza

(2005, p 1) notes, '[I]n the government, media, and public mind the relationship between "race" and education is overwhelmingly negative'. The findings of the Stephen Lawrence Inquiry (Macpherson, 1999), with its emphasis on the devastating effects of 'institutional racism' in the Metropolitan Police, provoked a similar defensiveness and hostility to that which had occurred 20 years earlier in relation to Rampton and Swann but, nonetheless, Home Secretary Jack Straw accepted the report in its entirety. Macpherson made 70 recommendations, four directed at education, which provided the basis of the Race Relations (Amendment) Act (2000) that requires that all public bodies have in place anti-discriminatory and 'race equality policies'. The Cantle Report pointed to residential and school segregation as a contributory factor in the riots it examined and Tomlinson (2005) suggests that this report influenced the 2002 Immigration and Asylum Act, which outlined new policies for citizenship and nationality. It also led to the setting up in 2002 of the Home Office Community Cohesion Unit. In 2007 Oldham LEA announced plans to replace seven ethnically segregated schools with three academies funded from the BSF programme that would have a 'multicultural make-up'. *The Independent* (29 March 2007) commented that 'there is political pressure to drive through the change, fuelled by concern that segregation is also affecting the Government's school performance targets'.

The primary trend in national equity policy has been both symbolic and rhetorical – non-performative. Much of the policy activity around 'race' issues in education has been in the form of 'sound bites' and a good deal of activity has taken the form of taskforces, policy groups, websites and conferences (see Box 4.5), rather than legislation. Tomlinson (2005, p 182) describes efforts to 'eliminate racial and gender inequalities' as 'patchy and uneven', and generally there has been a reluctance to address issues of racism directly.[3] The pace of policy had been slow and halting in contrast to the haste apparent elsewhere and has, as noted already, depended heavily on local and institutional initiatives, many of which Conservative education policies from 1988 onwards tended to interrupt, discourage or deliberately inhibit. Troyna (1995, p 142) referred to this period as marked by the rise of 'equiphobia' and the correlative demise of anti-racism in the agendas of LEAs and individual schools. In particular, the 1988 national curriculum worked directly against attempts to develop a 'multicultural' curriculum in schools. Indeed, the report of the multicultural task group set up by the NCC in 1989 was neither published, nor were any of its recommendations put into practice. The national curriculum, at least in its first iteration, was used to calm 'fears that children will not learn about British heritage' (John Patten, quoted in Tomlinson and Craft, 1995, p 5) and 20 years on 'there is still no integral anti-racist training for teachers. A total of 70% of newly qualified teachers say they do not feel equipped to teach pupils from different ethnicities' (Mirza, 2005, p 14). Moreover, during the 1990s, use of Section 11 grants, introduced in 1966 to allow LEAs to make special provision in the exercise of their functions in the consequence of the presence in their areas of substantial numbers of immigrants from the Commonwealth whose language or customs differed from those of the community, was subject to increasingly tight direction so that, for instance, neither community languages nor minority arts could be funded. Section 11 was replaced in 1997 by ethnic minority achievement grants.

Box 4.5: Some New Labour 'race' equality initiatives

- Ethnic Minority Achievement Unit established in DfES.
- 1998 Social Exclusion Unit report on over-representation of Black boys in school exclusions and truancy.
- DfES consultation 'Aiming High: Raising achievement of minority ethnic pupils' (DfES, 0183/2003, www.dfes.gov.uk/).
- Aiming High includes: the Black Pupils' Achievement Programme, the Ethnic Minority Achievement Programme and Raising the Achievement of Gypsy Traveller Pupils.
- The Goal Programme is being piloted by the National Academy of Gifted and Talented Youth between 2006 and 2009. It will support the development of high-potential pupils from disadvantaged backgrounds, including Black and minority ethnic pupils.

- DfES since 2002 has run a National Advisory Group for the Strategy to raise the achievement of minority ethnic students.
- QCA ran a Race Strategy Group (2000-06).
- State school status has been made available to some Muslim, Hindu and Greek Orthodox schools.

What is being suggested here is that equity issues in English education are marked, more than anything else, by a history of policy avoidance. While in some respects New Labour has been more active in and attentive to 'race' issues than preceding governments (see Box 4.5 and also Chapter Two), its approach in general has been incoherent and piecemeal and 'dominated by short-term high-profile initiatives that have not achieved a great deal' (Heidi Safra Mirza, a member of the government's Schools' Standards Task Force, personal communication). In contrast to other fields of education policy, exhortation, rather than intervention, has been used, with the exception of the 2000 Race Relations (Amendment) Act, a Home Office measure involving a 'hands-off approach' (Heidi Safra Mirza). Policy itself remains unaddressed, as a source or carrier of racism (see Box 4.6), and issues addressed by 'race' and education policies are also inflected and distorted by discourse and preoccupations from 'elsewhere', as currently, for example, by things like gun crime, religious and cultural practices, immigration, asylum and terrorism. There are also more general policy ambivalences around 'race' relations that have implications for education. In particular these have concerned: the need for skilled labour, as noted in Chapter One, as against 'problems' associated with non-White immigration; and valuing of cultural diversity, as against renewed emphasis, especially post-9/11 and 7/7, on national identity, English language skills and the meaning of citizenship. Gillborn's (2005, p 499) overall assessment of New Labour education policy is that '[T]he evidence suggests that, despite a rhetoric of standards for all, education policy in England is actively involved in the defence, legitimation and extension of White supremacy'.

Box 4.6: New Labour, 'race' and education

The DfES (2004) 'five year strategy for children and learners' mentions minority ethnic pupils only once, in one 25-word paragraph. Racism, prejudice and discrimination do not appear in the text at all.

A 2006 DfES report, as yet unpublished but obtained by the *Independent on Sunday* newspaper, into the exclusion of Black pupils, concluded that 'The exclusions gap is caused by largely unwitting, but systematic, racial discrimination in the application of disciplinary and exclusions policy'. The Report also noted that Black pupils were 'five times less likely to be registered as "gifted and talented"' (*Independent on Sunday*, 10 December 2006).

Finally, in this section, I want both to reiterate the complexity of issues concerning equity in education, the compounding effects of multiple forms of social exclusion and the need to appreciate the continuing and overwhelming significance of class and poverty in relation to educational performance and participation. Social class 'cuts across' and intersects with 'race' and gender inequalities, often with the effect of multiplying disadvantage. A review of research by Gillborn and Mirza (2000) (see Figure 4.1) concluded by indicating that in terms of educational performance the 'class gap' remains greater, but receives far less attention in policy, than either the gaps in 'race' or gender performances. Class as such currently has no place in the language of education policy – it has been displaced by social exclusion. Whatever advances may have been made in some aspects of women's and minority ethnic groups' educational achievements, class differences and inequalities seem firmly entrenched and may even be getting worse.

The report by the National Children's Bureau *Child poverty and education* (Ennals, 2004) found that the UK continues to have one of the biggest class divides in education in the industrialised world. It

Figure 4.1: 'Race', class and gender gaps in educational achievement

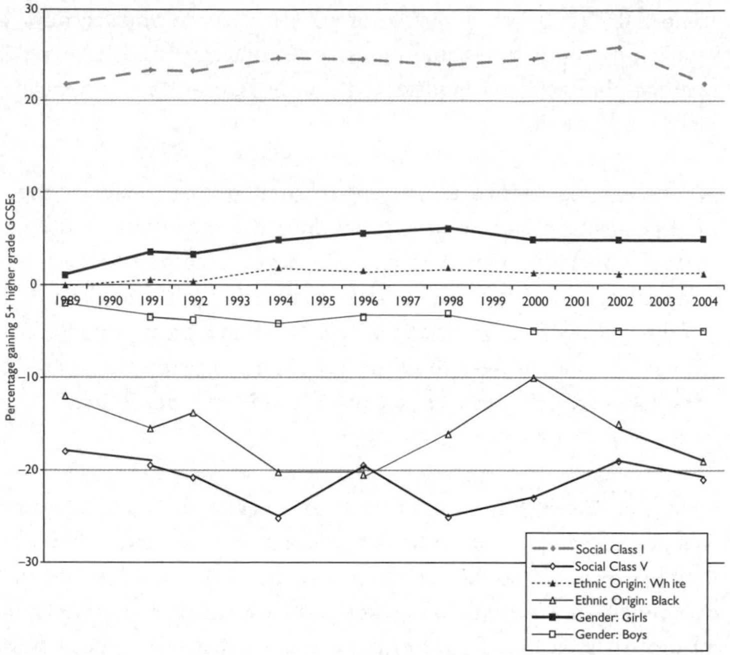

pointed to strong correlations between poverty, social class and poor educational attainment among children in the UK, revealing that:

- an attainment gap between poor and better-off children was evident as early as 22 months and widened as children got older. Poor children were still one third as likely to get five good GCSEs as their wealthier classmates;
- the rate at which the performance of children from different classes diverged during secondary schools was faster in areas where the 11 Plus system is retained;
- young people from unskilled backgrounds were over five times less likely to enter HE than those from professional backgrounds.

The report also argued that the effect of poverty on children went beyond test results. Poor children can be denied access to school trips, face problems in affording school uniform, suffer stigma from insensitive approaches to free school meals and feel socially excluded at school. In March 2007 figures from the Department for Work and Pensions showed an increase in the number of children living in relative poverty in the UK: 2.8 million, up by 100,000 from the previous year. The children's charity Barnardo's called the figures 'a moral disgrace' (www.barnardos.org.uk/news_and_events).

The ongoing policy engagement of New Labour with issues of social class (or rather social exclusion) and education is taken up in different ways in the next three sections of this chapter.

Parenting

As noted already, Prime Minister Tony Blair made an enormous personal investment in education policy, making many key policy announcements himself rather than leaving them to his Secretaries of State.[4] Education was a recurring theme in his speeches and press conferences, he made many visits to schools and personally praised and rewarded 'excellent' teachers. Blair also often spoke about education from the point of view of a parent. As he explained in one of his monthly news conferences during the passage of the 2006 Education and Inspections Bill:

> Whenever I look at education, I speak as a parent first and as a politician second. I know what I wanted for my own children, and that is what I expect other parents to want and our job should be to help them get it, not to stand in the way of them and say we know better than you do what's good for your child. (23 January 2006)

And yet it could be said that, in relation to parenting, knowing 'better than you do what's good for your child' is exactly what the government was saying through the provisions of the 2006 Education and Inspections Act and its other parenting initiatives. Clauses 90-92 of the Act extended previously established parenting contracts and orders 'so that they can be used more widely to ensure that parents take proper responsibility for their children's behaviour at school'. Parents were also to be required to take responsibility for excluded pupils and made subject to prosecution or penalty notices if excluded pupils were to be found in a public place during school hours without a reasonable excuse. This built on existing regulations, which in March 2004 saw Oxfordshire parent Patricia Amos imprisoned for the second time over her daughter's truancy, and other legislation on 'anti-social behaviour'. In 2002 proposals were announced that included fixed penalty fines of £50 for those parents with children who regularly truanted (see Box 4.7). In 2003, 5,381 parents were taken to court, and 80% of them were found guilty.

Box 4.7: Failure to cut truancy makes ministers get tough on parents

> Ministers announced tougher sanctions against parents of persistent truants in October 2002. The latest figures show the level of unauthorized absence has once again refused to budge.
>
> The Government's target of cutting truancy by a third this year has been comprehensively missed. But truancy did fall in areas supported by the Excellence in Cities scheme.
>
> Now a new fast-track process will allow parents just one term to make sure their child attends school or face prosecution that could lead to fines of up to £2,500 or jail. But the Prime Minister has scrapped plans to withdraw child benefit from the parents of truants.

The new procedure will be piloted in six local education authorities in England from November 2002. (*TES*, 11 October 2002)

In New Labour policy discourses, parents are key figures in regenerating social morality and lack of parental discipline is linked to problems of truancy, anti-social behaviour, offending and obesity. Alongside legal procedures regarding 'failing' parents, efforts have also been made to offer parents professional health and child-rearing help and support, particularly through Sure Start schemes and Parentline (a confidential telephone counselling service aimed at providing professional support for parents and others who have the care of children), while those deemed to be in need can also be sanctioned to attend parenting education classes (Home Office, 2003). LEAs can apply through magistrates' courts for civil parenting orders against parents of excluded children who are deemed 'unwilling to engage with the school or the LEA to improve their child's serious misbehaviour' (DfES press release, 2004/0053). Also in 2004 the National Attendance and Behaviour Strategy was announced, funded at a cost of £470 million (www.dfes.gov.uk/). In earlier measures the Labour government introduced summer schools, homework guidelines and after-school homework centres. More generally all of this can be traced back to New Labour's 'new moralism' agenda, or what McCaig (2001) calls 'social authoritarianism' and the attempt at a 'remoralisation' of society by strengthening civil institutions like the family. This is also very much third way practice where the 'proactive state' addresses itself to 'causes' rather than 'effects', prevention rather than 'repair':

> We can then, in the jargon, 'intervene'. Intervention can sound very sinister. Actually, in the great bulk of cases it means that extra help and support can be provided. It might mean that a more intense health-visitor programme is arranged. Or it might mean parenting classes are offered; or help with drug or alcohol abuse. Or placing families within projects

> like the Dundee project where the family is given help but within a proper, disciplined framework.... The answer for these families is that a rising tide of material prosperity will not necessarily raise all ships. A cash transfer, at least on its own, is not what is needed. What is needed, instead, is proper structured help, where a due sense of responsibility may be part of the mix, and at a stage early enough to make a difference. (Blair, 2006b)

In Foucault's (1979) terms Blair is deploying 'dividing practices', a procedure that objectifies subjects (feckless parents) as socially and politically irresponsible, the 'others' of policy who need to be 'saved' from their uncivilised lives through expert 'interventions'. They are incapable of being responsible for themselves and their children. Forms of expertise are brought to bear. In effect this is the same model of governing as that applied to institutions, a certain sort of freedom is offered, a virtuous, disciplined and responsible autonomy which, if not taken up appropriately, provokes 'intervention', as is the case in 'failing schools'. We even see here further extension of 'contracting' as a way of representing relationships between institutions, between individuals and institutions, and between individuals one with another, in the form of 'home–school contracts'. Also deployed here is another form of reculturation wherein promoting 'a culture of achievement' means 'changing attitudes' and harnessing parents to the drive to raise standards in education. As David Blunkett argued:

> We need teachers who are forward looking, ready for change and committed to continuous improvement. We need parents who are prepared to take responsibility for supporting their child's education and we need a culture which values education and demands the best. (Blunkett, 1999, DfES News Centre, 3 September, www.dfes.gov.uk)

Gewirtz (2001, p 366) identifies these policies and initiatives as the 'latest stage in a long history of state-sponsored attempts to transform the parenting behaviour of working-class parents', describing this as 'New Labour's resocialization programme', an attempt 'to make all families like middle-class families, or at least the ideal-typical middle-class family of much educational research … clones of Tony and Cheri Blair'.

In fact, different aspects of the 2006 Act articulate two very different forms of relation between families and state. The first is a neoliberal or market relation based on more choice and voice (Chapter Three) and the use of 'parent power' through complaints mechanisms and the possibility of setting up their own schools, although this also has elements of the bolstering of civil society through participation. The other indicates a disciplinary relationship of normalisation, or what is sometimes termed 'responsibilisation' (Rose, 1996). Here, again, the causes of 'failure' and inequality are posited as cultural and moral rather than structural. In the first instance the emphasis is on 'rights' and the second on 'responsibilities'. Again this is a significant shift from Old to New Labour perspectives where 'the state as a donor and the citizen as a recipient' is regarded as no longer viable; and rather 'civic society, the space between the state and the individual must be expanded' (*The Guardian*, 16 January 2007, quoting Prime Minister Tony Blair). Giddens (1998b, p 65; emphasis in original), indeed, argues that: '*no rights without responsibilities*' is 'a prime motto for the new politics'. Indeed the third way represents a 'dual commitment to the values of opportunity and personal responsibility' (White, 1998, p 6), which 'fits' with the New Labour version of equity in education as meritocracy.

Meritocracy

> I want a Britain where there is no cap on ambition, no ceiling on talent, no limit to where your potential will take you and how far you can rise. (Brown, 2007)

The idea of meritocracy was introduced in Michael Young's (1958) satire *The rise of the meritocracy*, an account of a future society in which IQ was the sole determinant of position and opportunity. The book formed part of a more general reaction against the use of intelligence testing in education, particularly the exaggerated belief about the part it could play in an 'equitable' allocation of grammar school places. The New Labour version of meritocracy expunges the critique and gives a positive value to the notion through various programmes and initiatives which, as Gillborn and Youdell (2000) argue, display traces of a 'new IQism', that is, the idea that ability is a fixed and definable and measurable quality of individual students which, they suggest, is being 'strengthened by contemporary policy and practice' (p 212) and which in schools 'provides an opportunity for teachers to identify the winners and losers at the earliest possible stage' (p 212). This kind of thinking was evident, somewhat chillingly, in the 2005 White Paper *Higher standards: Better schools for all* (DfES, 2005a), which stated that 'we must make sure that every pupil – gifted and talented, struggling or just average – reaches the limits of their capability' (p 20, para 1.28). John White identified a similar IQism, and ideas about fixed intelligence in relation to the Gifted and Talented Programme, part of the EiC initiative:

> The Gifted and Talented initiative can be seen as the latest manifestation of Galton's project, taken up by Terman, Burt and many others, of identifying an intellectual elite and making educational provision for them. (White, 2006, p 144)

This and other policies involve identification or seeking out of those students *who are gifted and talented*: 'It means shifting the focus decisively from the institution to the individual, irrespective of geography or birth, so that every gifted pupil will be stretched and special needs met' (Blunkett, 1999). In 2002 the government established the National Academy for Gifted and Talented Youth based at the University of Warwick to provide extra-curricular activities for students between 11 and 19 years of age, accepting students from all schools, whether state, CTCs, grammar or private, deemed to be in the top 5% (of what is not clear). In 2007 the Academy is running a 'talent search' to identify gifted students aged 11-16 who are required to provide evidence of their ability. '"World Class Tests" offer an ideal means of demonstrating ability for entry to the Academy' (World Class Arena website, National Academy for Gifted and Talented Youth, 9 February 2007, www.nagty.ac.uk/).

Giddens refers to these policy orientations as about the 'redistribution of possibilities' rather than of resources but he also acknowledges that in 'such a social order, the privileged are bound to be able to confer advantages on their children – thus destroying meritocracy' (Giddens, 1998b, p 102; for a discussion of the issues involved here see Hills and Stewart, 2005). As already noted, Blair is also openly critical of comprehensive education and in favour of ability grouping in schools and Rentoul (1997, p 132) contends that '[I]t was Blair who floated the idea of "accelerated learning", a marginal policy of largely symbolic value which means moving able children up a whole year in subjects in which they excel'. The principle which runs through New Labour's vision of equality, especially in relation to education policy but also more generally within the third way, is that of opportunity, removing barriers and providing possibilities for those with energy and talent, rather than universal provision.[5] This is a manifestation of the political underpinnings of the third way which, as Giddens explains, involves combining social solidarity with a dynamic economy, strives for equal opportunities not equal outcomes, promotes pluralism in welfare supply and concentrates on wealth and income creation, not their distribution. This involves, according to Lister, a 'paradigm shift in Labour Party thinking on "welfare"' which 'can be summed up as a move away from an equality agenda to one comprising the trinity of Responsibilities, Inclusion and Opportunity (ie RIO)' (Lister, 2000). Roy Hattersley, an 'Old Labour' critic of government education policy, suggested that Tony Blair's 'destiny is to create a meritocracy', adding that now 'my party not only pursues policies with which I disagree; its whole programme is based on a principle that I reject' (*The Observer*, 24 June 2001).

Figure 4.2: A genealogy of meritocracy

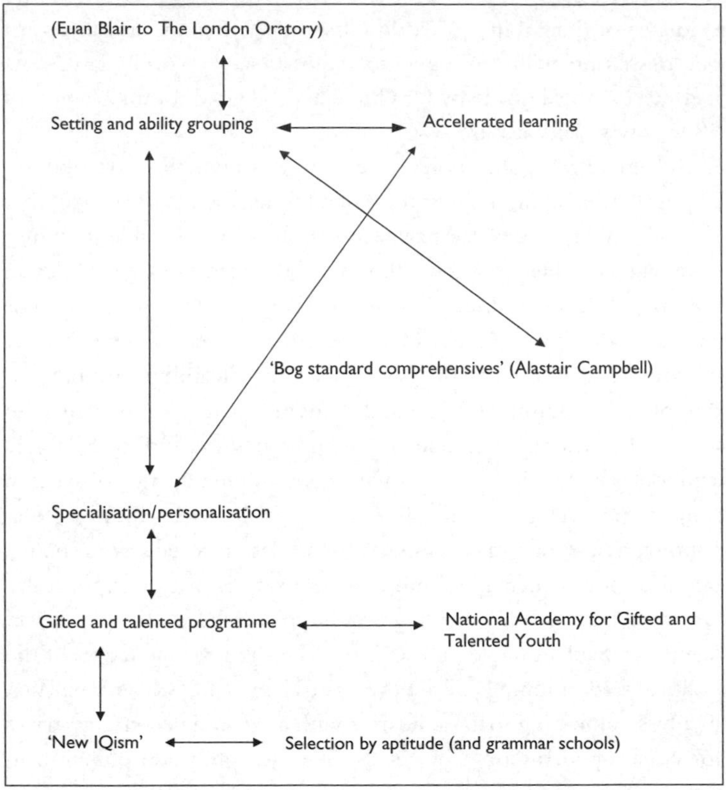

Academies, trusts and privatisation

The final 'take' on equity in this chapter explores a range of issues related to the academies programme. The academies programme, or 'city academies' at that time, was introduced in March 2000 by David Blunkett, in a speech to the Social Market Foundation entitled 'Transforming secondary education'. The first projects were announced in September of that year in a programme specifically linked to 'under-performance' and schools in cities working in 'difficult circumstances'. In his speech Blunkett argued:

> We need a dramatic increase in the number of successful schools in our cities. Far too many schools are under-performing in terms of the outcomes for their pupils. Many of these schools are working very hard and doing good things in difficult circumstances. But that is not enough if the outcomes for the young people do not fit them for further education and the world of work. No single approach will solve all problems, but radical innovation in the creation of new schools is one option. City academies will provide for this.

Other key New Labour policy themes are represented here: the importance of radical innovative ideas; the need to increase participation post-16; and preparation for the world of work. The DfES Green Paper *Schools: Building on success* (DfES, 2001a), proposed that the city academy programme would raise standards by innovative approaches to management, governance, teaching and the curriculum with a specialist focus on one area. The programme builds on the Conservatives' CTCs initiative, which was in turn informed by the development and experience of charter schools in the US (PWC, 2005). The programme is expensive – the House of Commons Education and Skills Select Committee (2005) estimated a cost of £5 billion. There was an initial target of 200 such schools by 2010, 60 in the London boroughs. In November 2006 Tony Blair announced that the target would be raised to 400; by September 2007 82 academies were open in 51 local authorities.

Academies are run by their sponsors on the basis of a funding agreement with the DfES, negotiated separately in each case. This 'quasi-contractual' model of working has distinct parallels with the creation of 'executive agencies' within the civil service initiated through the Next Steps programme in the 1990s. The academies are 'publicly funded independent schools' (DfES, 2005a) outside LEA control that relate directly to the DfES (now DCSF) academies division. They have, as the 2005 White Paper described it, 'freedom to shape their own destiny in the interest of parents and children' (DfES, 2005a, p 24). Sponsors provide 10% of the capital costs (or now a 'cash' fund) up to a maximum of £2 million, although actual building costs are much more. The average cost of an academy is £25-£30 million (against a typical new LEA community school cost of £20-£25 million). The most expensive, the Bexley Business Academy, sponsored by property developer and Labour Party financial backer David Garrard, cost £38 million. Sponsors may choose their own headteacher and staff and appoint the majority of governors. There is one LEA governor and one elected by parents. Addressing potential sponsors the DfES/Academy Sponsors Trust brochure states that 'issues of ethos, specialism and uniform are entirely for you' (www.standards.dfes.gov.uk/academies/pdf/Academiesprospectus2006.pdf). They are exempt from the specific requirements of the national curriculum 'and are free to adopt innovative approaches to the content and delivery of the curriculum' (DfES Standards site, www.standards.dfes.gov.uk/) but are subject to Ofsted inspections. As noted previously they also have the opportunity to set aside existing national agreements on pay, conditions and certification of teachers; that is to say, they can employ non-qualified individuals, a significant move in the 'flexibilisation' of the teaching workforce building on a more general policy impetus for the 'modernisation' of the school workforce and 'workforce remodelling' (Chapter Three).

In many respects the programme stands as a *condensate* of New Labour education policies, an experiment in and a symbol of education policy beyond the welfare state and an example and indicator of more general shifts taking place in governance and regulatory structures (see the move from government to governance). Innovation, inclusion and regeneration are tied together in the academies rhetoric and, to some extent, at least, are realised in practice, and are intended to address local social problems and inequalities and histories of 'underachievement'. A National Foundation for Educational Research (NFER) study (Chamberlain et al, 2006), based on the first 17 academies, found they were more socially diverse in terms of children receiving free school meals than the make-up of the locality in which they were set but admitted more children who did not achieve level 4 in Key Stage 2 maths tests, that is, who were performing below their expected level in national tests. Academies are also intended to enact a new set of potential relations between education and the economy within which schools are required to take much more responsibility for fostering 'knowledge cultures' as part of economic regeneration programmes in 'entrepreneurial localities' and in relation to the requirements of the digital workplace. In the most recent versions of the academies programme it is intended that they should become the hubs of local school networks geared to relevant sectors of the local economy. They are to stand in open relation to their communities and often provide community facilities of various kinds. Finally, they are intended to blur welfare state demarcations between state and market, public and private, government and business and, as noted already, introduce and validate new agents and new voices within policy itself and into processes of governance; they are indicative of a 're-agenting' (Jones, 2003) of education policy. Specifically academies draw in and on the 'energies' of entrepreneurial and policy 'heroes' and social entrepreneurs and mobilise business philanthropy. In various ways through the academies programme, specialist schools, Teach First and other means philanthropy is becoming reincorporated into state policy as a way of avoiding both bureaucratic and market difficulties in bringing about change, and facilitating 'faster', less durable and often very personal policy action.

Academies also specialise; they are, in effect, specialist schools writ large, with 'business and enterprise' the most popular variant (Woods et al, 2007). Academies involve a self-conscious attempt to promote entrepreneurism and competitiveness, 'the enterprise narrative', involving, in some cases, both curriculum content and an organisational orientation towards entrepreneurism in terms of commercial exploitation of innovations and in relationships with commercial companies. Sponsors of academies include 'philanthropic' individuals (for example, Eric Payne, Jack Petchey, John Aisbitt, Clive Bourne), companies (for example, Tarmac, HSBC, West Bromwich Albion), charities (for example, United Learning Trust (ULT), EduAction, ARK), religious groups (for example, the Church of England, the Catholic Church, Oasis Trust), and some universities (for example, Brunel,

Manchester, University of the West of England, Wolverhampton). The largest sponsor in terms of number of schools is the Church of England charity, ULT. Many individual sponsors are what we might call 'hero entrepreneurs', who embody key values of New Labour, particularly the possibilities of meritocracy, of achieving individual success from modest beginnings and wealth creation from innovative ideas and knowledge. These include Alex Reed (Reed Recruitment), Frank Lowe (Lowe Group advertising agency), Roger de Haan (Saga Holidays) and Rod Aldridge (Capita). In effect these are proselytisers for a new kind of capitalism, 'responsible capitalists', espousing new values, 'putting something back in the community'. Not all sponsors are Labour supporters, however (for example, Robert Edmiston, EIM; Lord Harris of Peckham, Carpetright). These actors can be understood in Jessop's terms as bearers of a new accumulation strategy having 'increasing participation … in shaping education mission statements' (Jessop, 2002, p 167). We may also see here increasing reliance on getting policy done through new 'linkage devices' and 'lead organisations' – trusts and agencies like the Academy Sponsors and Specialist Schools Trusts (now merged) – which operate somewhere between and are funded by both state and private sources.

However, the programme has neither gone smoothly nor unopposed. At the local level several proposed academies have been 'seen off' by groups of local parents and trade union campaigns, including two in London proposed by ARK (Absolute Return for Kids), a charity founded by hedge-fund millionaire Arpad Busson; one in Coniston put forward by Peter Vardy (evangelical Christian car dealer who has opened three other academies in North-East England); and another proposed by fashion designer Jasper Conran. Several academy proposals, including those in Merton, Islington and the Isle of Sheppey, have been subject to legal challenge coordinated by lawyers from Matrix, the human rights chambers that includes Cherie Blair, on behalf of parents, and at least one has gone to judicial review (*The Guardian*, 13 June 2006).

In a very direct sense the academies programme is another example of the third way approach. These schools are neither state nor private, outside LEA oversight (although LEAs are now being drawn into the programme as the flow of sponsors dries up), and intended to draw on the energies and ideas of the private and voluntary sectors. They are presented as an innovative response to the failures of public sector schooling and traditional forms of governance. The academies may also be understood as a further, dramatic step in the 'break-up' of the state education system, a form of 'disarticulation' which was begun under the Conservatives with CTCs and grant-maintained schools and involving the 'progressive dismantling of comprehensive education and the reinvention of grammar schools as specialist schools' (Hulme and Hulme, 2005, p 46). This disarticulation was taken a stage further in the 2006 Education and Inspections Act. However, as a result of 'back-bench revolts' and resulting compromises, the Act did not go as far in the process of fragmentation as was signalled in the 2005 White Paper *Higher standards: Better schools for all* (DfES, 2005a). The Act created a new category of trust schools, much like grant-maintained schools but with additional freedoms. Outlining the rationale for trust schools, Ruth Kelly, Secretary of State for Education, explained at a DfES press conference:

> Specialist schools have become a mass movement for higher standards, now outperforming non-specialists by 11 percentage points at GCSE. Attainment at academies, which have replaced failing schools, is rising at a much faster rate than in other schools. These schools and their pupils have benefited from greater autonomy, greater freedom, a strong individual ethos, and the involvement of community partners from business, charities and higher education institutions.... The time is right to move to the next level building on these achievements and enabling every school to adopt these benefits to raise standards.

Trust schools as initially conceived in the 2005 White Paper (DfES, 2005a) would have had unprecedented freedoms from central and local authority control in almost all areas of their functioning. In effect, the White Paper proposed that all local authority schools would be academies, voluntary-aided, foundation or trust schools. LEAs would be left to work alongside a newly created national schools commissioner to promote choice, diversity and better access for disadvantaged groups to good schools. Even now trust schools will own their own assets, may contract or procure their own building projects and may be established by or, in the case of existing schools, may establish partnerships with 'a foundation' and 'allow that foundation to appoint a majority of governors' (DfES, 2005a). Any school may become a trust school and schools may join together to form a trust (for example, proposals for the Aspire Trust Wakefield to bring together three schools within a charitable trust involving Bearing Point, a US management services and consultancy company, Hi Tec Ltd, Leeds Metropolitan University and Wakefield District Housing). There is no single blueprint for becoming a trust – schools can choose who they work with in order to 'best meet the needs of their pupils' (DfES, 23 February 2006). Again, through this mechanism new 'agents' can become involved in the running of state schools – private companies, charitable foundations, religious organisations, voluntary associations, local community groups or groups of parents. According to the 2005 White Paper (DfES, 2005a) such relationships would offer to trust schools 'external support and a success culture, bringing innovative and stronger leadership to the school, improving standards and extending choice' (DfES, 2005a, pp 24-5). Once again, two key dynamics of New Labour's reforms come together here – autonomy, flexibility and businesslike innovation, on the one hand, and consumer choice and the freedom to respond to parent 'demand' in terms of substance or scale, on the other. While these kinds of possibilities were signalled in earlier legislation which, for instance, gave non-statutory organisations the right to 'bid' to establish new state schools, the major precedent and driver for this development is clearly the academies. As noted previously, new policy 'moves' build on and extend and advance previous ones.

Conclusion

It is not easy to make sense of all this. 'Cutting through the thickets of rhetoric to discern the actual path is not always easy, particularly when the two seem to be pointing in different directions' (Lister, 2000). The organising theme for this chapter has been policy and equity, but it should be very clear that under New Labour in particular policies rarely have a single purpose or a single focus, although initiatives like EAZs, EiC, academies and New Deal for Communities were targeted at least initially at areas of social deprivation and the particular problems of the inner cities. Equity issues are very often subsumed within more general policy strategies and are tied to goals concerned with workforce skills, flexibility, efficiency and effectiveness, reform of teachers and the modernisation of the public sector generally. Within third way policy making, modernisation and reform, raising achievement and equity are tightly interrelated. However, Whitty (2002, p 119) argues that 'these policies have so far been relatively weak in respect to overcoming disadvantage and tackling inequalities', and points out that 'there was initially a reluctance to confront the possibility that, even if its policies succeed in raising standards overall, they might exacerbate inequalities' (p 119). In contrast, Tomlinson (2001, p 169) suggests that New Labour's 'short-term ameliorative policies in socially disadvantaged areas … had positive effects for many individuals', but goes on to note 'the negative consequences of educational reforms during the 1980s and 1990s which give pride of place to the obsession with selection and segregation' (p 168) and later makes the point that:

> New Labour has been able to square the circle between anxiety that the lower classes and disadvantaged were not participating fully in education, with policies that gave distinct advantages to those from higher social groups. (Tomlinson, 2003, p 202)

Whitty (2002, p 121) is more positive about New Labour's 'relational thinking' and their 'willingness to look beyond the "failures" of schools at families and communities in explaining and tackling underachievement'. The idea of 'relational thinking', or 'joined-up policy' as it is called, has been pursued through initiatives like *Every Child Matters*. This, as part of the response to the death of Victoria Climbié, encourages a holistic approach to children and young people, with the possibility of support for parents and carers through 'universal services such as schools, health and social services and childcare' (*Every Child Matters* summary document, p 2). Local integration of services and administration was initiated through the creation of local authority children's services departments, incorporating education, and a new Minister for Children, Young People and Families was created within the DfES prior to the restructuring of the department in 2007. *Every Child Matters* also proposes certain common outcomes, skills and knowledge across all child-related settings. These are:

- staying safe
- being healthy
- enjoying and achieving
- making a positive contribution
- economic well-being.

So, over and against or alongside the moves towards disarticulation noted above, there is intended to be a process of integration and joining up; over and against an emphasis on choice, diversity and personalisation there is a statement of common goals and entitlements; and through Sure Start there is by design the creation of a new welfare-based system of preschool care and education. However, policies such as *Every Child Matters* and Sure Start, and academies, are also, as I have tried to stress, composites. Sure Start is educational in that it is about giving children a 'good start' in their learning and development; it is about children's health in providing advice and support to parents in relation to their children's physical development; it is also disciplinary; it is about early interventions into 'dysfunctional families'; and it is a form of economic policy in that, combined with Child Tax Credits, it is intended to enable more mothers to return to the workforce. Again, equity is related to and subsumed within other goals and purposes, and policy seeks to address these different goals together. *Every Child Matters* is aimed at 'reducing levels of educational failure, ill health, substance misuse, teenage pregnancy, abuse and neglect, crime and anti-social behaviour' (*Every Child Matters* summary document, p 7, www.standards.dfes.gov.uk/). Equity is no longer a value in its own right within policy; indeed Lister (2000) argues that New Labour's overall approach to social problems constitutes 'a marked retreat from greater equality as an explicit goal.... In their place is the objective of "redistribution of opportunity", through education, training and paid employment'.

Notes

[1] The Prime Minister set up the Social Exclusion Unit in 1997. Since then the Unit has led policy thinking in addressing difficult social problems. Initially part of the Cabinet Office, the Unit moved to the Office of the Deputy Prime Minister in May 2002 and now works closely with other parts of the Office such as the Neighbourhood Renewal Unit and the Homelessness and Housing Support Directorate to tackle deprivation.

[2] The Aiming High document itself outlines the government's commitment to continuing to raise standards for all young people whatever their ethnic or cultural background and ensuring that all education policies truly address the needs of every pupil in every school. (DfES Standards website, www.standards.dfes.gov.uk/)

[3] Schools participating in Aiming High build on the frameworks set out in the primary and secondary national strategies, adopting a whole-school approach to raising pupils' achievement. They focus on areas shown to be especially effective, including:

- strong leadership
- high expectations

- demonstrating respect for pupils
- valuing ethnic diversity in the curriculum
- intolerance of racism, bullying and poor behaviour
- engagement with parents and the wider community
- monitoring of pupils' attainment, with effective interventions for individuals and groups at risk of falling behind (see www.findoutmore.dfes.gov.uk).

[4] Chancellor Gordon Brown has emulated Tony Blair's approach and commitment. In his 2006 pre-budget report (6 December 2006) he announced a spending and policy package that he said was part of a programme to make Britain 'the most educated nation in the world' so that it could challenge the emerging powers of China and India. Education was the top priority 'now and into the future' (www.hm-treasury.gov.uk).

[5] It may be that Giddens' social theory is one of the influences here.

5

A sociology of education policy: past, present and future

This account and interpretation of education policy will be concluded in two ways by focusing on a set of general issues that have arisen and recurred in the foregoing text: first, by looking at 'dissolutions and conservations' within current education policy. Second, by thinking about how education and education policy are being reconfigured in space and time. Ongoing trends will also be discussed.

Dissolutions and conservations

What is sometimes called the 'discourse of endings' is a popular tactic in social science thinking and analysis. This discourse takes the concatenation of social and economic changes at a particular point in time as signalling the end of one epoch and the beginning of another – it is argued that changes are so many, varied and profound that taken together they actual constitute something new, a new kind of society. The philosopher John Gray (1999) indulged in this in his book *Endgame* when he argued that: 'We live amid the ruins of the projects of the modern age and at an historical moment when the dissolution of modern societies' most distinctive beliefs and practices is immutably under way'. There is actually a case to be made that this is an appropriate way of thinking about education and social policy and some of that argument will be rehearsed below, drawing on developments outlined in previous chapters. However, over and against this I also want to emphasise that in order to achieve a proper grasp of contemporary education policy it is necessary to understand both what has changed and what has stayed the same, that is, what was called in Chapter One 'dissolution *and* conservation' within education policy.

Some of the dissolutions within recent education policy can be summed up in terms of what writers like Tomlinson (2001) and Gewirtz (2002) call the shift from a 'welfarist' to 'post-welfarist' education 'settlement' or more simply 'changing times' (Clarke et al, 2007) or 'new times' (Kenway et al, 2007). There are two major dimensions to this; one is substantive, that is, changes in the organisation and structure of schools, teaching and the curriculum (see pp 197-201); the other is regulatory, changes in the form of governance and control in and over education. This latter again has two aspects: (1) changes in the form and modalities of the state; for example, Urry (2000) emphasises the shift of the role of the state from a gardener state to a gamekeeper state – that is, to use another metaphor, from rowing to steering; and (2) changes in the organisational forms of educational institutions themselves, from bureau-professionalism to entrepreneurial-managerialism and concomitant changes in the status, conditions and identities of educational workers. Both sets of changes have been outlined in some detail in previous chapters. I shall also suggest later that we need to think about learners as different from before.

In a period of 20 years the system and structure of English education has changed from what Ainley (2001, p 475) describes as 'a National System Locally Administered to a Local System Nationally Administered'. More generally, this is part of what Glennerster et al (1991) call a 'decisive break' that cuts across the entire spectrum of UK social policy and is certainly how New Labour has represented its approach to education policy – as a process of transformation, and an adaptation to the necessities of the global economy (as discussed in Chapter One), that is, the development of a new form of education – creative, risk-taking, innovative, entrepreneurial and 'personalised' in response to 'consumer' needs, whatever that might mean (see Clarke et al, 2007) – a new form of public service, based on a 'mixed economy' of provision, 'appropriate' to new social and economic conditions. Nonetheless, we do need to be aware that the political rhetoric of reform may well exaggerate or misrepresent the effects or impact of change, that is, the extent of 'real' change in 'real' schools. Policy in practice is subject to recontextualisation and reinterpretation and different policies may be in contradiction when 'joined up' in practice. Rhetorical claims are easy to make but the enactment of policy is complex and difficult. The conditions of change faced by different institutions make the enactment of policy more or less difficult. Policy makers often assume the best of possible conditions when they imagine policies and policy effects in their head. Some of the ways in which current education policies require divergent responses from teachers and schools has also been indicated at various points in the preceding chapters.

However, despite the undeniable and very basic reforms in the ways in which education is governed, structured and organised it is still possible to see the contemporary traces, and current re-emergence (see Box 5.1), of social patterns and organisational forms and preoccupations within education policy that have been inherent in the English education system since its beginnings in the 19th century. In particular, as should be evident from previous chapters, the social differentiations that were part of the basic building blocks of state education in the 19th century, especially those involving social class, continue as significant features of the policies and politics of education. For example, in what Tomlinson (2001, p 168) calls the 'obsession with selection and segregation of children into different schools or different curricula within schools', this has been a distinct feature of post-1988 education policies and is evident now in the increasing diversity of types of schools and the re-establishing of separate vocational and non-school-based curriculum routes for some students post-14. The government intends that at age 14 around 40% of students will end their general education and follow a vocational programme. These programmes will each be based on a particular industry (for example, health and social care, hospitality and catering, hair and beauty, creative and media) and will lead from 2008 to Specialised Diplomas rather than GCSEs. These new developments will literally be built into the future of schooling. BSF funding is targeted at building schemes that 'demonstrate that they will make a contribution to implementing 14-19 reform' (DfES, 2005, para 3.48, www.bsf.gov.uk/).

Box 5.1: *Higher standards: Better schools for all*

Simon Jenkins writing about the 2005 Education White Paper *Higher standards: Better schools for all*, suggested: It is hardly conceivable that the government is about to take Britain back not to 1944 but to 1934, to pre-war institutional apartheid based essentially on class. The Blair/Adonis plan is a reenactment of the old grammar/elementary divide, with a privileged Whitehall sector creaming off the best pupils and a despised local sector left on short rations. It is Britain as a 30s educational theme park. (*The Guardian*, 25 January 2006)

Also as in the 19th century we can see many elements of current education policy having a dual focus. On the one hand, on problems of the management of 'dangerous' urban populations – the socially excluded – and, on the other hand, problems of class and minority ethnic underachievements, as well as issues around immigration, citizenship and national identity. Policies like EAZs, EiC and academies were initially responses to the education problems of cities, but also in practice may contribute to increased social segregation as parents exercise their choice of school strategically. Individual or family choices do not necessarily operate to the benefit of all. As Lipsey (2005, p 27) notes, 'when everyone in the public sector tries to maximise their personal welfare through the exercise of individual choice, it may have unpredictable consequences on institutions like schools and hospitals. The effect may be to give people *less* of what they want'. On the other hand, the emphasis given to choice within policy is clearly addressed to the social and cultural expectations of the middle classes. Further, running through all of this is emphasis on a new form of individualism that draws at least in part on 19th-century liberal political philosophy in terms of 'self-making', responsibility, flexibility, choice, family values and entrepreneurship. Indeed, this individualism 'in' and 'through' policy is evident in the change in the language and tactics of policy, a move away from concern with 'inequality' to 'social exclusion', with a focus on the cultural rather than the structural bases of exclusion.

It could be argued that despite the 'flirtation' with comprehensive education in the 1960s and 1970s no government, Conservative or Labour, has been willing to take seriously the idea of a common system of education and that the current trend within policy towards a fragmentation and differentiation of school types, as an alternative to 'bog-standard' comprehensives, within a weakly articulated common framework, is a return to the historic basis of English education. In a further parallel with the 19th century faith schools remain and indeed have been reinforced as having a key role in social differentiation, and faith organisations are also prominent among academy sponsors (Chapter Four) We are also seeing the re-emergence of a variety of providers and participants in education provision and policy in the form of charitable organisations, philanthropists (often 'entrepreneurial heroes') and commercial sponsors and in parts of education 'for-profit' organisations. These new voices and participants in policy are set over and against the whittling away of the powers and roles of local government and the dissolution of local, democratic control over schooling. The 'marketising' of relations between schools (Chapter Three) is also part of 'the fragmentation of national and state systems of common schooling' (Whitty, 2002, p 97), although at the same time schools are being 'joined up' in new ways in federations and networks).

Space and time

One useful way of thinking about the new necessities of education policy and their solutions in the work of educational organisations is through the concepts of space and time, that is: (1) the respatialisation and rescaling of education policy and a general 'speeding up' and urgency of policy that reflects the space and time compressions of globalisation itself; and (2) the spatial and temporal reconfiguration of educational processes.

Among many spatial dimensions of policy there is most obviously the subordination of education to the competitive pressures of the global market and the attempt in England, and elsewhere, to facilitate a 'knowledge economy' within which surplus value is generated by new kinds of 'labour'. This new kind of labour is itself spatially particular, working in and through IT networks of 'continual interactivity' (Hardt and Negri, 2000, p 291). However, as noted in Chapter One, the extent of the 'knowledge economy' in terms of actual employment is generally exaggerated. IT plays another role in the reformulation of the time–space relations of education in that increasing numbers of students are being 'home schooled' or are virtually 'connected' to a digital schooling community (in the US a small number of virtual high schools are now run by private education management companies). For both older and younger learners the home is increasingly a significant site of learning, via the internet or software materials or other kinds of e-learning. For some learning and recreation are blurred into new forms of 'edutainment', and state education is being supplemented by some parents (who can afford it) by bought-in tuition, expert services or enrichment activities for their children (Vincent and Ball, 2006).

Students can choose among diverse providers and curricular offerings across national boundaries, particularly in the post-compulsory sector, through distance learning programmes. There is a borderless economy of education from within which student consumers can pick and choose, and within the digital curriculum the spaces of knowledge itself are reorganised, as sequences of knowledge gobbets ('Bytesize' as it is on the BBC revision website), which can be transferred as 'credits' and combined in novel ways with no guarantee of internal coherence. This is a 'cut and paste curriculum', as Robertson (2000) calls it, which may have no principles of integration. In such changes, students are rendered as active consumers, what Clarke et al (2007, p 1) call the 'strange' new figure in the remaking of public services, but also perhaps passive learners, although also 'responsible' and 'lifelong learners'. They have to be responsible individually for much of the organisation and discipline of their own learning – another kind of fragmented but restricted autonomy. In England there was a brief but unsuccessful experiment with Individual Learning Accounts (ILAs) on which learners could draw to pay for their education and training as and when they saw fit.

Lifelong learning is itself a new, open-ended temporal framework for education and education policy (Falk, 1999); that is, to adapt to change and to new economies we must be constantly learning and 'updating' ourselves, making ourselves relevant, having the right skills, making ourselves employable. Increasingly again this is a responsibility passed from the state to the learner, but those who fail to remain relevant may find themselves required to undertake 'activation' courses.

Schools are also becoming new kinds of spaces and places as they are rebuilt and redesigned, figuratively and literally – through PFI and BSF schemes. They stand for and are icons of reform and new modalities of learning – the products of the 'reimagineering' of education. This is particularly so in the academies programme. Many of the first wave of academies were designed by architects with international reputations for innovative building – such as Richard Rogers and Norman Foster. The academies and other new schools have new kinds of social and architectural ecologies, which promise new kinds of learning experience, in technologically rich, flexible learning environments. The Gilbert Report (DfES, 2006) recommends that 'personalised learning' should 'influence' the design of school buildings and that technology should be used to 'enhance pupils' access to learning resources and key software packages from home' (p 45). These new schools represent learning in new kinds of ways, with flair and dynamism, a break from, policy texts tell us, both the lumpen commonalities and class-ridden divisions of previous education policy regimes. And some of these new schools are no longer part of the infrastructure of the state at all, in the sense that they are not state-owned. PFI schools are financial assets, owned by construction companies or private equity funds (national and foreign). They provide long-term income flows to the private sector (as well as ensuring borrowings savings to the Treasury) and they are built for flexible use, and the contracts by which they are leased and run are bought and sold in financial markets. Furthermore, academies and trust schools are spaces in which new kinds of policy actors can act out their ideas and personal commitments (social, moral and religious) about education. New generation schools (like academies and extended schools) are also joined up with and open to their communities, with facilities (swimming pools and post offices, etc) and services (health and business centres, etc), 'wrap-around child care', 'parenting and family support' and 'adult and family learning'. They are open for longer hours, and have shared public spaces like cyber-cafes and conference centres. The DfES is spending £680 million on extended schools during 2006-08. The school day itself is reconfigured – there are now many 'breakfast clubs' and 'after-hours clubs' available at school, some run by private providers (making it possible for more mothers to return to the workforce). Variously in these ways education is both more global and more local, creating new patterns of social access and exclusion – a highly complex social differentiation set alongside new forms of 'activation' and intervention within an increasingly disarticulated system.

Perhaps also what we are seeing here are some general indications of a 'new correspondence' (Whitty, 2002) between schooling and capital in terms of the ways in which schooling processes are being reworked by technology and through new forms of temporal and spatial arrangements for learning – new flexibilities. Furthermore, the management of schools and school leadership are now modelled on the social relations, incentive systems and practices of business organisations. Schools are less and less specific institutions but rather are organised and look and operate like businesses.

Schools are more 'open' in other senses. In the context of competitive and contract funding, there is, as noted already, an individuation of schools *and* of the school workplace and its workers involving more and more 'skill mixes', short-term projects, freelancers, consultants, unqualified staff and agency workers with fixed-term contracts. Educational labour is being 'flexibilised' and made more amenable to the requirements of competition between institutions and the generation of 'profit'. This further contributes to the dissolution of older moral obligations and identities of professionalism and the invention of new ones around institutional competition and individual performance, related to pay and promotion. Again in these respects educational institutions increasingly look like, act like and have social and organisational arrangements like those of firms.

The spaces in which policy is thought and done have also changed. There are shifting 'geographies of power' (Robertson and Dale, 2003). The places that matter for policy are both more focused and more dispersed – focused, for example, in the powers held by the Secretary of State and embodied in the person of the Prime Minister as a model for new leadership. But, as outlined in Chapter One, policy is also being formed in new places by different people, both locally, nationally and internationally The creation of a European 'education space', for example, and the competition and free trade policies of the WTO insinuate themselves into, or at times simply override, 'national' policy-making agendas, and all of this is contributing to the development of a new kind of post national state. Policy is also being dispersed internally. There are new school autonomies but these are mainly budgetary and are offset against the loss of older autonomies that enabled decisions about curriculum and pedagogy. There are new networked federations of schools and colleges and universities and multiple partnerships, both local and dispersed, relating institutions together through digital communication and economies of scale. There is a proliferation of new non-governmental agencies, lead and link organisations and trusts, most of which are also required to act entrepreneurially to fund themselves. Many of these also act internationally to disseminate, to learn and to sell their methods or expertise – through networks. There are new players, as noted above, individual and corporate, who sit at the tables of policy making, who seek influence and favour, and who 'do' or 'sell' policy by contract and in relation to outcome measures and performance payments. These new policy contexts are, paradoxically, both more transparent and less visible. There are more and a wider variety of participants in the policy process but it is sometimes difficult to know which voices count most, or where and how key decisions are arrived at. Think-tanks, advisers and entrepreneurial actors are able to speak about and speak to policy, through new social networks that cross between public, private and voluntary and philanthropic spaces.

Policy discourse flows through these new places, gathering pace and support and credibility as it moves. Together all of this constitutes a new but unstable policy settlement or 'spatio-temporal fix', as Jessop (2002) calls it, but as I have been at pains to emphasise, it is 'made up' out of a mix of different kinds of policy ideas – old and new.

In relation to all of this the state itself is increasingly dispersed and in some respects smaller, as it moves from public sector provision to an outsourcing, contracting and monitoring role, from rowing to steering, but also at the same time more extensive, intrusive, surveillant and centred. In particular, as already signalled, the sphere of 'economic policy' is greatly expanded and the state is increasingly proactive in promoting competitiveness and scaffolding innovative capacities – collective and individual – in education and elsewhere through focused funding and strategic interventions where individuals or organisations are 'failing' to meet their 'responsibilities' – 'failing schools', 'inadequate parents' or 'inactive workers'.

Next steps

Futurology is a mysterious and dangerous art and I shall do no more than signal some features and trends in education policy that may have significance in the immediate future.

I have tried to make clear that there is currently a great deal of education policy, and the flow and volume of policy is unlikely to relent. Also the reach of education policy, or perhaps more accurately now, *learning policy*, is extensive and expanding. More and more of the life of learners is subject to policy, as indicated above. Policy is expanding through the day, through the extension of compulsory schooling and through the life course. What this flood of policies articulates is the production of a new kind of worker, citizen, learner with new dispositions and qualities; it is 'developing not only a "sense" of how to be, but also "sensibility": requisite feelings and morals' (Colley et al, 2003, p 471). Our 'learning' is also expanding to include health, fitness and sexual behaviour, and citizenship and entrepreneurship. We appear to be moving inexorably towards 'the learning society', a society in which 'every adult possess[es] a personal learning plan, written down and monitored with a chosen mentor; every organisation seek[s] to become a learning organisation' (Keep, 1997, p 457). In Bernstein's terms (2001) these are the outlines of a 'totally pedagogised society' and they involve the wholesale 'pedagogisation of life' in which learning is an activity that is conducted endlessly, and 'in which the State is moving to ensure that there's no space or time which is not pedagogised' (Bernstein, 2001, p 377). The totally pedagogised society works to mobilise subjects in ways that promote self-reliance and enterprise, enabling them to develop capacities, constantly remaking themselves, a form of continuous 'optimisation'. We are expected to make the most of ourselves – to be creative, innovative and entrepreneurial. As outlined in Chapter One, this is driven by the subordination of social policy to the demands of labour market flexibility and/or employability and the perceived imperatives of international competitiveness through which and in the name of which 'the individual and "its" society become ever more interwoven' (Tuschling and Engemann, 2006, p 452). Individual and institutional actors and their dispositions and responses are tied to the fate of the nation within the global economy.

However, alongside this expansion of policy in relation to individuals the *disarticulation* of the English system of education is likely to continue. Trust schools are beginning to take off and there are already a wide variety of potential participants emerging. More academies are due to open and new forms of relationships between schools, locally and at a distance, are developing. Parent-led schools are a possibility and the conditions necessary for private providers to bid for school management contracts covering groups of schools may soon be in place. The latter would be one further example of the more general *commercialisation* of education, as private providers of all kinds take up the market opportunities created by lifelong learning and extended school initiatives within the increasingly competitive conditions of the struggle for educational advantage. Over and against this the EU education goals suggest that a further *regionalisation and harmonisation* of education policy is likely even if only in modest ways.

The *personalisation* process is relatively new on the education policy agenda but has been given some impetus by the Gilbert Report (DfES, 2006) and the 2006 Education and Inspections Act, and in July 2007 the new Schools Secretary Ed Balls announced an extra £150 million for personalisation. The extent to which the rhetoric of personalisation is translated into institutional and classroom practices remains to be seen but it will provide new opportunities for forms of differentiation and social advantage-seeking that interested parents will undoubtedly pursue. As noted in Chapter Three personalisation is one instance of an emphasis within social and education policy on individualism, the making of the individual within and the subject of policy. This is perhaps a particular manifestation of what Beck (1992) calls the 'second modernity' or 'reflexive modernization' with its 'disembedding mechanisms' (Giddens, 1991) that dissolve traditional parameters and social and political institutions and their 'protective frameworks' and generate a 'social surge of individualism' with the effect that 'people have been removed from class commitments and have to refer to themselves in planning their individual labour market biographies' (Beck, 1992, p 87). However, the bewildering imperative of self-determination, which is represented for example in the policies of 'responsibilisation' noted above, produces its own particular inequalities. Those deemed unfit within these conditions of freedom are subject to interventions of remediation, and enforced 'activation' within workfare social policies that are aimed at cultivating appropriate personal attributes – such as self-esteem, self-confidence, self-motivation, ambition and efficacy. Individuals are required 'to make something of their lives and use their ability and potential to the full' (Blair, 2002). All of this encourages individualistic engagements with and responses to policy, for instance parental choice. In other words, as Monahan (2005, p 113) puts it, policy design 'embeds the values of its process into its outcomes'.

One dimension of this trend of individualisation, the use of individual learning access and home-based learning, indicates again a general extension of the *digitalisation* of education – the use of ICT as a medium for learning and for selling education. In relation to this, within education policy students of all sorts have been explicitly reconstituted as 'customers', a development that further reinforces the idea that their learning experience is itself a commodity that (hopefully) can be exchanged at some point of entry into the labour market. As part of this, individual learners may find themselves alone and lonely in an e-world devoid of community and commitment within which, increasingly, social relations are valued solely for their extrinsic worth. This kind of shift is pointed up in the increasing perception of social relationships as social capital, a form of investment in social relations for individuals and for the state. Here social relations themselves are a commodity, something to be 'invested in', that produces 'returns'. Furthermore, Monahan (2005, p 152) suggests that the digitalising of public institutions brings about a 'loss of public space for democratic interchange'. The public sphere and the public responsibility to which some versions of citizenship refer are both diminished. We are expected to take responsibility for ourselves but not to be responsible for others, and more and more of our social life is segregated or privatised.

Contemporary education policy faces two ways: towards an imaginary past of a British heritage, traditional values and social order and authority, within which social boundaries are reinforced, and towards an imaginary future of a knowledge economy, high skills, innovation and creativity and a meritocracy within which social boundaries are erased. The first rests on a set of fixed national and social identities, the second envisages a post-national, post-social, but connected world that is flexible and fluid, within which identities can be continually remade.

References

Adonis, A. and Pollard, S. (1997) *A class act: The myth of Britain's classless society*, London: Hamish Hamilton.

Ahmed, S. (2004) 'Declarations of Whiteness: the non-performativity of anti-racism', in *borderlands e-journal*, vol 3.

Ainley, P. (2001) 'From a national system locally administered to a national system nationally administered: the new leviathan in education and training in England', *Journal of Social Policy*, vol 30, pp 457-76.

Amin, A. (1997) 'Placing globalisation', *Theory, Culture and Society*, vol 14, pp 123-37.

Archer, L., Hutchings, M. and Ross, A. (2003) *Higher education and social class: Issues of exclusion and inclusion*, London: RoutledgeFalmer.

Apple, M. (1996) 'Power, meaning and identity: critical sociology of education in the United States', *British Journal of Sociology of Education*, vol 17, pp 125-44.

Archer, M. (1979) *Social origins of educational systems*, London: Sage Publications.

Arnold, M. (1864/1969) 'A French Eton, or middle-class education and the state', in P. Smith and G. Summerfield (eds) *Matthew Arnold and the education of a new order*, Cambridge: Cambridge University Press.

Arnot, M. and Phipps, A. (2003) 'Gender, education and citizenship', in *Document préliminaire pour le Rapport mondial de suivi sur l'EPT 2003/4*, Paris: UNESCO.

Baker, K. (1993) *The turbulent years: My life in politics*, London: Faber.

Ball, S.J. (1990) *Politics and policymaking in education*, London: Routledge.

Ball, S.J. (1994) *Education reform: A critical and post-structural approach*, Buckingham: Open University Press.

Ball, S.J. (1997) 'Policy sociology and critical social research: a personal review of recent education policy and policy research', *British Educational Research Journal*, vol 23, pp 257-74.

Ball, S.J. (2003) *Class strategies and the education market: The middle class and social advantage*, London: RoutledgeFalmer.

Ball, S.J. (2007) *Education Plc: Understanding private sector participation in public sector education*, London: Routledge.

Banks, O. (1955) *Parity and prestige in English secondary education*, London: Routledge and Kegan Paul.

Barber, M. (1994) *The making of the 1994 Education Act*, London: Cassell.

Barber, M. (2005) *The virtue of accountability*, Boston, MD: Boston University.

Barber, M. (1997a) *The learning game: Arguments for an education revolution*, London: Indigo.

Barber, M. (1997b) *How to do the impossible: A guide for politicians with a passion for education*, London: Institute of Education.

Barber, M. and Phillips, V. (2000) 'Fusion: how to unleash irreversible change (lessons for the future of system-wide school reform)', Paper to the DfEE Conference on Education Action Zones, March.

Barnett, C. (1986) *The audit of war*, London: Macmillan.

Bauman, Z. (1991) *Modernity and ambivalence*, Oxford: Polity Press.

Beck, U. (1992) *Risk society: Towards a new modernity*, Newbury Park, CA: Sage Publications.

Bell, L. and Stevenson, H. (2006) *Policy in education: Processes, themes and impact*, London: Routledge.

Bentley, T. (1998) *Learning beyond the classroom: Education for a changing world*, London: Routledge.

Bentley, T. (1999) *The creative age: Knowledge and skills for a new economy*, London: Demos.

Bernstein, B. (2001) 'Video conference with Basil Bernstein', in A. Morais, I. Neves, B. Davies and H. Daniels (eds) *Towards a sociology of pedagogy*, New York, NY: Peter Lang.

Best, G. (1973) *Mid-Victorian Britain 1851-1875*, New York, NY: Schocken Books.

Bevir, M. and Rhodes, R.A.W. (2003) 'Searching for civil society: changing patterns of governance in Britain', *Public Administration*, vol 81, pp 41–62.

Blair, T. (1998a) 'Foreword and introduction', in DSS (Department of Social Security), *New ambitions for our country: A new contract for welfare*, Cm 3805, London: The Stationery Office.

Blair, T. (1998b) 'Foreword', in DfEE (Department for Education and Employment), *The Learning Age: A renaissance for a new Britain*, London: The Stationery Office.

Blair, T. (2000) 'Knowledge 2000', Conference on the knowledge-driven economy, 7 March (www.number 10.gov.uk).

Blair, T. (2001) Speech on public sector reform, 16 October (www.direct.gov.uk).

Blair, T. (2002) Labour Party Annual Conference, September, Blackpool.

Blair, T. (2005a) Speech on education, Sedgefield, 18 November.

Blair, T. (2005b) Labour Party Annual conference, September, Brighton.

Blair, T. (2005d) Monthly press conference, October.

Blair, T. (2006a) Speech to the Labour Party's Centenary Conference, Blackpool, 10 February.

Blair, T. (2006b) 'Our nation's future – social exclusion', Lecture, 5 September.

Blunkett, D. (1999) Statement to the House of Commons, 22 March.

Bonal, X. (2002) 'Plus ça change...: The World Bank global education policy and the post-Washington consensus', *International Studies in Sociology of Education*, vol 12, pp 3-21.

Bottery, M. (2000) 'The directed profession: teachers and the state in the third millennium', *Journal of Inservice Education*, vol 26, pp 475-86.

Brehony, K. (1985) 'Popular control or control by experts? Schooling between 1880 and 1902', in M. Langan and B. Schwarz, *Crisis in the British state 1880-1930*, London: Hutchinson.
Brown, G. (2007) Mansion House speech, 21 June.
Burgess, S., Briggs, A., McConnell, B. and Slater, H. (2006) *School choice in England: Background facts*, CMPO Working Paper Series No 06/159, Bristol: University of Bristol, September.
Busher, H. (2006) *Understanding educational leadership*, Buckingham: Open University Press.
Cabinet Office (1999) *Modernising government*, Cm 4310, London: The Stationery Office.
Cabinet Office (2006) *The UK government's approach to public service reform*, London: Prime Minister's Strategy Unit, Public Service Reform Team.
Campbell, D. (2006) *The Observer*, 22 October.
Cardini, A. (2006) 'An analysis of the rhetoric and practice of educational partnerships: complexities, tensions and power', *Journal of Education Policy*, vol 21, pp 393-415.
Carnoy, M. (2000) 'School choice? Or is it privatization?', *Educational Researcher*, vol 29, pp 15-20.
Cerny, P. (1990) *The changing architecture of politics: Structure, agency and the future of the state*, London: Sage.
Chamberlain, T., Rutt, S. and Fletcher-Campbell, F. (2006) *Admissions: Who goes where? Messages from the statistics*, Slough: National Foundation for Educational Research.
Chitty, C. (1989) *Towards a new education system: The victory of the New Right?*, Lewes: Falmer Press.
Clarke, J., Cochrane, A. and McLaughlin, E. (1994) *Managing social policy*, London: Sage Publications.
Clarke, J., Gewirtz, S. and McLaughlin, E. (eds) (2000) *New managerialism, new welfare?*, London: Sage Publications.
Clarke, J., Smith, N. and Vidler, E. (2006) 'The indeterminacy of choice: political, policy and organisational implications', *Social Policy and Society*, vol 5, pp 1-10.

Clarke, J., Newman, J., Smith, N., Vidler, E. and Westmarland, L. (2007) *Creating citizen-consumers: Changing publics and changing public services*, London: Sage Publications.

Coffield, F. (2006) 'Running ever faster down the wrong road: an alternative future for education and skills', Inaugural lecture, Institute of Education, University of London, 5 December.

Colclough, C. and Lewin, K. (1993) *Educating all the children*, New York, NY: Oxford University Press.

Colley, H., James, D., Tedder, M. and Diment, K. (2003) 'Learning as becoming in vocational education and training: class gender and the role of vocational habitus', *Journal of Vocational Education and Training*, vol 55, pp 471-96.

Coopers & Lybrand (1988) *Local management of schools: A report to the Department of Education and Science*, London: Coopers & Lybrand.

Considine, M. (1994) *Public policy: A critical approach*, Melbourne, Australia: Macmillan.

Cowen, R. (1996) 'Last past the post: comparative education, modernity and perhaps post-modernity', *Comparative Education*, vol 32, pp 151-70.

Cox, C.B. and Boyson, R. (1975) *Black Papers on education*, London: Critical Review Quarterly.

Cox, C.B. and Boyson, R. (1977) *Black Papers on education*, London: Critical Review Quarterly.

Cox, C.B. and Dyson, A.E. (1969) *Crisis in education*, London: Critical Quarterly Society.

Crowther Report, The (1959) *15 to 18*, London: Minister of Education's Central Advisory Council.

Crump, S. and See, R. (2005) 'Robbing public to pay private?: two cases of refinancing education infrastructure in Australia', *Journal of Education Policy*, vol 20, pp 243-58.

Dale, R. and Ozga, J. (1993) 'Two hemispheres – both New Right?', in R. Lingard, J. Knight and P. Porter (eds) *Schooling reform in hard times*, Lewes: Falmer Press.

David, M. (1993) *Parents, gender and education reform*, Cambridge: Polity Press.

Davies, B. and Ellison, L. (eds) (1997) *School leaderships for the 21st century*, London: Routledge.

Davies, M. and Edwards, G. (1999) 'Will the curriculum caterpillar ever learn to fly?', *Cambridge Journal of Education*, vol 29, pp 265-77.

Davis, J. (2004) 'The Inner London Education Authority and the William Tyndale Junior School affair, 1974-1976', *Oxford Review of Education*, vol 28, pp 275-98.

Denham, M. and Garrett, M. (2001) *Keith Joseph*, Chesham: Acumen.

DES (Department of Education and Science) (1985) *Better schools*, White Paper, Cmnd 9469, London: HMSO.

DfEE (Department for Education and Employment) (1996) *Self-government for schools*, London: The Stationery Office.

DfEE (1997) *Excellence in schools*, White Paper, London: DfEE.

DfEE (1998a) *The Learning Age: A renaissance for a new Britain*, London: The Stationery Office.

DfEE (1998b) *Teachers meeting the challenge of change*, London: DfEE.

DfES (Department for Education and Skills) (2001a) *Schools: Building on success*, Green Paper (www.eric.ed.gov).

DfES (2001b) *Schools: Achieving success*, White Paper, Cm 5230, London: DfES.

DfES (2003) *Raising standards and tackling workload*, London: DfES.

DfES (2004) *Five-year strategy for children and learners*, London: DfES.

DfES (2005a) *Higher standards: Better schools for all – More choice for parents and pupils*, White Paper, Cm 6677, London: DfES.

DfES (2005b) *The 14-19 Education and Skills Implementation Plan*, London; DfES.

DfES (2006) *Report of the Teaching and Learning in 2020 Review Group: Gilbert Report*, London: DfES.

Drucker, P. (1966) *The effective executive*, New York, NY: Harper Row.

DTI (Department of Trade and Industry) (1998) *Our competitive future: Building the knowledge driven economy*, London: DTI (www.dti.gov.uk/comp/competitive/wh_int1.htm).

du Gay, P. (1996) *Consumption and identity at work*, London: Sage Publications.

Dunleavy, P. and B, O'Leary (1987) *Theories of the state*, London: Macmillan.

Eagle, A. (2003) *A deeper democracy: Challenging market fundamentalism*, London: Catalyst.

Edwards, R. (2002) 'Mobilizing lifelong learning: governmentality in educational practices', *Journal of Education Policy*, vol 17, pp 353-65.

Edwards, R., Nicoll, K. and Tait, A. (1999) 'Migrating metaphors: the globalization of flexibility in policy', *Journal of Education Policy*, vol 14, pp 619-30.

Elliott, A. and Lemert, C. (2006) *The new individualism: The emotional costs of globalisation*, Abingdon: Routledge.

Elliott, J. (1996) 'Quality assurance, the educational standards debate, and the commodification of educational research', BERA Annual Conference, University of Lancaster.

Ennals, P. (2004) *Child poverty and education*, London: National Children's Bureau.

EU (European Union) (2000) *Lisbon European Council, Presidency conclusions*, Brussels: European Parliament, 23-24 March.

Evans, J., Rich, M., Allwood, R. and Davies, B. (forthcoming: 2008) *British Educational Research Journal*.

Falconer, P. and Mclaughlin, K. (2000) 'Public–private partnerships and the "New Labour" government in Britain', in S. Osborne (ed) *Public–private partnerships: Theory and practice in international perspective*, London: Routledge.

Falk, C. (1999) 'Sentencing learners to life', *Theory, Technology and Culture*, vol 22, pp 19-27.

Fejes, A. (2006) 'The planetspeak discourse of lifelong learning in Sweden: what is an educable adult', *Journal of Education Policy*, vol 21, pp 676-716.

Fielding, M. and Bragg, S. (2003) '"New wave" student voice and the renewal of civic society', *London Review of Education*, vol 2, pp 197-217.

Floud, J., Halsey, A.H. and Marton, F.M. (1956) *Social class and educational opportunity*, London: Heinemann.

Foucault, M. (1979) *Discipline and punish*, Harmondsworth: Peregrine.

Fullan, M.G. (2001) *Leading in a culture of change*, San Francisco, CA: Jossey-Bass.

Furlong, J. (2001) 'Reforming teacher education, re-forming teachers', in R. Phillips and J. Furlong (eds) *Education, reform and the state: Twenty-five years of politics, policy and practice*, London: RoutledgeFalmer.

Gee, J. and Lankshear, C. (1995) 'The new work order: critical language awareness and "fast capitalism" texts', *Discourse*, vol 16, pp 5-20.

Gee, J., Hull, G. and Lankshear, C. (1996) *The new work order: Behind the language of the new capitalism*, Boulder, CO: Westview Press.

Gewirtz, S. (2001) 'Cloning the Blairs: New Labour's programme for the re-socialization of working class parents', *Journal of Education Policy*, vol 16, pp 365-78.

Gewirtz, S. (2002) *The managerial school: Post-welfarism and social justice in education*, Buckingham: Open University Press.

Gewirtz, S., Ball, S.J. and Bowe, R. (1995) *Markets, choice and equity in education*, Buckingham: Open University Press.

Giddens, A. (1991) *Modernity and self-identity*, Cambridge: Polity.

Giddens, A. (1994) *Beyond Left and Right: The future of radical politics*, Stanford, CA: Stanford University Press.

Giddens, A. (1996) *Introduction to sociology*, New York, NY: W.W. Norton.

Giddens, A. (1998a) 'After the Left's paralysis', *New Statesman*, vol 127, no 4383, pp 37-40.

Giddens, A. (1998b) *The third way: The renewal of social democracy*, Cambridge: Polity.

Gillborn, D. (1997) 'Racism and reform: new ethnicities/old inequalities', *British Educational Research Journal*, vol 23, pp 354-60.

Gillborn, D. (1998) 'Racism, selection, poverty and parents: New Labour, old problems?', *Journal of Education Policy*, vol 13, pp 717-35.

Gillborn, D. (2005) 'Education policy as an act of white supremacy: whiteness, critical race theory and education reform', *Journal of Education Policy*, vol 20, 485-505.

Gillborn, D. and Mirza, H.S. (2000) *Educational inequality: Mapping race, class and gender: A synthesis of research evidence*, London: Office for Standards in Education.

Gillborn, D. and Youdell, D. (2000) *Rationing education: Policy, practice, reform and equity*, Buckingham: Open University Press.

Glass, D.V. (ed) (1954) *Social mobility in Britain*, London: Routledge.

Glennerster, H., Power, A. and Travers, T. (1991) 'A new era for social policy: a new enlightenment or a new leviathan', *Journal of Social Policy*, vol 20, pp 398-414.

Gray, J. (1999) *Endgame*, Cambridge: Polity.

Green, A. (1991) 'The peculiarities of English education', in CCCS Education Group (ed) *Education limited: Schooling and training and the New Right since 1979*, London: Unwin Hyman.

Grieshaber-Otto, J. and Sanger, M. (2002) *Perilous lessons: The impact of the WTO Services Agreement (GATS) on Canada's public education system*, Ottawa, Canada: Canadian Centre for Policy Alternatives.

Gurney-Dixon Report, The (1954) *Early leaving*, London: HMSO.

Hall, S. and Schwarz, B. (1985) 'State and society, 1880-1930', in M. Langan and B. Schwarz (eds) *Crises in the British state 1880-1930*, London: Hutchinson.

Halpern, D. (2005) *Social capital*, Cambridge: Polity Press.

Halpern, D. and Misokz, D. (eds) (1998) *The third way: Summary of the Nexus on-line discussion*, London: Nexus.

Halsey, A.H., Heath, A. and Ridge, J. (1980) *Origins and destinations*, Oxford: Clarendon Press.

Hampden-Turner, C. and Trompenaars, F. (1994) *The seven Cultures of capitalism: Value systems for creating wealth in the United States, Britain, Japan, Germany, France, Sweden and the Netherlands*, London: Piatkus.

Hardt, M. and Negri, A. (2000) *Empire*, Cambridge, MA: Harvard University Press.

Hargreaves, D. (1998) *Creative professionalism*, London: Demos.

Hargreaves, D. (2003a) *Education epidemic*, London: Demos.

Hargreaves, D. (2003b) *Transforming secondary schools through innovation networks*, London: Demos.

Hargreaves, D. (2005) *About learning*, London: Demos.

Harvey, D. (1996) *Justice, nature and the geography of difference*, Oxford: Blackwell.

Hatcher, R. (2000) 'Profit and power: business and Education Action Zones', *Education Review*, vol 13, pp 71-7.

Henry, M., Lingard, B., Fizvi, F. and Taylor, S. (2001) *The OECD, globalisation and education policy*, Amsterdam: IAU Press Pergamon.

Hill, M. (2005) *The public policy process*, Harlow: Pearson Longman.

Hills, J. and Stewart, K. (2005) 'A tide turned but mountains yet to climb?', in J. Hills and K. Stewart (eds) *A more equal society?* Bristol: The Policy Press.

Hoggett, P. (1994) 'The modernisation of the UK welfare state', in R. Burrows and B. Loader (eds) *Towards a post-Fordist welfare state?*, London: Routledge.

Home Office, The (2003) *The Respect Programme* (www.respect.gov.uk).

Hoppen, K.T. (1998) *The Mid-Victorian generation 1846-1886*, Oxford: Oxford University Press.

Hulme, R. and Hulme, M. (2005) 'New Labour's education policy: innovation or reinvention', in Powell, M., Bauld, L. and Clarke, K. (eds) *Social Policy Review 17*, Bristol: The Policy Press, for the Social Policy Association.

Hunte, C. (2004) 'Inequality, achievement and African-Caribbean pupils', *Race Equality Teaching*, vol 22, pp 31-6.

Husbands, C. (2001) 'Managing performance in performing schools', in D. Gleeson and C. Husbands (eds) *The performing school: Managing, teaching and learning in a performance culture*, Buckingham: Open University Press.

Huxham, C. and Vangen, S. (2000) 'What makes partnerships work?', in S. Osborne (ed) *Public-private partnerships: Theory and practice in international perspective*, London: Routledge.

Hyman, P. (2005) *1 out of 10*, London: Verso.

Jakobi, A.P. (2005) 'The knowledge society and global dynamics in education politics', *European Educational Research Journal*, vol 6, pp 39-51.

Jessop, B. (1998) 'The narrative of enterprise and the enterprise of narrative: place marketing and the entrepreneurial city', in T. Hall and P. Hubbard (eds) *The entrepreneurial city: Geographies of politics, regime and representation*, Chichester: John Wiley.

Jessop, B. (2002) *The future of the capitalist state*, Cambridge: Polity Press.

Johnson, M. (2004) *Personalised learning: An emperor's outfit?*, London: Institute for Public Policy Research.

Johnson, R. (1991) 'A new road to serfdom? A critical history of the 1988 Act', in CCCs Education Group 2 (ed) *Education limited*, London: Unwin Hyman.

Jones, K. (2003) *Education in Britian: 1944 to the present*, Cambridge: Polity Press.

Jones, P.W. (1992) *World Bank financing of education: Lending, learning and development*, London: Routledge

Jones, P.W. (2007) *World Bank financing of education: Lending, learning and development*, 2nd edn, London: Routledge.

Joseph, K. (1975) *Reversing the trend*, London: Centre for Policy Studies.

Kavanagh, D. (1987) *Thatcherism and British politics: The end of consensus*, Oxford: Oxford University Press.

Keep, E. (1997) '"There's no such thing as society ...": some problems with an individual approach to creating a learning society', *Journal of Education Policy*, vol 12, pp 457-71.

Kelly, J. (2002) 'Business people may run state school federations', *Financial Times*, 15 September, p 4.

Kenny, M. and Smith, M.J. (2001) 'Interpreting New Labour: constraints, dilemmas and political agency', in S. Ludlam and M.J. Smith (eds) *New Labour in government*, London: Macmillan.

Kenway, J. (1990) 'Education and the Right's discursive politics', in S.J. Ball (ed) *Foucault and education*, London: Routledge.

Kenway, J. and Bullen, E. (2001) *Consuming children: Education-entertainment-advertising*, Buckingham: Open University Press.

Kenway, J., Bigum, C., Fitzclarence, L., Collier, J. and Tregenza, K. (2007) 'New education in new times', in S.J. Ball, I.F. Goodson and M.M. Maguire (eds) *Education, globalisation and new times*, London: Routledge.

Knight, C. (1990) *The making of Tory education policy in post-war Britain 1950-1986*, Lewes: Falmer Press.

Kooiman, J. (2003) *Governing as governance*, London: Sage Publications.

Labour Party (1995) *Diversity and excellence: A new partnership for schools*, London: Labour Party.

Labour Party (1997) Manifesto, London: Labour Party.

Labour Party Policy Unit (1998) 'Pledges into action: education and employment', Briefing paper, Annual Conference, Blackpool, September.

Lawton, D. (1980) *The politics of the school curriculum*, London: Routledge and Kegan Paul.

Leadbeater, C. (2000a) *Living on thin air: The new economy*, London: Penguin.

Leadbeater, C. (2000b) 'Three forces are driving modern economies – finance, knowledge and social capital', *Guardian Unlimited*, 1 February.

Leadbeater, C. (2004) *Personalisation through participation*, London: Demos.

Le Grand, J. and Bartlett, W. (eds) (1993) *Quasi-markets and social policy*, Basingstoke: Macmillan.

Levin, B. (1998) 'An epidemic of education policy: what can we learn for each other?', *Comparative Education*, vol 34, pp 131-42.

Levin, B. (2004) 'Media-government relations in education', *Journal of Education Policy*, vol 19, pp 271-83.

Lingard, R. and Rawolle, S. (2004) 'Mediatizing educational policy: the journalistic field, science policy, and cross-field effects', *Journal of Education Policy*, vol 19, pp 361-80.

Lingard, B. and Rizvi, F. (2000) 'Globalisation and the fear of homogenisation in education', in S.J. Ball (ed) *Sociology of education: Major themes, Volume IV: Politics and policies*, London: RoutledgeFalmer.

Lingard, B., Ladwig, J. and Luke, A. (1998) 'School effects in postmodern conditions', in R. Slee, G. Weiner with S. Tomlinson (eds) *School effectiveness for whom? Challenges to the school effectiveness and school improvement movements*, London: Falmer.

Lipsey, D. (2005) 'Too much choice', *Prospect*, December, pp 26-9

Lister, R. (2000) 'To Rio via the 3rd Way: Labour's welfare reform agenda', *Renewal: a Journal of Labour Politics (Online)*, vol 8, pp 9-20.

Lowe, R. (2004) 'Education policy', in A. Seldon and K. Hickson (eds) *New Labour, Old Labour: The Wilson and Callaghan governments, 1974-79*, London: Routledge.

Lyotard, J.-F. (1984) *The postmodern condition: A report on knowledge*, Manchester: Manchester University Press.

McCaig, C. (2001) 'New Labour and education, education, education', in S. Ludlam and M.J. Smith (eds) *New Labour in government*, London: Macmillan.

McCulloch, G. (2006) 'Education and the middle classes: the case of English grammar schools, 1868-1944', *History of Education*, vol 35, pp 689-704.

Maclure, S. (1987) *Promises and piecrust*, Southampton: The Community Unit.

Maguire, M.M. (1996) 'Open days and brochures: marketing tactics in the post 16 sector', BERA Annual Conference, Lancaster.

Maguire, M.M. (2004) 'The "modern" teacher: a textual analysis of educational restructuration', in S. Lindblad and T. Popkewitz (eds) *Educational restructuring: International perspectives on traveling policies*, Greenwich, CT: IAP.

Mahony, P., Menter, I. and Hextall, I. (2004) 'Building dams in Jordan, assessing teachers in England: a case study in edu-business', *Globalisation, Societies and Education*, vol 2, pp 277-96.

Mahony, P., Menter, I. and Hextall, I (2004) 'The emotional impact of performance-related pay on teachers in England', *British Educational Research Journal*, vol 30, pp 435-56.

Major, J. (1999) *John Major: The autobiography*, London: HarperCollins.

Marquand, D. (1988) *The unprincipled society: New demands and old politics*, London: Jonathan Cape/Fontana Press.

Milburn, A. (2006) 'New Labour: a new agenda for the next decade. Empowering citizens will be the key political challenge of the next decade', *The Sovereign Debates*, 14 September.

Mirza, H. (2005a) 'Race, gender and educational desire', Inaugural professorial lecture, Middlesex University.

Mirza, H. (2005b) '"The more things change, the more they stay the same": Assessing Black underachievement 35 years on', in B. Richardson (ed) *Tell it like it is: How our schools fail Black children*: Stoke-on-Trent: Bookmark Publications and Trentham Books.

Monahan, T. (2005) *Globalization, technological change, and public education*, New York, NY: Routledge.

Morris, E. (2002) 'Why comprehensives must change', *The Observer*, 23 June.

Newman, J. (2001) *Modernising governance: New Labour, policy and society*, London: Sage Publications.

Newman, J. (2005) 'Enter the transformational leader: network governance and the micro-politics of modernization', *British Journal of Sociology*, vol 39, pp 717-34.

Norwood Report, The (1943) *Curriculum and examinations in secondary schools*, London: HM Stationery Office.

Novoa, A. (2002) 'Ways of thinking about education in Europe', in A. Novoa and M. Lawn (eds) *Fabricating Europe: The formation of an education space*, London: Kluwer, pp 131-55.

OECD (Organisation for Economic Co-operation and Development) (1995) *Governance in transition: Public management reforms in OECD countries*, Paris: OECD.

OECD (1998) *Civil society and international development*, Paris: OECD.

OECD (2004) *Education at a glance*, Paris: OECD.

Olssen, M., Codd, J. and O'Neill, A.-M. (2004) *Education policy: Globalization, citizenship and democracy*, London: Sage Publications.

O'Neill, O. (2002) *A question of trust: The BBC Reith Lectures 2002*, Cambridge: Cambridge University Press.

Osborne, D. and Gaebler, T. (1992) *Re-inventing government*, Reading, MA: Addison-Wesley.

Paterson, L. (2003) 'The three educational ideologies of the British Labour Party, 1997-2001', *Oxford Review of Education*, vol 29, pp 167-86.

Perkin, H. (1969) *The origins of modern society, 1780-1880*, London: Routledge.

Peters, T. and Waterman, R. (1982) *In search of excellence*, London: Harper Row.

Power, S. and Whitty, G. (1999) 'New Labour's education policy: first, second or third way', *Journal of Education Policy*, vol 14, pp 535-46.

Power, S., Edwards, T., Whitty, G. and Wigfall, V. (2003) *Education and the middle class*, London: RoutledgeFalmer.

PricewaterhouseCoopers (2005) *Academies Evaluation: Second Annual Report*, London: DfES.

Putnam, R. (1995) 'Tuning in, tuning out: the strange disappearance of social capital in America', *PS: Political Science and Politics*, vol 28, pp 664-83.

QCA (Qualifications and Curriculum Authority) (1998) *The Crick Report: Education for citizenship and the teaching of democracy in schools*, London: QCA.

Quah, D.T. (1998) *UNESCO courier*, December.

Reay, D. (1998) 'Micro-politics in the 1990s: staff relationships in secondary school', *Journal of Education Policy*, vol 13, pp 179-95.

Reich, R. (1991) *The work of nations: A blueprint for the future*, New York, NY: Vantage.

Rentoul, J. (1997) *Tony Blair*, London: Warner Books.

Reynolds, D., Sullivan, M. and Murgatroyd, S. (1987) *The comprehensive experiment: A comparison of the selective and non-selective system of school examination*, Lewes: Falmer Press.

Riddell, S. and Salisbury, J. (2000) 'Introduction: educational reforms and equal opportunities programmes', in S. Riddell and J. Salisbury (eds) *Gender, policy and educational change: Shifting agendas in the UK and Europe*, London: Routledge.

Rinne, R., Kallo, J. and Hokka, S. (2004) 'Too eager to comply? OECD education policies and the Finnish response', *European Educational Research Journal*, vol 2, pp 454-85.

Robertson, D. (2000) 'Students as consumers: the individualization of competitive advantage', in P. Scott (ed) *Higher education reformed*, London: Falmer Press.

Robertson, R. (1995) 'Glocalization: time-space and homogeneity-heterogeneity', in M. Featherstone, S. Lash and R. Robertson (eds) *Global modernities*, London: Sage Publications.

Robertson, S. (2002) 'Changing governance/changing equality? Understanding the politics of public–private partnerships in education in Europe', European Science Foundation – Exploratory Workshop, Barcelona, 3-5 October.

Robertson, S. and Dale, R. (2003) 'New geographies of power in education: the politics of rescaling and its contradictions', in British Association for International and Comparative Education (BAICE)/British Educational Research Association (BERA), *Globalisation, culture and education*, Bristol: University of Bristol.

Rose, N. (1996) 'Governing "advanced" liberal democracies', in A. Barry, T. Osborne and N. Rose, *Foucault and political reason: Liberalism, neo-liberalism and rationalities of government*, London: UCL Press.

Saltman, K.J. (2005) *The Edison schools: Corporate schooling and the assault on public education*, New York, NY: Routledge.

Sayer, A. (1995) *Radical political economy: A critique*, Oxford: Basil Blackwell.

SCAA (School Curriculum and Assessment Authority) (1996) *Desirable outcomes for children's learning on entering compulsory education*, London: SCAA.

Scott, A. (1996) 'Bureaucratic revolutions and free market utopias', *Economy and Society*, vol 25, pp 89-110.

Scott, J. (1997) *Corporate business and capitalist classes*, Oxford: Oxford University Press.

Shore, C. and Wright, S. (1999) 'Audit culture and anthropology: neo-liberalism in British Higher Education', *The Journal of the Royal Anthropological Institute*, vol 5, pp 557-75.

Simon, B. (1991) *Education and the social order, 1940-1990*, London: Lawrence and Wishart.

Simon, B. (1994) *The state and educational change: Essays in the history of education and pedagogy*, London: Lawrence and Wishart.

Simon, B. and Rubenstein, D. (1969) *The evolution of the comprehensive school*, New York, NY: Routledge and Kegan Paul.

Slater, D. and Tonkiss, F. (2001) *Market society*, Cambridge: Polity Press.

Slaughter, S. and Leslie, L. (1997) *Academic capitalism: Politics, policies and the entrepreneurial university*, Boston, MD: Johns Hopkins University Press.

Smyth, J., Dow, A., Hattam, R., Reid, A. and Shacklock, G. (2000) *Teachers' work in a globalising economy*, London: Falmer Press.

Sparks, D. (2003) 'Change agent: an interview with Michael Fullan', *Journal of Staff Development*, winter, vol 24, no 1 (www.nsdc.org/publications/articleDetails.cfm?articleID=452).

Spens Report, The (1938) *Secondary education with special reference to grammar schools and technical high schools*, London: HM Stationery Office.

Stedman Jones, G. (1984) *Outcast London: A study of the relationship between classes in Victorian society*, Harmondsworth: Penguin.

Stiglitz, J. (2002) *Globalization and its discontents*, London: Penguin.

Tabb, W. (2000) 'The World Trade Organization? Stop world takeover', *Monthly Review*, vol 5, pp 1-18.

Tawney, R.H. (1931) *Equality*, London: Unwin

Taylor, S., Rizvi, F., Lingard, B. and Henry, M. (1997) *Educational policy and the politics of change*, London: Routledge.

Thrupp, M. and Willmott, R. (2003) *Education management in mangerialist times: Beyond the textual apologists*, Buckingham: Open University Press.

Timmins, N. (2001) *The five giants: A biography of the welfare state* (new edn), London: HarperCollins.

Tod, I. (1874) *On the education of girls of the middle classes*, London.

Tomlinson, S. (2001) *Education in a post-welfare society*, Buckingham: Open University Press.

Tomlinson, S. (2003) 'New Labour and education', *Children and Society*, vol 17, pp 195-204.

Tomlinson, S. (2005) *Education in a post-welfare society*, 2nd edn, Buckingham: Open University Press.

Tomlinson, S. and Craft, M. (1995) 'Education for all in the 1990s', in S. Tomlinson and M. Craft (eds) *Ethnic relations and schooling: Policy and practice in the 1990s*, London: Athlone.

Troman, G. (2000) 'Teacher stress in the low-trust society', *British Journal of Sociology of Education*, vol 21, pp 331-53.

Troyna, B. (1995) 'The Local Management of Schools and racial equality', in S. Tomlinson and M. Craft (eds) *Ethnic relations and schooling: Policy and practice in the 1990s*, London: Athlone.

Tuschling, A. and Engemann, C. (2006) 'From education to lifelong learning: the emerging regime of learning in the European Union', *Educational Philosophy and Theory*, vol 38, pp 451-69.

Urry, J. (2000) *Sociology beyond societies: Mobilities for the twenty-first century*, London: Routledge.

van Zanten, A. (1997) 'Schooling immigrants in France in the 1990s: success or failure of the Republican model of integration?', *Anthropology and Education Quarterly*, vol 28, pp 351-74.

Vernon, R. (1977) *Storm over the multinationals*, London: Macmillan.

Vincent, C. and Ball, S.J. (2006) *Childcare, choice and class practices; Middle-class parents and their children*, London: Routledge.

Wade, R. (2001) 'Showdown at the World Bank', *New Left Review*, no 7, second series, pp 124-137.

Warmington, P. and Murphy, R. (2004) 'Could do better? Media descriptions of UK educational assessment results', *Journal of Education Policy*, vol 19, pp 293-9.

Watson, M. and Hay, C. (2003) 'The discourse of globalisation and the logic of no alternative: rendering the contingent necessary in the political economy of New Labour', *Policy & Politics*, vol 31, pp 289-305.

Weiss, L. (1997) 'Globalization and the myth of the powerless state', *New Left Review*, no 225, pp 3-27.

White, J. (2006) *Intelligence, destiny and education: The ideological roots of intelligence testing*, London: Routledge.

White, S. (1998) *Interpreting the 'Third Way': A tentative overview*, Cambridge, MA: MIT, Department of Political Science.

Whitfield, D. (2001) *Public services or corporate welfare*, London: Pluto Press.

Whitty, G. (2002) *Making sense of education policy*, London: Paul Chapman.

Whitty, G. and Edwards, T. (1998) 'School choices policies in England and the United States: an exploration of their origins and significance', *Comparative Education*, vol 34, pp 211-27.

Willmott, H. (1993) 'Strength is ignorance; slavery is freedom: managing culture in modern organizations', *Journal of Management Studies*, vol 30, pp 215-52.

Willmott, H. (1995) 'Managing the academics: commodification and control in the development of university education in the UK', *Human Relations*, vol 48, pp 993-1027.

Witte, J. (2001) *The market approach to education: An analysis of America's first voucher program*, Princeton, NJ: Princeton University Press.

Wittel, A. (2001) 'Towards a network sociality', *Theory, Culture and Society*, vol 18, pp 51-76.

Woods, P.A., Woods, G.J. and Gunter, H. (2007) 'Academies, schools and entrepreneurialism in education', *Journal of Education Policy*, vol 22, pp 237-59.

World Bank (1986) *Financing education in developing countries: An exploration of policy options*, Washington, DC: World Bank.

Young, M. (1958) *The rise of the meritocracy*, Harmondsworth: Penguin.

Index

E

G

H

M

O

P

S

T

Y